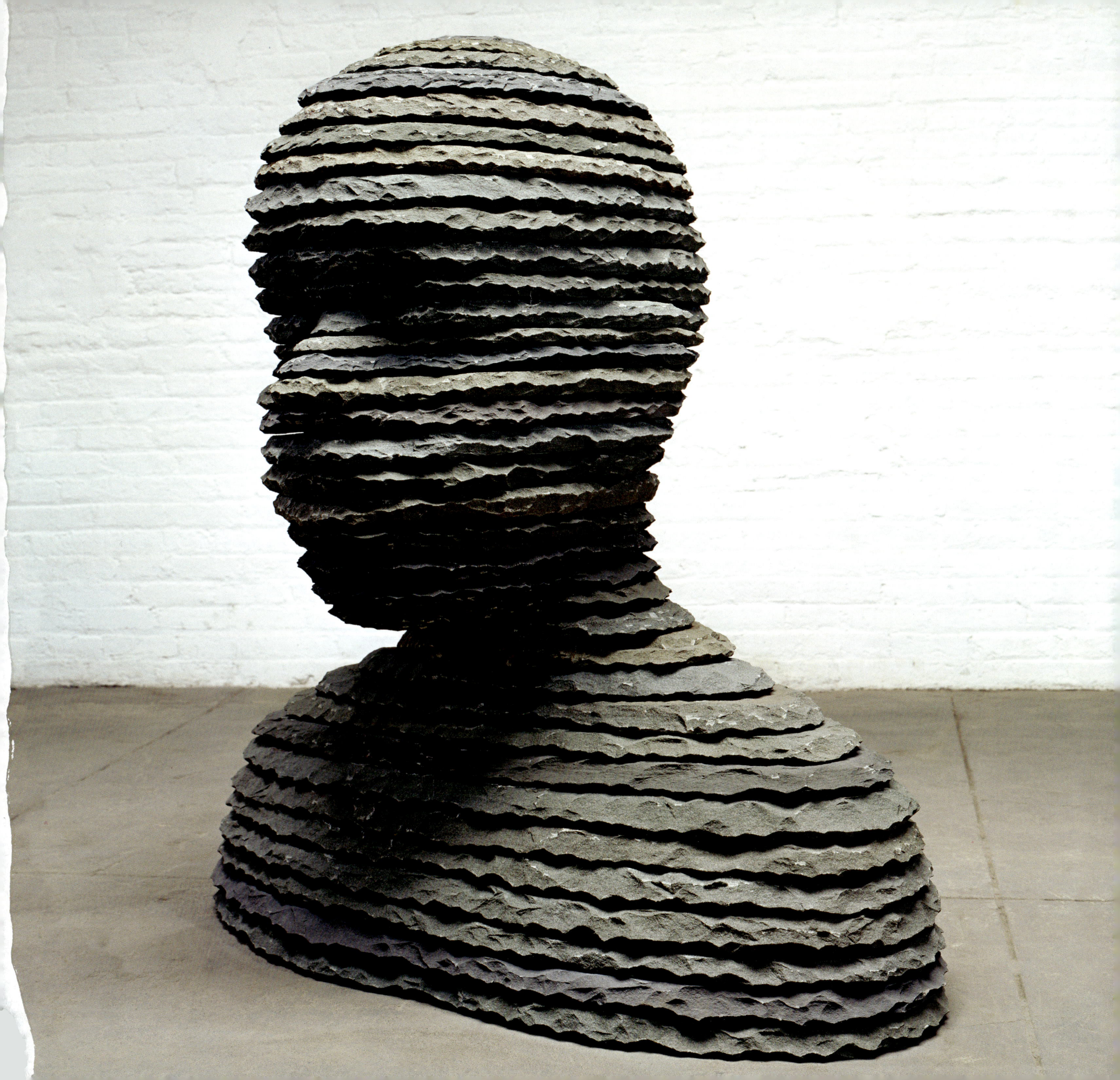

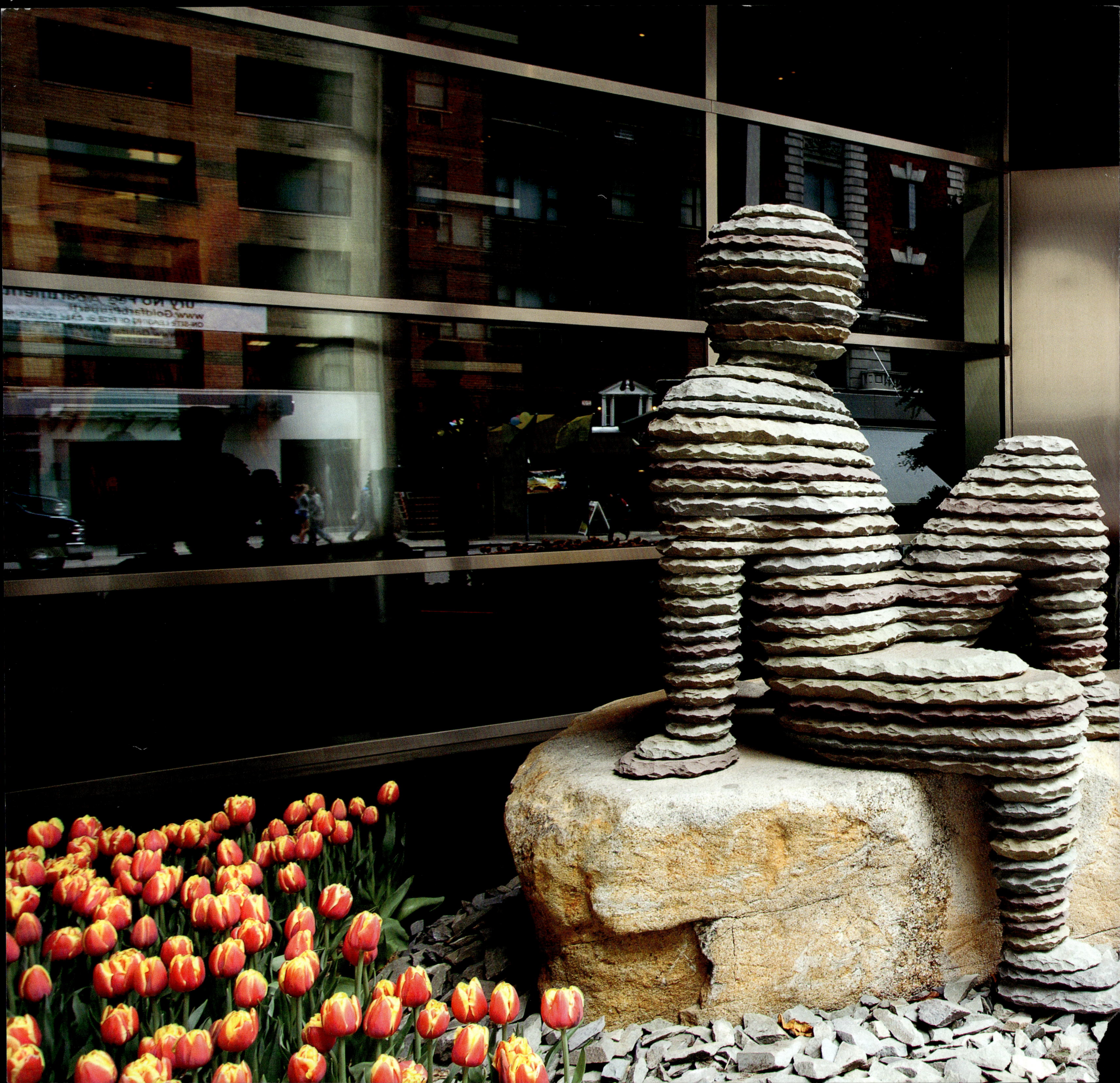

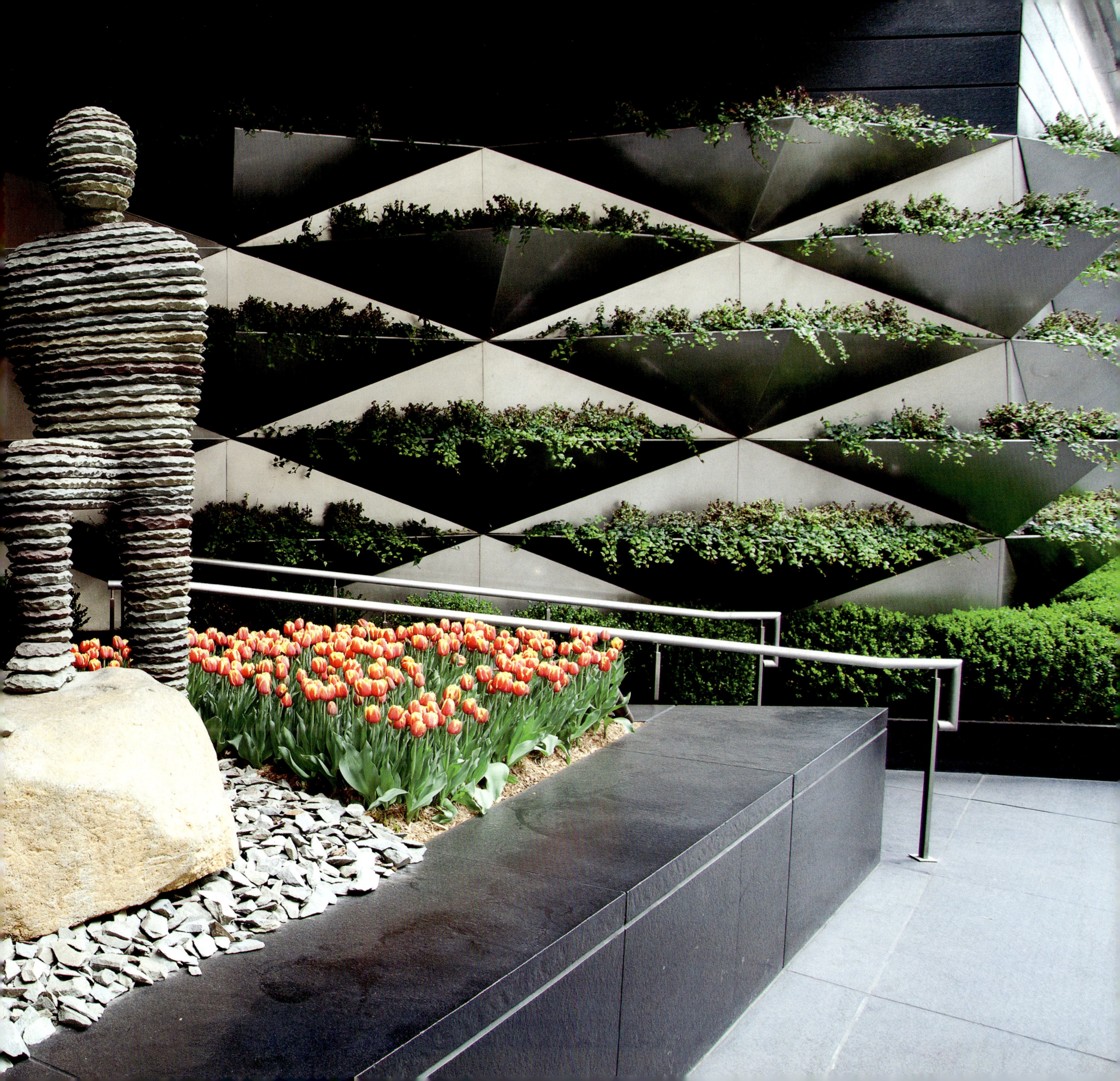

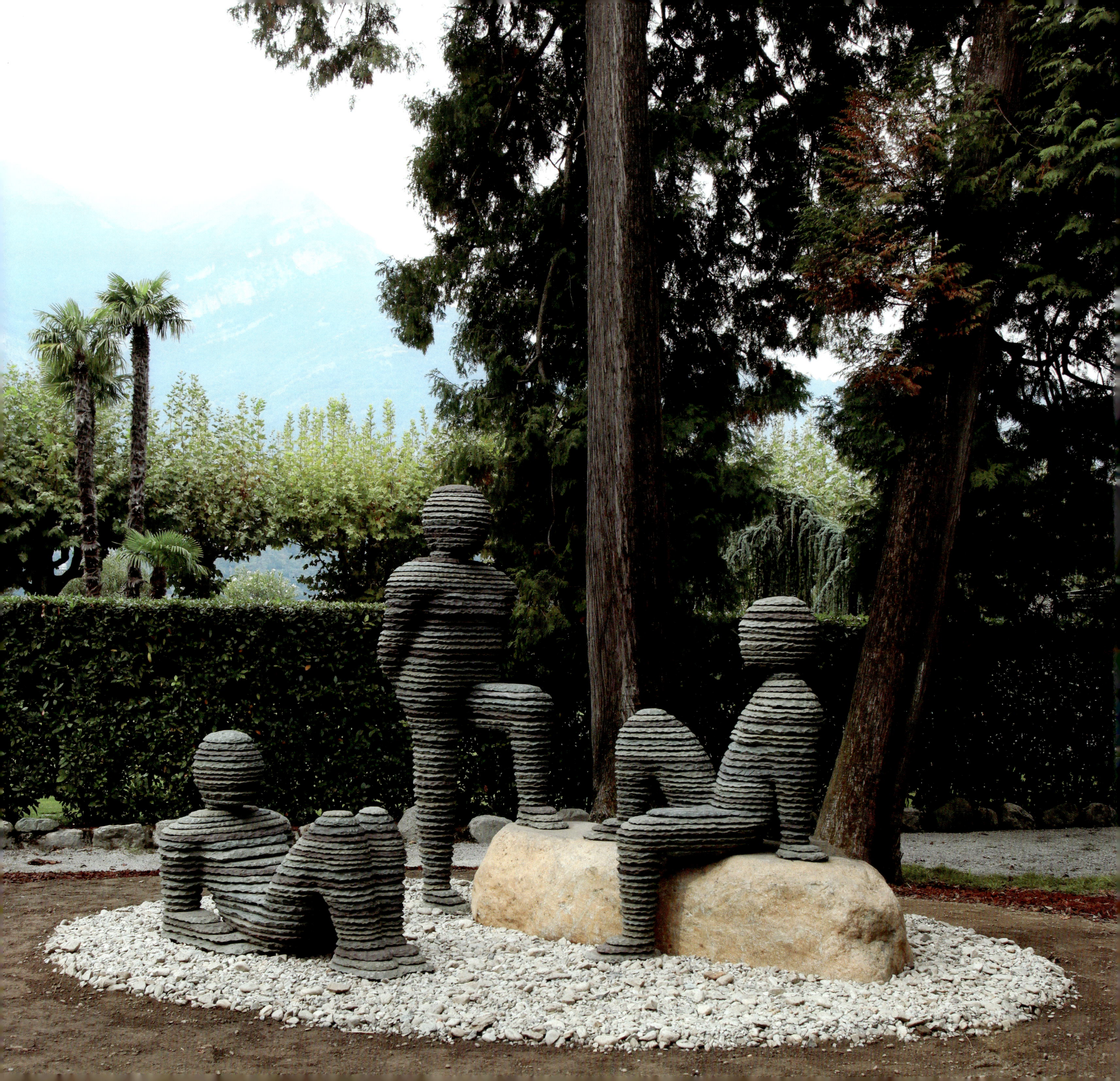

Boaz Vaadia: Sculpture

ESSAY BY WENDY STEINER

FOREWORD BY TOM MORAN

GROUNDS FOR SCULPTURE

THE ARTIST BOOK FOUNDATION

NEW YORK   NORTH ADAMS   LONDON

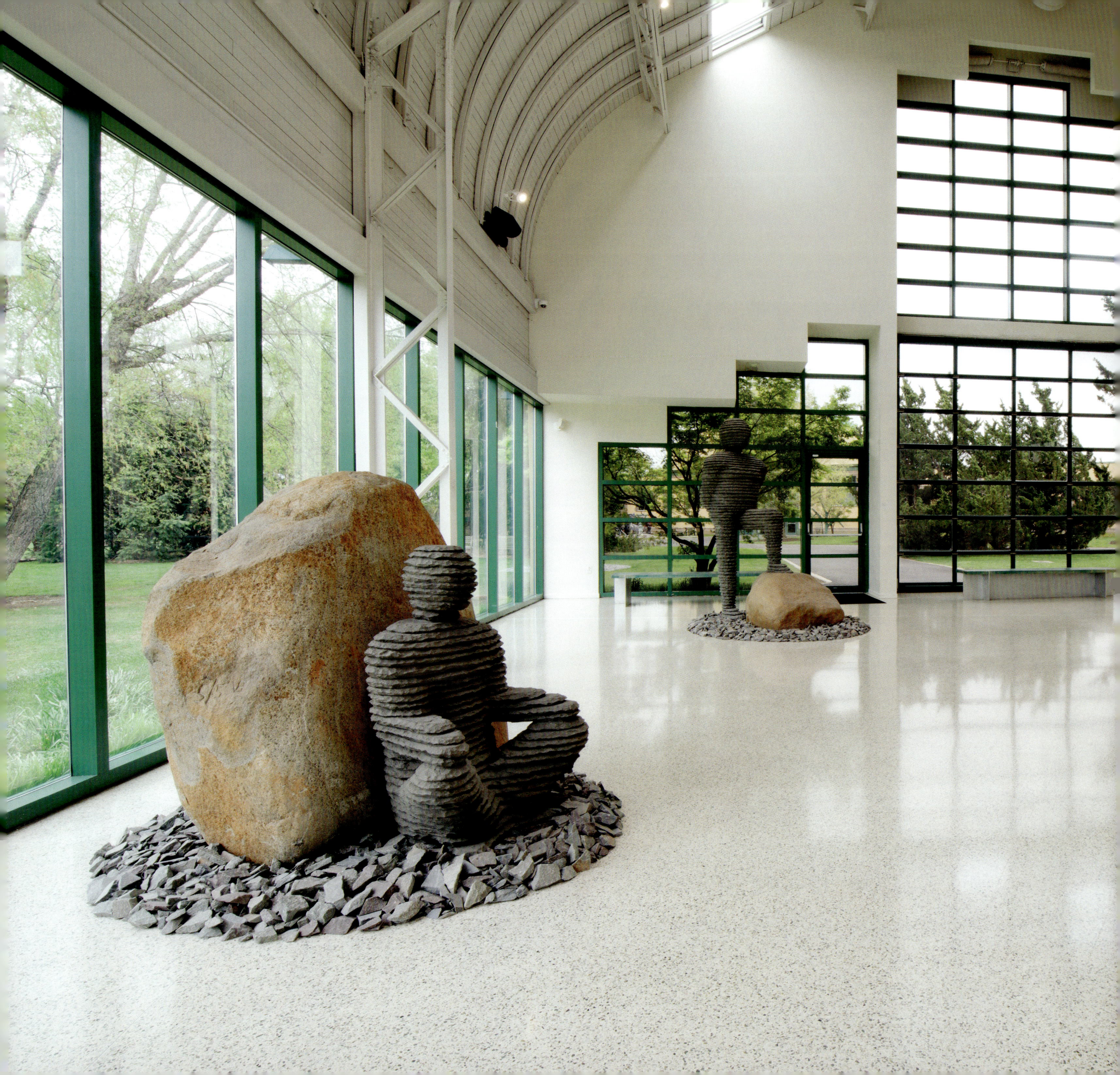

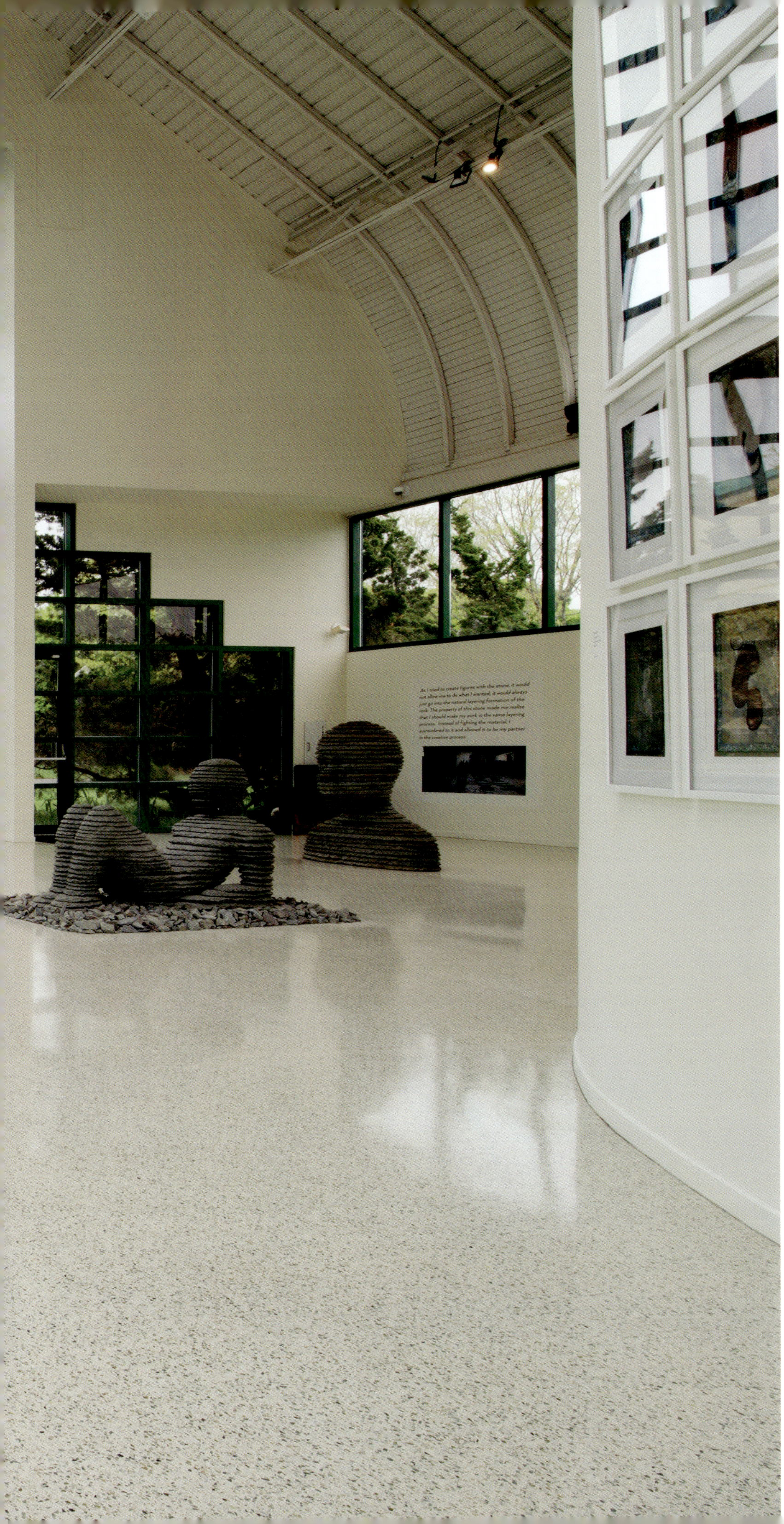

Contents

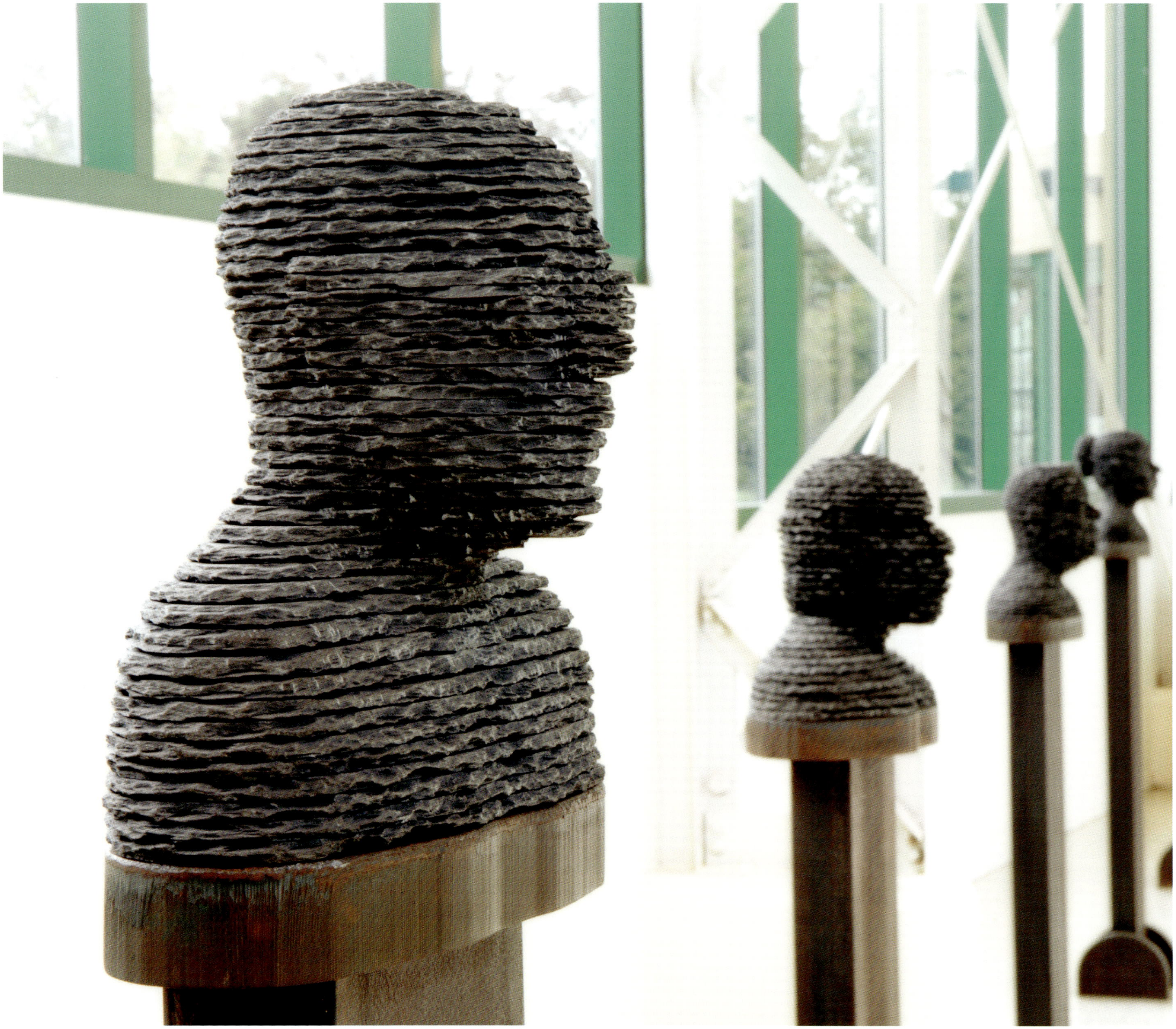

Acknowledgments

I WOULD LIKE TO THANK the following people for their contributions and help with the production and organization of this major exhibition. I am very grateful to have worked with Gary Garrido Schneider and all the staff at Grounds For Sculpture who made this show possible. Special thanks to Tom Moran; together we collaborated seamlessly to produce this show, and to Faith McClellan who provided the necessary organization. I would also like to thank Wendy Steiner for lending her words to this catalogue with her insightful essay. Thanks also to Jennifer Lewis for working with me so tirelessly on so many aspects of this show, and to Harry Gordon for his care in the shipping and installation of this extensive body of work.

My deepest gratitude is extended to Ivan Karp for his integrity, honesty, and support, and for launching my career. I feel I was very lucky to work with a dealer of his caliber.

It is with great pride that I am happy to acknowledge the support and generosity of the Consulate General of Israel in New York for their contribution to this catalogue as well as their promotion of Israeli culture. As well, I'd like to recognize the Connaught Brown gallery, which has, in the last decade, increased the presence of my work internationally. And my thanks to Sponder Gallery, Imago Galleries, Jim Kempner Fine Art, and Vered Gallery for their generous support for this publication.

In addition, I would like to thank all of my family and friends for being there for me; all of the art dealers and galleries that have shown my work and supported me throughout the years; all of the public and private collectors who have invested in me throughout my career; all of the foundries I work with for casting my bronze sculptures; all of the people at The Artist Book Foundation who helped with the publication of the catalogue; and my assistants Vincent Tiley and Dax Sommerfeld, as well as all of my past assistants for their help.

Lastly, to the love of my life Kim, my real rock; and to the sunshine of my life, my daughters Rebecca and Sara who kindly leant their collection to this exhibition.

BOAZ VAADIA
WILLIAMSBURG, BROOKLYN, NEW YORK
MAY 2016

Installation at
Main Museum Gallery,
Grounds For Sculpture,
Hamilton, NJ, 2016.

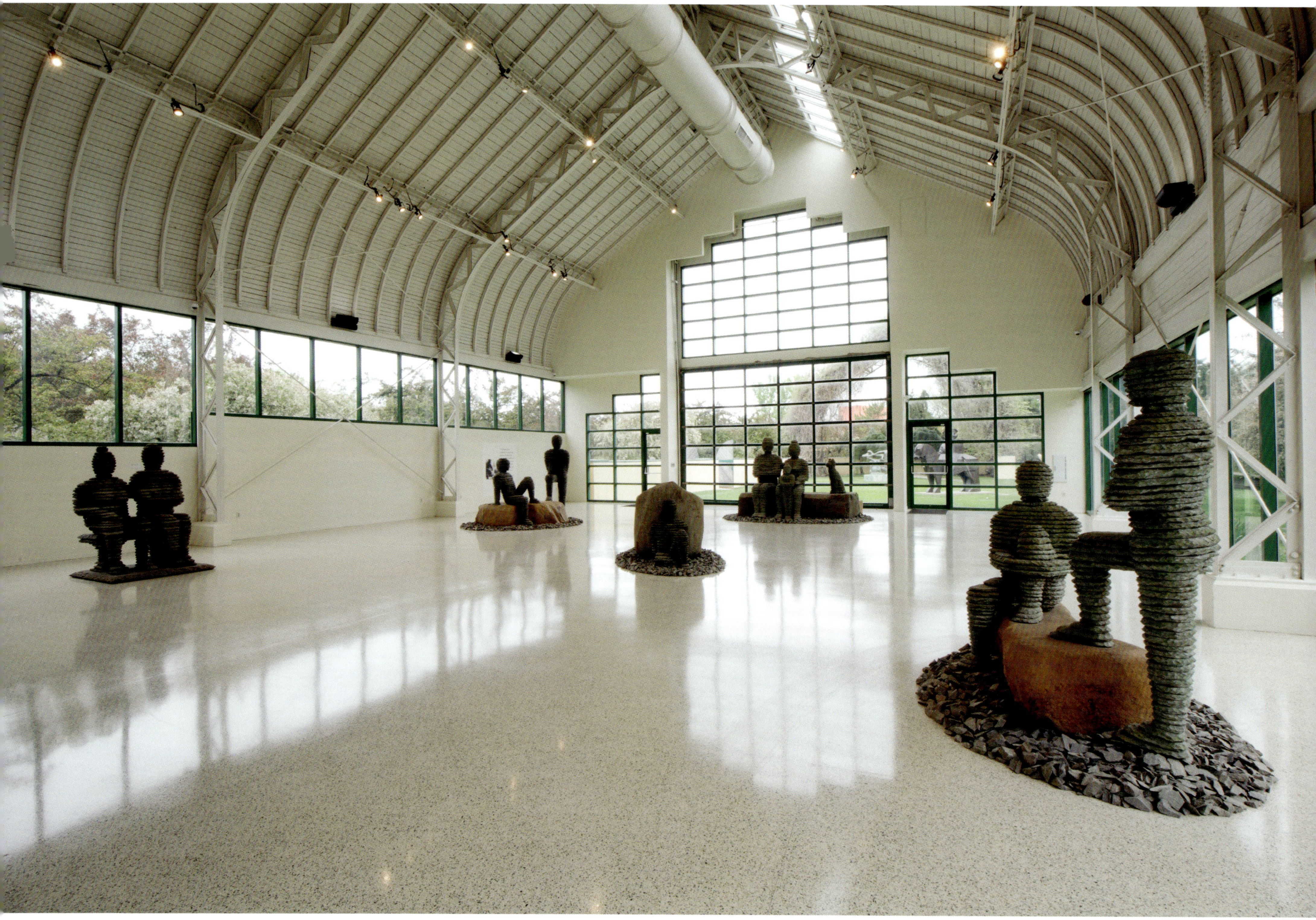

Boaz Vaadia: Sculpture

Foreword

BOAZ VAADIA arrived in SoHo in the excitement of the 1970s. Artists were building their loft studios and the galleries that would eventually show their work became plentiful over time. The international boutiques and design stores had not yet arrived. Trucks hit the big potholes on the overburdened cross streets with a loud bang. New York City was on the verge of bankruptcy. Vaadia found a place to live and work and, like many artists, raided dumpsters for his material.

Boaz's early exhibitions consisted of works made primarily from the materials he found. He transformed such finds into distinctive artworks comprised of wood, bone, hair, and other mixed mediums; they were ritualistic in manner and resembled highly personal ex-votos. He assembled sculptures made of branches stripped of their bark and bound together with rope or leather. In some of these works, he found resourceful ways to suspend a large stone serving as an integral compositional element. He used the weight of the stone to provide the necessary gravitational force that would allow the piece to stand. Recognizing the physical truths revealed in the process of making this body of work, Vaadia moved toward deeper explorations of three-dimensional concepts and focused on his interest in structure, balance, and gravity.

Boaz Vaadia: Sculpture celebrates his art and his important contribution to the advancement of sculpture over a long and prolific career. All stages of the artist's work since the 1970s appear in this extensive exhibition, which includes more than 125 of his pieces installed in two major buildings. The exhibition as a whole amplifies the critical understanding of Vaadia's career, and coincidentally, traces a pathway from abstraction to figuration. However, neither was ever the main point. The limitations he imposed upon himself instead concerned the natural forces of gravity and balance; a reliance on natural materials even after they had become part of a cityscape; and, a sense of offering—of veneration. Seven of his bronze sculptures are on view outdoors in the beautiful gardened landscape of Grounds For Sculpture. The exhibition includes many of the artist's earliest works as well as his large bluestone sculptures and the bronzes he casts from them. On view along with the large bronze and stone sculptures are intimate

Installation at
Main Museum Gallery,
Grounds For Sculpture,
Hamilton, NJ, 2016.

groupings of his smaller works made of multiple strata of roofing slate mounted atop wooden pedestals Vaadia made out of huge beams he found. Early examples of work, including some created in his birth country of Israel, reveal the important first steps he took that led to the vast crescendo of works on view these many years later. In Vaadia's relentless advancement of his art, the exhibition debuts four of his most recent bas-relief sculptures in slate, signaling an exciting new development in his oeuvre.

The story of Boaz Vaadia's journey into art is as rich in texture and depth as his sculptures. He was born in a small village in Israel. His father was a farmer who worked the fields of the family farm. From the time he was a boy, Vaadia did chores on the farm and dreamt about art. In time, he would travel alone by bus to attend art classes in a town some distance away from home and return before dark. He became familiar with the incredible ancient treasures of his homeland, including architecture and sculpture. He eventually worked on the restoration of some of these structures during breaks while serving in the army. Vaadia's memories of his early years in Israel form a strong personal identity about his origins and the connection of his art to his roots and his love and respect of nature.

He exhibited the series of his early fetishistic works during his first years in New York, and then began working with bulky rectangular slabs of bluestone and slimmer pieces of discarded slate roofing tiles that he rescued by the dozens from the dumpsters in SoHo. To Boaz, finding such a cache of usable stone was at once triumphant and prophetic. Once he undertook the development of the sculptural approach he would use, he realized that working with these sedimentary materials linked him personally and spiritually back to the earth. Not long after this, the debut of his distinctive figurative work in stacked stone was on view at Ivan Karp's SoHo gallery. Vaadia never looked back.

From the mid-1980s and over the past three decades, Vaadia has been fixated on harnessing the natural forces of balance and gravity explored in his earlier works to new sculptural works depicting the human figure. Even though using the figure as a subject in his work had been of interest to him for some time, Vaadia seized it as a subject in the next phase of his work to highlight the true source of his inspiration and focus, the material. His concept centers on stacking thick, quarried bluestone slabs in carefully planned and organized renditions of the figure, constructed in such a way that the force of gravity is in harmony with the balanced layers forming the composition. When complete, the apparition of the figure consists of an intricate myriad of stone layers that stand in harmonious respect for the natural formation of the ancient sedimentary stone he uses. The same intent carries through Vaadia's multitude of smaller sculptures executed in slate. In all of his stone-layered works, Vaadia still meticulously hand-carves the perimeter edge of each piece bringing final form to the work using a technique so specific to his eye that he alone does the carving.

He often incorporates large glacial boulders in his compositions. Many of these works contain groupings of figures that make the overall composition of each piece enormously heavy. The origins of how he came to use such large stones dates back to when he purchased a building in the Williamsburg neighborhood of Brooklyn, which now serves as his studio. Arriving there one day, he found the entire street dug up for an extensive city sewer project. Recognizing yet another twist of fate in his favor, Vaadia was able to secure and stockpile a large number of the glacial boulders excavated during the project for use in his works.

Boaz Vaadia has created a body of work that is distinctive in the continuum of sculpture. The exhibition stands as evidence of Vaadia's powerful will to achieve mastery in harnessing natural materials within a personally defined and meticulously focused genesis of form. By using both an additive and subtractive process in stone, he has created sculptures that connect deeply felt natural processes that he recognizes in nature. The definitive collection of the works in the exhibition is a profound testimony to Vaadia's artistry and his connection with the earth and the human condition.

TOM MORAN
CHIEF CURATOR
GROUNDS FOR SCULPTURE
HAMILTON, NEW JERSEY
MAY 2016

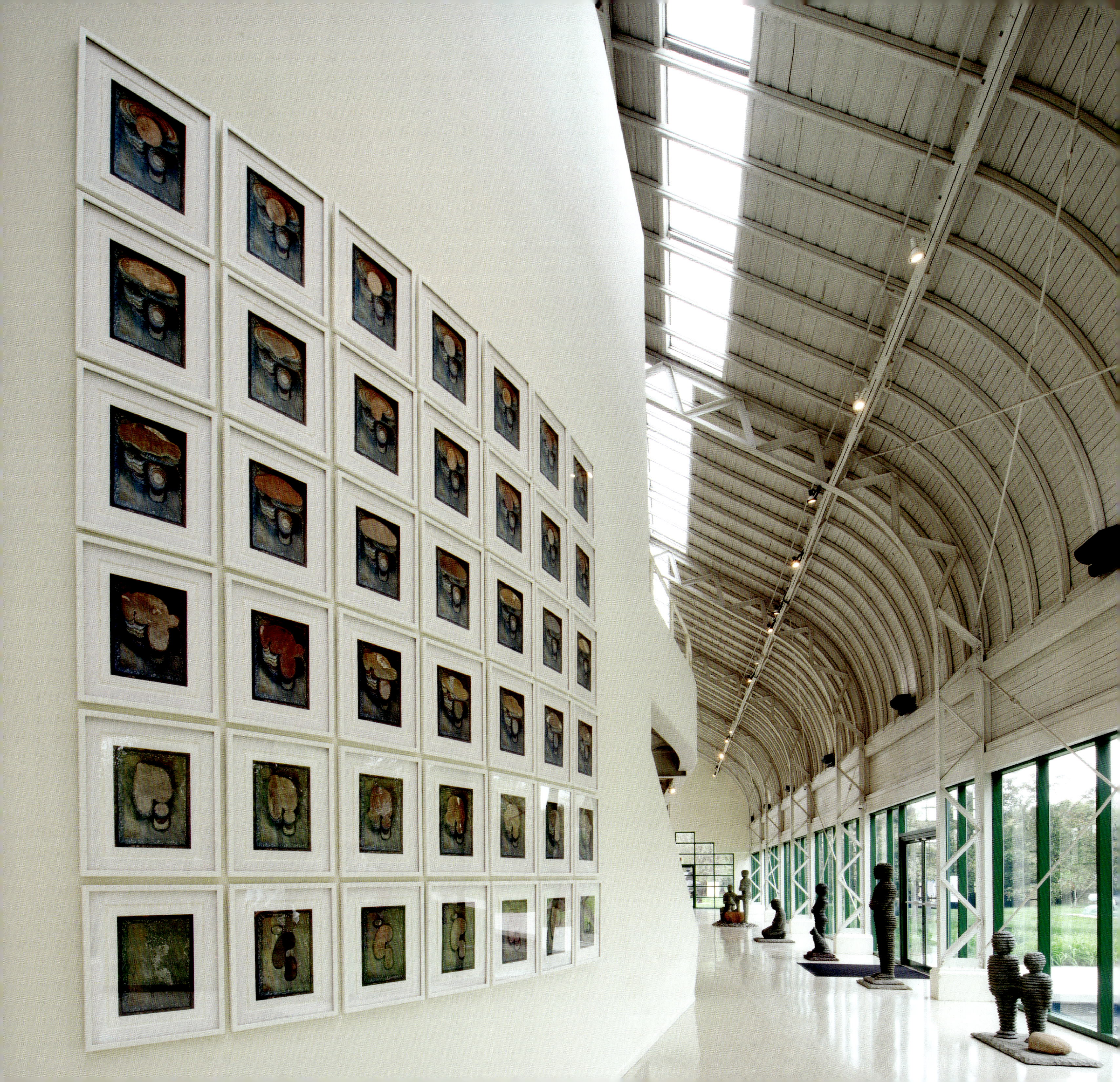

Boaz Vaadia: Grounds For Sculpture

BY WENDY STEINER

GROUNDS FOR SCULPTURE, a former industrial fairground in Hamilton, New Jersey, is the site of the first retrospective survey of Boaz Vaadia's career. It is a match made in heaven. The Grounds are a twenty-first-century update of the scene in Georges Seurat's *A Sunday Afternoon on the Island of La Grande Jatte* (1884): a leisure park nestled within the ferment of fast-forward, high-tech exurbia. Here, the most sophisticated sculptures seem as accessible as the tall grasses and trees of the gardens and the light-filled, human-scale architecture of the galleries. Exploring Grounds For Sculpture by foot and by thought, we cannot help but marvel at the democratic case it makes for art.

Boaz Vaadia's work could also be described as "grounds for sculpture." Methodically, curiously, humanely, he investigates the preconditions of his practice and its reason for being. We might picture him as *Ahiam 2nd* (plate 102), daydreaming against an ancient boulder on a bed of stony shards. The sedimentary strata that make up his feet and forearms lead down like steps to the earth, showing the way back to their beginnings. Oblivious to heavy machinery and high technology alike, *Ahiam 2nd* lies lost in thought, a hand-wrought vision of repose.

The earliest grounds for his sculpture, Vaadia tells us, lay in his family's farm in Israel. "Simple and primal," it inspired an enduring connection to the earth that demanded sacrifice and reverence on his part. "My father was a basic farmer. He thought that heavy equipment was raping the land, and he used to plow with a mule."[1] Vaadia uses the word "rape" again when he speaks of the graffiti artists who spray the boulders he stores in a lot in the Williamsburg neighborhood of Brooklyn, New York. The paint ruins the patina on the rocks, and it takes years for the exquisite skins to return. Vaadia's art making, in contrast, is an act of humility: "Your entire life is only a second in the lifetime of a stone formation. So I have that respect for the materials I work with; I have respect for nature, natural forces, and for what I learn from the processes [I use]."[2]

In Israel, Vaadia grew up surrounded by ancient architecture and sculpture. During breaks in his military service, he worked on an archaeological restoration team, learning stoneworking

Wall installation at
Main Museum Gallery,
Grounds For Sculpture,
Hamilton, NJ, 2016.

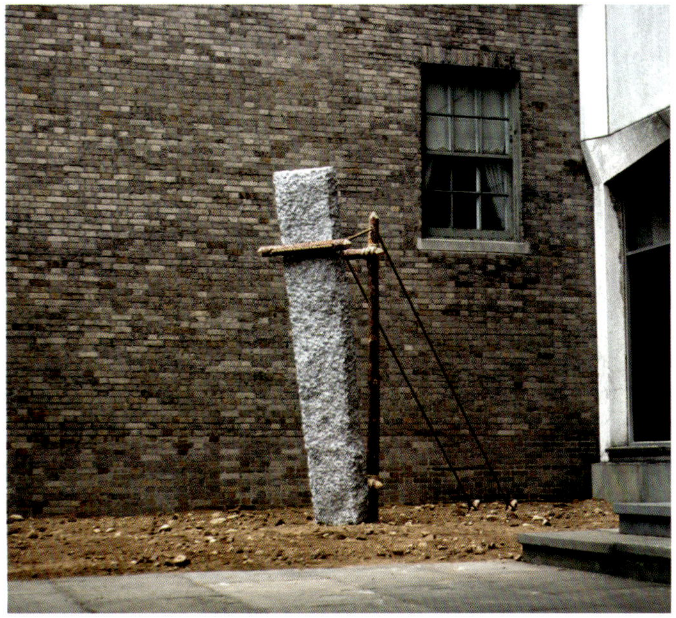

FIG.1. Photograph of *The Left Pillar in the Porch of the Temple*, 1978.
Stone, wood, rope, and soil,
108 x 147 x 32 in. (274.3 x 373.8 x 81.3 cm).
Installation at The Jewish Museum, New York, NY, 1978.

techniques dating back to biblical times. He was moved by the crosses that pilgrims scratched on stone shrines. Unlike graffiti, these marks seemed to him a positive offering, the human equivalent of weathering. They taught him that artworks grew and changed through interaction with their viewers, developing like living things, but in slow motion. An artist formed them, but viewers brought out their beauty and aura. Holiness, Vaadia claims, is the energy people bring to what they revere.

For his 13th birthday, Vaadia asked his parents for an African fetish, and they found him one. Later, caring for his mother in her final illness, he imagined creating fetishes to house her spirit and the spirits of his departed grandparents. He decided that his sculptures would be "sites that encourage veneration."[3] He began with the elemental materials on the farm—sticks, stones, leather, fur, feathers, string, rope, sand, human hair—tying and wrapping them into form. In the presence of these aesthetic fetishes, altars, and shrines, he says, people would experience "something beyond themselves."[4] Even the welded industrial parts of his earliest piece, *Untitled*, 1971 (plate 1), are filled with a pent-up energy, the sphere almost popping out of its constraining pipes. This and the other works in the exhibition that were made between 1971 and 1975 slept for more than forty years in the family barn, numinous artifacts waiting to be wakened to life by viewers.

Attending art school in Israel, Vaadia acquired another ground for his work: twentieth-century sculpture. The use of fur and the technique of wrapping recall Meret Oppenheim's surrealist teacup. The stone, aluminum, and iron penis and testicles of *Untitled*, 1973 (plate 2), drooping over a forked stick suggest Dalíesque dreamscapes, and there is a whiff of Arte Povera in Vaadia's assemblages of humble materials. But his thinking differs from those artists: he uses these materials to discover the rules and limits they impose on his practice.

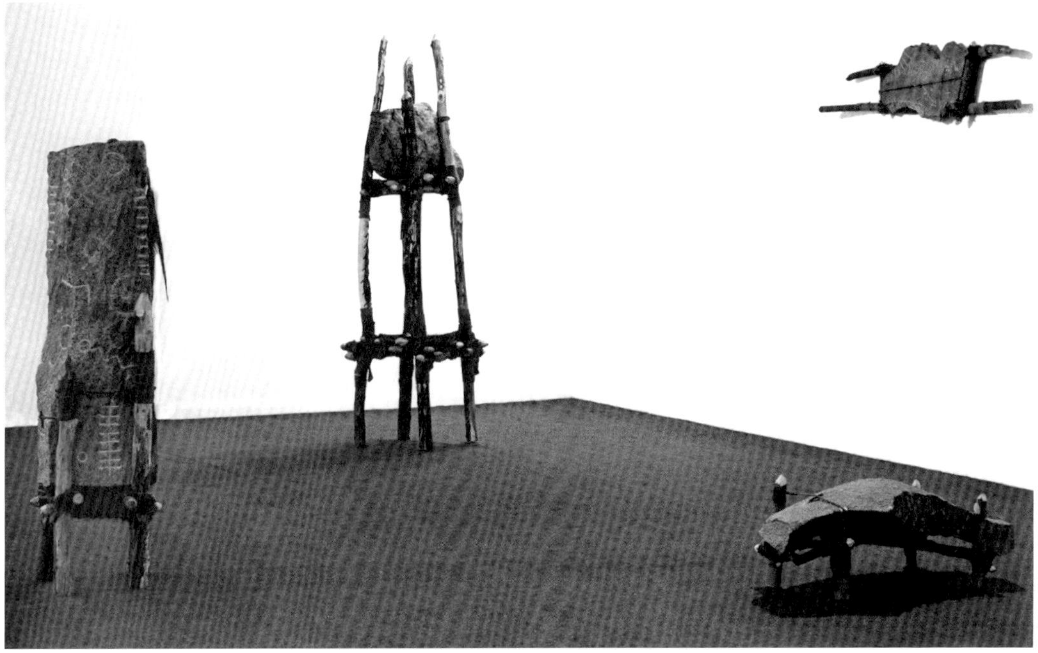

FIG.2. Installation at Hundred Acres Gallery, New York, NY, 1976.

Vaadia's severe dyslexia had already taught him a lot about limits.[5] Unable to read about art, he says, he was free to feel it deeply and he consciously defined himself through this accident of his cognitive makeup. In 1978, The Jewish Museum of New York selected one of his pieces for a group show: a massive slab of curbstone pitched at a precarious angle over stony rubble. The slab was held back from falling—indeed, held back from any motion but this ominous leaning—by a framework of restricting poles and ropes. Although Vaadia had previously labeled all his works *Untitled*, the museum insisted on a descriptive title, and he sent them one: *The Left Pillar in the Porch of the Temple* (fig. 1). It was a private joke: in the Bible, that pillar's name is "Boaz." In effect, Vaadia had made a self-portrait, and this "portrait of the artist as a young man" was an image of tense restriction.

Still, limitation was not a misfortune, as he saw it. The artists Vaadia most admired—Alberto Giacometti and Isamu Noguchi—accepted the rules imposed by time, gravity, and the characteristics of their materials. "Finding ways to work within those parameters," Vaadia states, is "what eventually shapes each individual artist's work. So you can call them 'boundaries' or you can call them 'limitations.' But that is the scope within which we work."[6] For Vaadia, limits are defining grounds for artistic creativity, freedom, and self-realization.

This idea was at work in his first U.S. solo exhibition, held at Hundred Acres Gallery in 1976 (fig. 2). The abstract pieces in this show (*Untitled*, 1976, plates 28 and 29) caged massive stones in structures of poles lashed together with leather thongs. "Caged," however, is too negative a term. The scaffoldings support the stones and frame them, or raise them up to display their numinous beauty. Vaadia sometimes incised marks on the stone, like the pilgrims' scratchings he had seen in Israel's holy sites.

In a 1979 group show in Washington, DC, called *Other Gods: Containers of Belief*,[7] critics responded to his works as fetishes. Julia Keydel registered the power of this sculpture, which engages us on the level of elemental awareness: "Shaped by Vaadia [the materials] evoke…the earliest expressions of human beings—ceremonial objects, tools, and rudimentary structures. Particularly striking about Vaadia's current work is the directness with which these pieces communicate a sense of involvement with primal forces without demanding initiation into a private magical ritual for complete understanding."[8]

Vaadia landed in the ferment of New York City in 1975 with a scholarship from the America-Israel Cultural Foundation. Hundreds of artists were converting abandoned warehouses into studio lofts, and the sidewalks were torn up, with broken pavement piled at every corner—bluestone slabs in subtle shades of gray, blue, green, purple, and brown. Dumpsters overflowed with broken roofing slates and cedar poles, the discarded props for the saplings the city had been planting. A postmodern *bricoleur*, Vaadia scavenged through SoHo, discovering in the process the materials that would determine his practice ever after.

For this reason, Grant Moser, a writer on the arts, has labeled Vaadia a "Sculptor of Coincidence."[9] But it is Vaadia's attitude toward chance that sets him apart. He viewed SoHo as his urban farm, and accepted the grounds it provided for his sculpture. The paving stones connected him to the earth's primordial past: "The bluestone I work with is a remnant of an ancient [river delta]—layers of sediment, compressed by thousands of pounds of pressure over millions of years—only to find its way into my studio."[10] But those stones, at the same time, were human artifacts intended for paving. Similarly, the slates were shaped for roofing and the poles for landscaping. Integral elements of the urban fabric, they had been unceremoniously torn out and abandoned, like the rubble in archeological sites in Israel that had been repeatedly razed and buried. In hand-fashioning the gifts of his new farm, Vaadia set out to show his respect. He followed an aesthetic ecology in doing so, salvaging urban waste for art.

It took Vaadia a while to understand the limits imposed by these materials. Gravity lays down sedimentary stone in layers, and the city of New York had delivered them up to him in manageable chunks. He responded by standing the layers on end and bolting them together as vertical parallels in his 1982 *Untitled* (plate 66). But soon it dawned on him that he was fighting gravity rather than respecting it. If he piled the layers one on top of the other, they would convey both the process of sedimentary rock formation and twentieth-century geometric abstraction. In fact, they would go on signifying their origins in stone and abstraction even if he stacked them into a shape that resembled something else entirely—something like a person, for example.

Now, Vaadia had a way of representing the human figure without turning his back on either the nature of his material or the history of twentieth-century art: "I had tried to work with figures before, but it felt too derivative. Then, I saw that I could reinterpret the human figure in a way that hadn't been done before. I surrendered to the stone."[11] Surrendering to the stone, Vaadia passed from abstraction to figuration. The year was 1985, and he never looked back.

He had a host of new limitations to explore. Bluestone forms in thicker layers than slate. Accordingly, he would make figures in two scales: life-size for bluestone, pedestal-size for

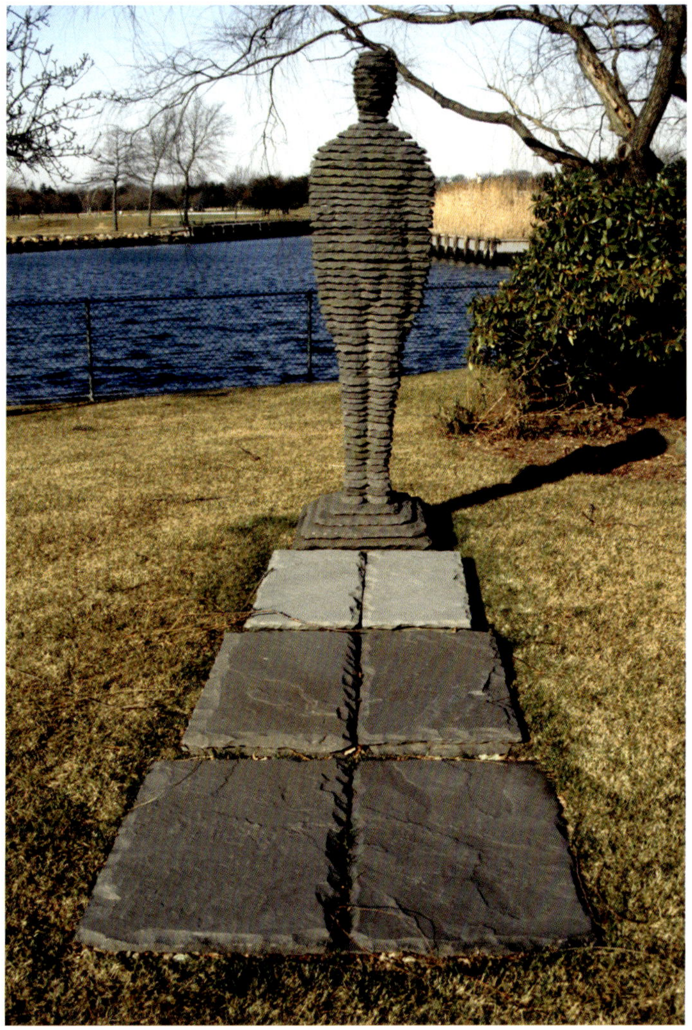

FIG.3. *Shemai'ah*, 1985.
Bluestone,
82 x 137 x 41 in. (208.5 x 348 x 104 cm).
Private collection, New York.

slate. Since gravity and the structure of stone are fatal for projecting limbs or precariously balanced masses, he would have to place his figures in compressed, stable poses. Finally, layers interfere with surface detail, and so his sculpture would represent not so much a person as "a person's shadow,"[12] the formal generalization of a human being. One of his artist friends, Gabi Benzano, wrote that Vaadia was creating a "symmetrical dialogue between the slices of stone and the image of man."[13]

Vaadia named his first figurative slate piece *Adam* (1985) after a guest who happened to be staying in his loft. *Shemai'ah* (fig. 3), the first life-size figure in bluestone, was named for another visitor. The titles were just a convenience, he claims—a way to distinguish one piece from another. The fact that they all came from the Old Testament was an accident: his visitors were usually Israelis, after all. However, "once someone pointed out the trend—I decided it was a good direction to go, so I now give Hebrew names to all my pieces.... I would finish a piece and name it after someone I knew, like a workman or a relative."[14]

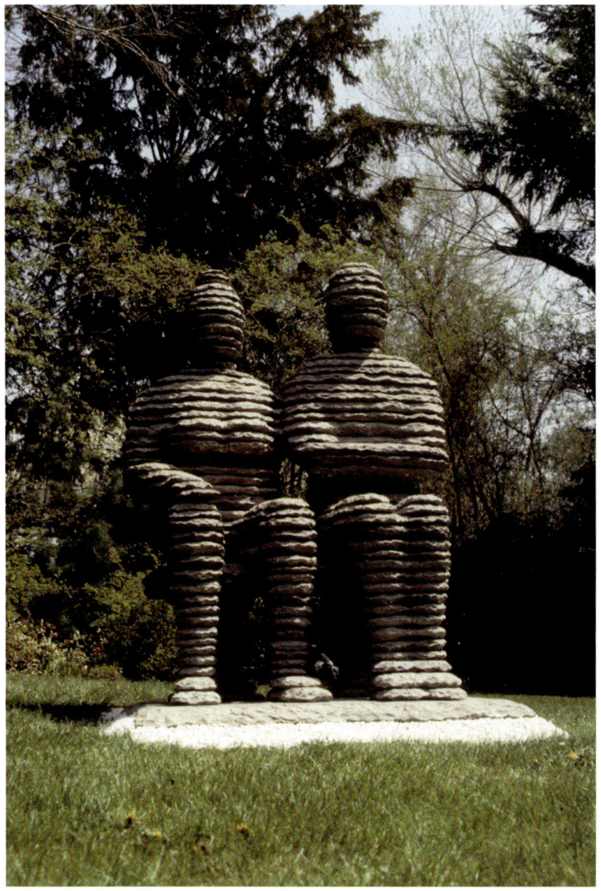

FIG.4. *Maakha and Rehavam*, 1988.
Bluestone,
66 x 47 x 45 in. (167.5 x 119.5 x 114.5 cm).
Private collection of Rebecca Vaadia and Sara Vaadia.

The bluestone *Shemai'ah* is a sturdy male with legs conjoined and arms flush with the sides of his body. There is a touch of Giacometti in *Shemai'ah*'s oversized feet, and indeed, Vaadia's figurative work makes many allusions to modernism. The figure in *Shemai'ah* stands at the end of a pavement of six slabs: *actual* paving stones that also *represent* paving stones. This is a common semiotic pun among modernists, as in Kazimir Malevich's 1915 painting, *Black Circle*, where the black circle, in being what it signifies, collapses reality and representation. Similarly, the wooden pedestals in Vaadia's slate sculptures echo Constantin Brâncusi's carved columns. They are sections of beams from demolished buildings that Vaadia salvaged from dumpsters, cleaned up, and finished by hand with beeswax.

In 1989, accident provided Vaadia with yet another material. He had just moved into a new studio in Williamsburg, where a sewer line was under construction on his block. Bulldozers were unearthing dozens of boulders deposited in Brooklyn during the last ice age. Vaadia found the granite monsters thrilling. "As a guy who was raised on a farm in Israel," he says, he responded strongly to their "primeval feel."[15] He was told he could have them for free; all he had to do was cart them away. Within hours he had acquired a forklift and was piling up boulders in his studio, although at this point he had no idea what he would do with them.

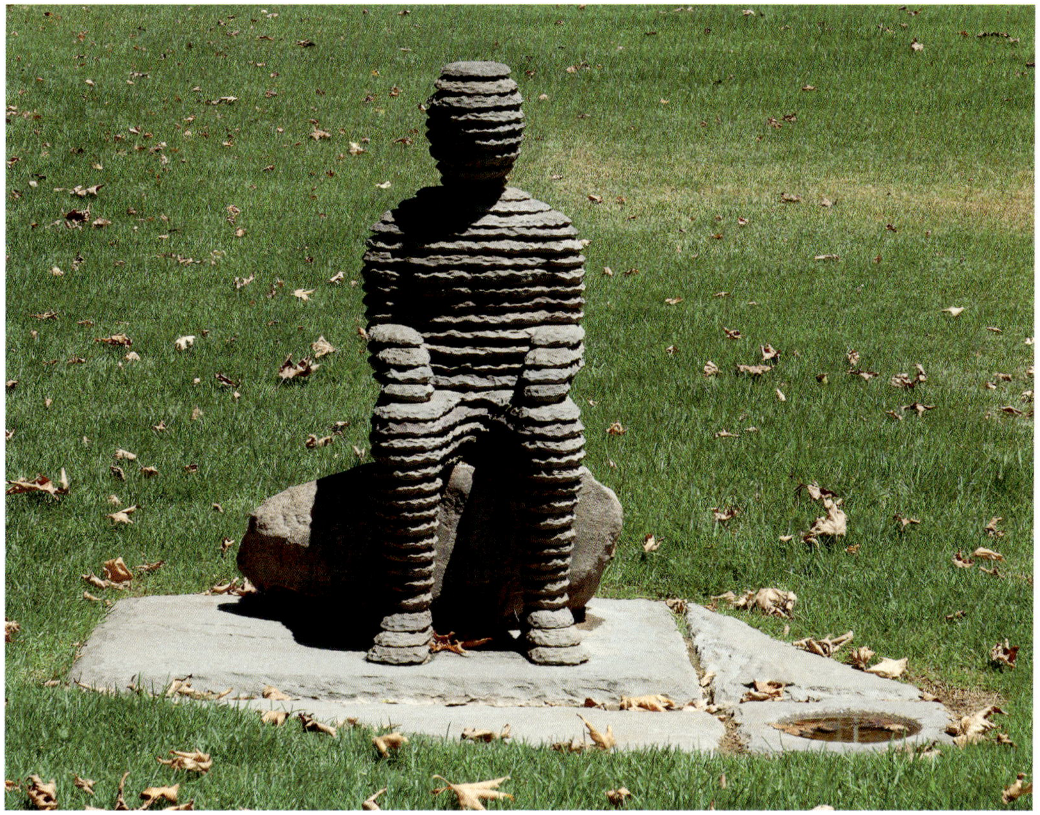

FIG 5. *Re'uven*, 1991.
Bluestone, boulder, and water,
46 x 64 x 52 in. (117 x 162.5 x 132 cm).
Collection of The Open Museum, Tefen, Israel.

The solution came, predictably, via accident. On a rainy day, Vaadia invited the sewer-line workmen inside the studio to eat their lunch. There were no chairs, and so they perched, leaned, and lounged against the boulders. Suddenly, Vaadia had a whole new repertoire of poses as well as a use for the boulders: they would serve as supports. In the past, when a pose had required a figure to be braced, as in *Maakha and Rehavam* (fig. 4), Vaadia created a bench, throne, or column made of the same stone layers as the figure. But from now on, the glaciers were the sculptors of his supports (with a little assistance from the artist). *Yoshiyyahu with Dog* (1989) was the first of many works, such as *Gilalay & Ginnetoy* (plate 85), in which the irregular shape of the igneous boulder contrasts with the orderly horizontal strata in the sedimentary bluestone of the figure.

By now, Vaadia was in his 40s, and the days of happy accidents would seem to have been over. To embark on a life-size figure—let alone a grouping of such figures—he had to plan the whole work in advance or risk wasting five tons of stone and many months of labor. But one day, as he was putting the finishing touches on *Re'uven* (fig. 5), a bird flew into the studio, and his sense of the sculpture changed completely. On the spot, he carved out a birdbath in the base, so that when *Re'uven* was installed outdoors, birds could continue to vary the composition. In a similar embrace of accident, Vaadia has been known to leave coins in a sculpture when they fall in, or drops of blood from a cut, a secret signature in DNA.

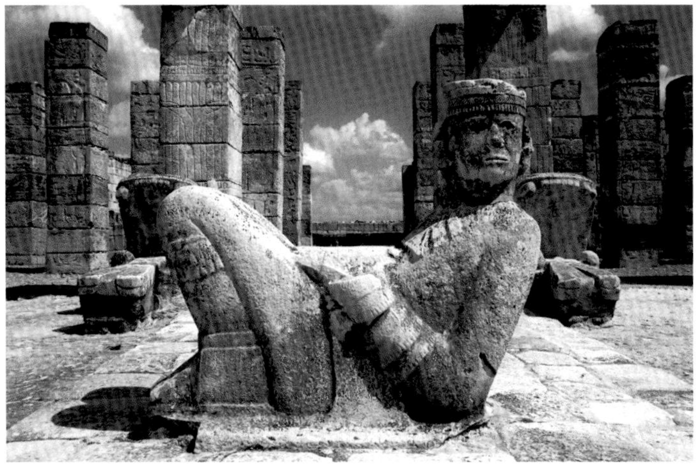

FIG.6. *Chac Mool*, c. 950–1539 CE. Stone, pre-Columbian Mesoamerican, post-classic Mayan civilization. Chichen Itza, Yucatan, Mexico. Image © Emilio Navarino.

These improvisations are minor, however, compared to the constraints he accepts from his medium. "I would never depict a ballerina," he says. "She wouldn't stand up."[16] "Degas's little dancer stands up," I object. Vaadia smiles: "You can do anything in bronze. One of my rules is that the stone figures must hold together solely by gravity—though I bolt them for safety." "But you could make a dancer who was crouching," I persist, "or a dancer taking a lunch break, like *Ahiam 2nd*." Obviously I am missing the point; it is not just stone that rules out ballerinas. They belong to a different aesthetic universe from Vaadia's, one where beauty exists in opposition to ordinary life. "I am in love with the everyday, the beauty of the everyday," he insists. His female figures, such as *Devora* (1986) or *Hulda* (plate 109), are attractive, but they do not spend their days in toe shoes. As Benzano has written, "Vaadia's sculptures remain simply human, democratic, secular, not pretentious and not elevating the person, [not] constructing classes."[17] Vaadia's figure groupings are domestic and often familial: parents with their children, owners with their dogs, couples together so long they do not look at each other anymore.

This insistence on the beauty of the ordinary relates to Vaadia's idea of honesty. It requires a surrender of the ego, he says, made not once but over and over again, since sculpture is a constant temptation to grandiosity. One must succumb instead to its limits. Vaadia's bluestone pieces are on a human scale, and his columns, as in *Shimshon and Delila* (plate 79), are simple Doric affairs rather than Corinthian extravaganzas. To resist the glamour of gleaming surfaces and reflections, he never polishes his sculpture. Not that he blames other artists seduced by polished stone—his revered Noguchi, for example—but it is an indulgence he does not permit himself. By effacing himself, Vaadia welcomes the viewer in. He cultivates what he calls a "precious commonality," which connects people; it cannot be forced or owned, but only honored.

Vaadia's sculpture is deeply grounded in humanism. At The Metropolitan Museum of Art, he points to an Egyptian statue of a kneeling slave, whose arms are bound behind his back. The compression of the pose has helped the sculpture survive intact for millennia, and for this reason Vaadia appropriated the pose for *Ma'aseyahu* (plate 110). However, his kneeling figure has his arms proudly crossed over his chest rather than tied behind him. The pose is as stable as the original, but the inhumanity of slavery has been excised.

This point returns us to *Ahiam 2nd*. Like *Ma'aseyahu*, *Ahiam 2nd*'s pose has an ancient prototype: the chac mool (fig. 6), a reclining figure found near Toltec, Mayan, and Aztec tombs throughout Central America. Vessels for human sacrifice were placed on their torsos, and Vaadia sees them as figures of surrender, exposing their hearts to the cruel appetites of the gods. The compactness of the pose preserved these works from damage, but Vaadia has devised a kinder fate for his chac mool. *Ahiam 2nd*'s head does not swivel round in terror at his approaching executioner, but gazes off into the distance in calm repose.

This air of repose is what initially struck me when I came across *Ovadyahu* in 2008 in the window of the Connaught Brown gallery in London (a pose repeated in *Ah'av and Ovadyahu* (plate 103). It was as if one of Georges Seurat's conté crayon drawings had morphed into three dimensions (fig. 7).[18] Seurat's figures, relaxing in a natural setting, are unself-consciously lost in thought. They are ordinary people in ordinary circumstances, but have a simplicity and inwardness that makes them seem archetypal.

In his study of eighteenth-century French domestic painting, the art historian Michael Fried terms such poses "absorption."[19] The figures appear unaware of anyone's presence—whether inside the virtual space of the painting or outside in the real world of the viewer.

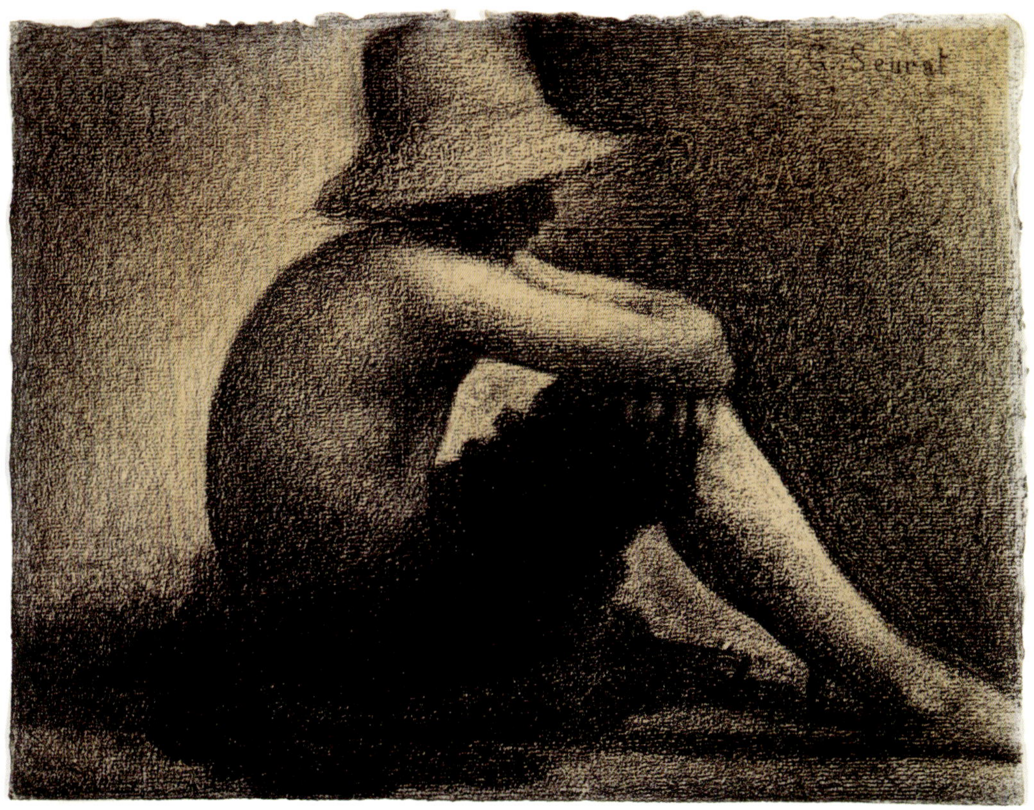

FIG. 7. Georges Seurat, *Seated Boy with Straw Hat*, 1883 (study for *Bathers at Asnieres*, 1883).
Black conté crayon on Michallet paper, 9½ x 12¼ in. (24.1 x 31.1 cm).
Yale University Art Gallery, Everett V. Meeks, B.A. 1901, Fund. Image © Yale University Art Gallery, New Haven, CT.

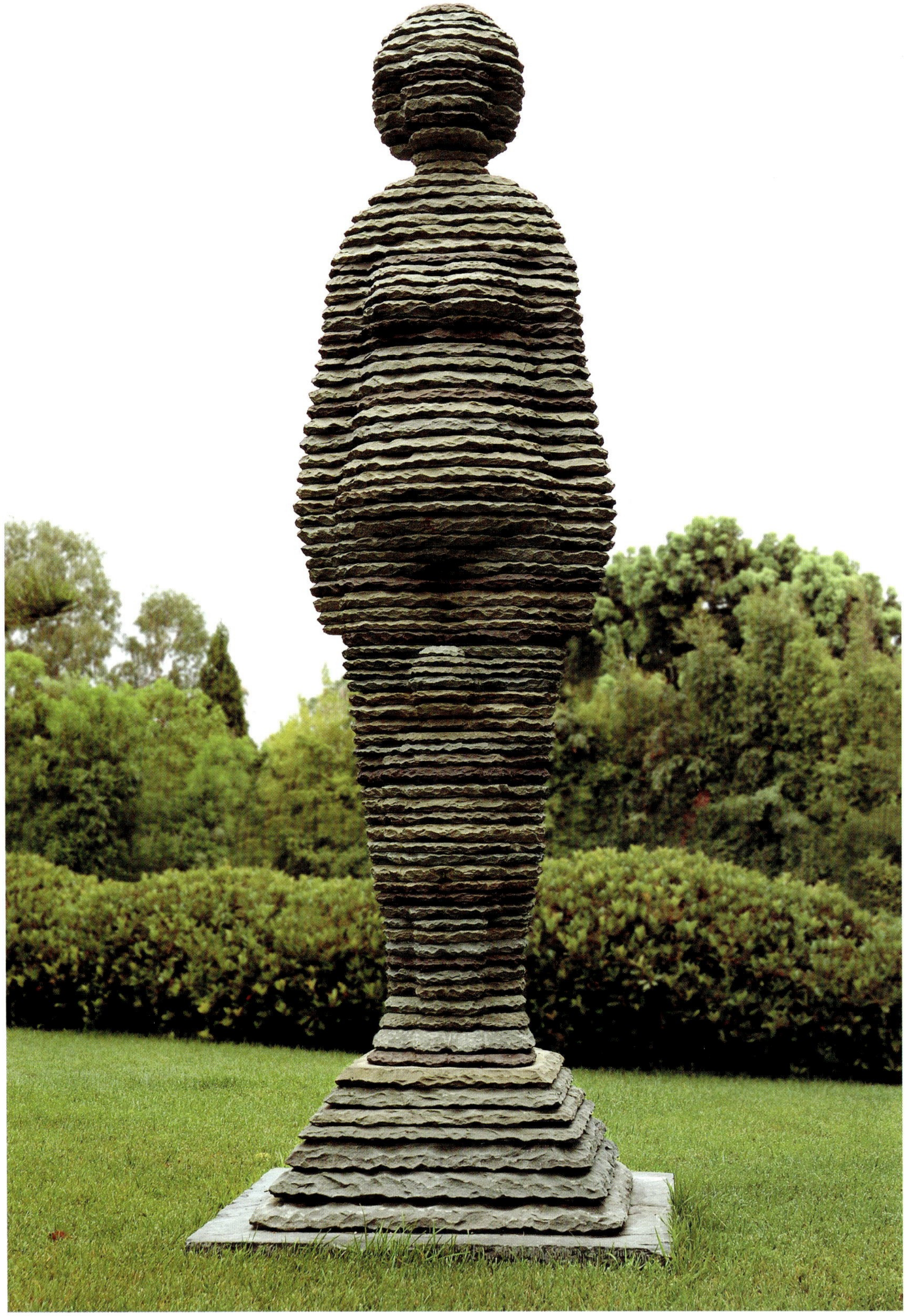

FIG. 8. *Rahel and Binyamin*, 1987.
Bluestone,
118 x 35 x 35 in. (300 x 89 x 89 cm).
Private collection, California.

For this reason, absorptive figures often represent moods or states of mind. Fried contrasts absorption with "theatricality," in which figures do just the opposite, indicating through their expression, pose, and orientation vis-à-vis the viewer that they are aware of being seen and are directing their attention toward others.

Seurat and Vaadia render both sorts of poses, but the social and formal abstraction of the absorptive figures draws special attention to the media of their arts. Stephen Sondheim registers this fact in "Sunday in the Park with George," a song about the Seurat painting, *A Sunday Afternoon on the Island of La Grande Jatte*: "On the green orange violet mass of the grass/ in our perfect park/ made of flecks of light/ and dark/ and parasols/ People strolling through the trees/…on an ordinary Sunday."[20] We might picture the descendants of these figures strolling, absorbed, through Grounds For Sculpture.

However, inward as Vaadia's figures may be, unlike Seurat's they are charged with muscular energy. In *Yizhaq & Eli'av* (plate 101), Yizhaq seems not so much resting his foot on a boulder as pressing it into the stone. His forearms, bound together as if in a straitjacket, are about to burst apart, and just as actively, they cage his chest inside their powerful grasp. The children in *Milka & Tirza* (plate 81) stand at attention like pint-size yogis straining in mountain pose. Such figures are not caught up in the drama of events, but in the drama of what could be called "life force."

It is interesting to compare them to *The Left Pillar in the Porch of the Temple*, where poles and cables keep the pitched diagonal slab from falling. April Kingsley, writing in 1979, compared this work to the Brooklyn Bridge, quoting its designer, John A. Roebling: "A force at rest is at rest because it is balanced by some other force or by its own reaction." This definition, Kingsley says, "condense[s] much of what Boaz Vaadia's structures are about…interactive tension and counterbalanced forces at rest. The very simplicity of the work's conception is what makes it seem spiritual."[21]

With Vaadia's later, figurative work, massive forces are certainly in play, most notably gravity. But although the poses sometimes seem tense with energy, the stone itself is "at rest." This stability is one of Vaadia's rules. For example, the point of contact between figures in a grouping or between a single figure and its support would normally be a site of counterposed forces. But Vaadia renders these contact points in a single slab of stone that runs through both figure and support, or through contiguous figures, as in *Milka & Tirza*. Vaadia's figures may represent opposed masses, but in the reality of the stone, no separate masses meet. Instead, we have the stability and stillness of continuous stone.

This bond across compositional elements is often expressively charged. *Rahel and Binyamin* (fig. 8, whose bronze study, *Hanna & Shemu'el*, plate 77, appears in the exhibition) shows a small child braced against his mother's legs. The common layers running through them at their points of contact convey the notion of security at many levels. In contrast, the figure in *Solomon* (plate 76) seems almost imprisoned in his throne, with so many layers running through it and his body. The zigzag shape, oversized feet, and elongation of the figure give it the gauntness of a Giacometti, and the open spacing of the layers compounds the air of psychic tension and agitation.

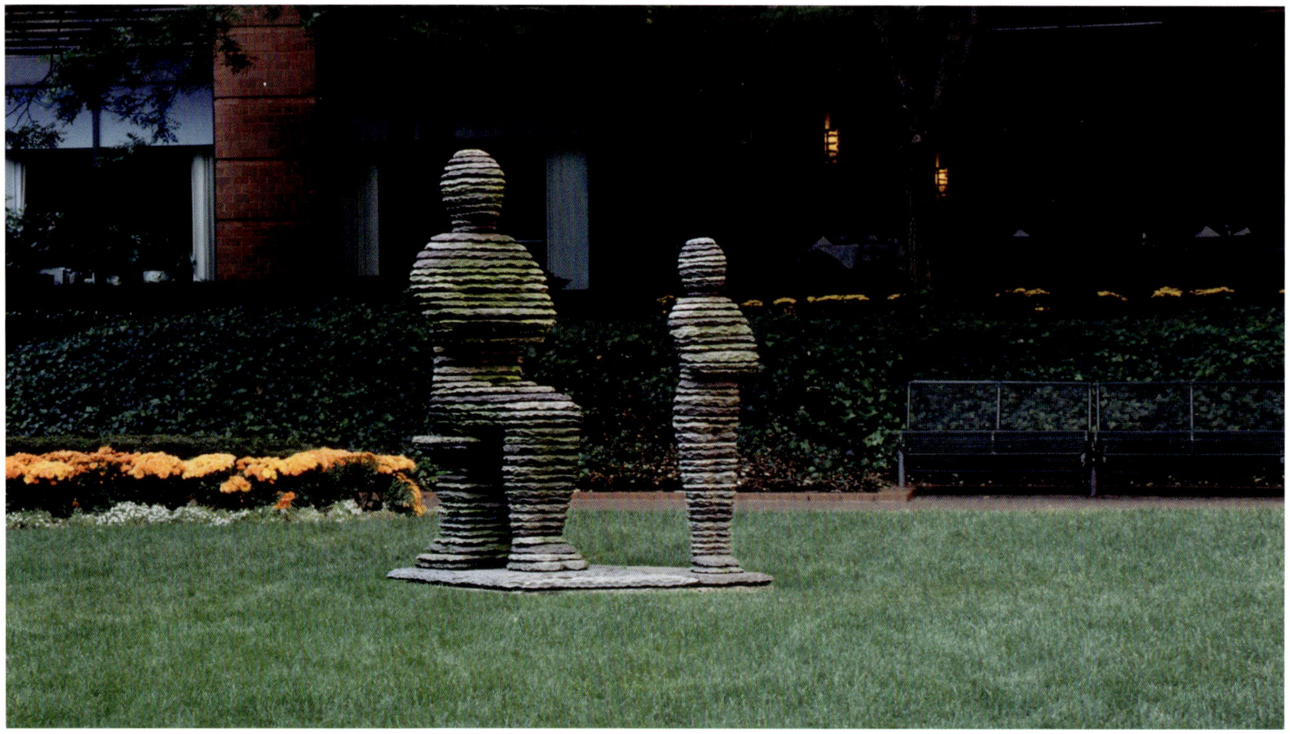

But as energetic as Vaadia's figures may be, such agitation is rare, even in group sculptures. His figures are nude, but they do not relate to each other passionately or evoke a sexual response in the viewer. Ultimately, they look like what they are: statuary. Still, that need not imply emotional disconnection. The boy in *Omri and Ah'av* (fig. 9) is echoing his father's proud pose, and we imagine the pleasure the father must be taking in his son's emulation. In contrast, in *Yokheved & Amram* (plate 105), the held-in strength and symmetry of the male figure speaks volumes next to the casually splayed legs of the plump female beside him; we cannot help but wonder how they feel about each other. With *Shimshon and Delila* (plate 79), separated by a column and facing in opposite directions, the relationship seems all too clear.

Figure groupings permit Vaadia to operate with larger scale and compositional complexity than do single figures. *Hanokh* (2011) and *Hattush* (2011), for example, identical except for their left-right inversion, function together as guardians; when they appear at the edges of a group, their mirror symmetry creates the formal enclosure of bookends.[22] Sometimes Vaadia uses bronze castings to experiment with combinations of figures, as in *Ammi'el & Amaryahu* (plate 86).[23] In *Avimelekh with Dog and 8 Lambs* (plate 83), the multiple lambs are hand-sculpted in stone, and *Avram with Dog and 10 Lambs* (fig. 10) goes further still. When the shepherd and his flock are sited out of doors, the entire landscape becomes Vaadia's composition.

In parks and gardens, Vaadia's stone sculptures seem to have come home. Rain deepens the variegated colors of the bluestone, and the seasons alter the light and vegetation that surround them, so that the sculptures seem to be constantly changing. Urban settings can be just

FIG. 9. *Omri and Ah'av*, 1987.
Bluestone,
74½ x 55 x 43 in. (189.5 x 139 x 109 cm).
Private collection, Florida. Photographed in Carnegie Park, New York, NY.

OPPOSITE

FIG. 10. *Avram with Dog and 10 Lambs*, 1992.
Bluestone and boulder,
7 x 46 x 13 ft. (2.13 x 14.02 x 3.96 m).
Private collection, New York.

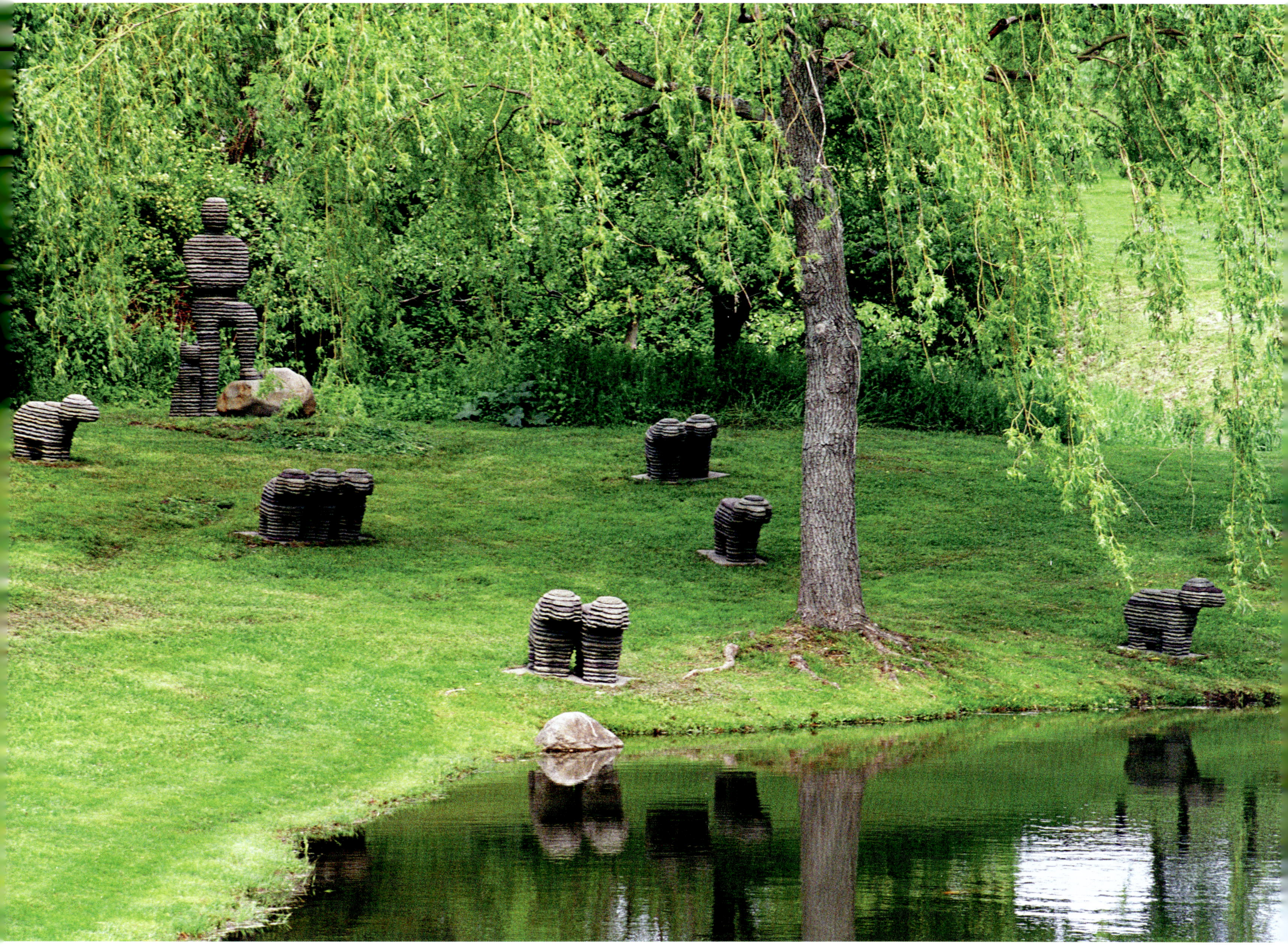

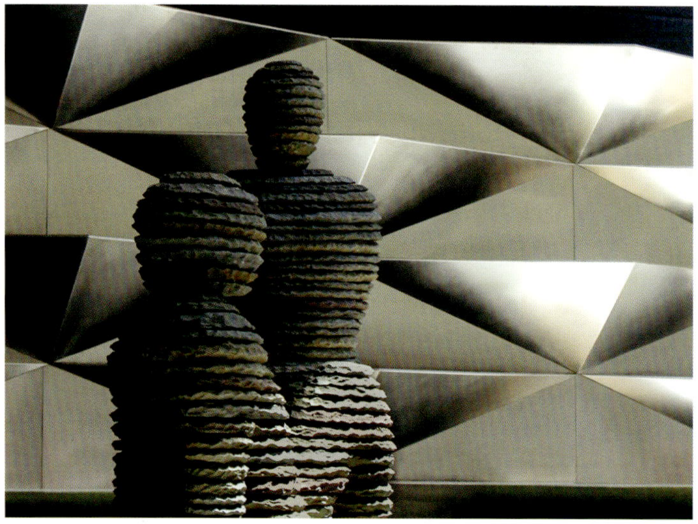

FIG. 11. Detail of *Asaf and Yo'ah*, 2001.
Bluestone and boulder,
78 x 110 x 80 in. (198.1 x 279.4 x 203.2 cm).
Private collection.
Permanent installation, Time Warner Center, South Tower, New York, NY.

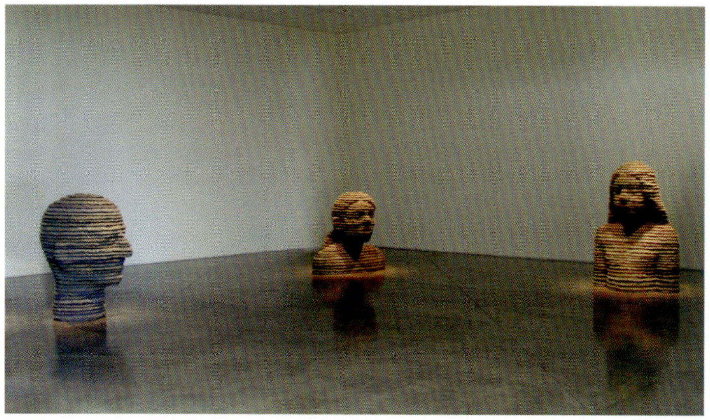

FIG. 12. Installation at Imago Galleries, Palm Desert, CA, 2003.

as powerful. The columnar limbs and right angles of *Asaf and Yo'ah* (fig. 11 and pages 2-3) echo the structural uprights and crossbeams of the Time Warner Building at their back; from the side, the figures look like space aliens basking in the sun against the abstract pattern in the building's metal cladding. (A bronze of this subject appears in the current exhibition, plate 92). Indoor settings can also affect the meaning of Vaadia's figures. The high polish on the floor of Imago Galleries made his portrait busts look like bathers immersed up to their chests in water (fig. 12); Grounds For Sculpture creates a similar effect with the portrait bust *ZAMIR* (plate 92).

Portraits were a new departure for Vaadia in 2002, after nearly two decades of faceless figures. The genre had always appealed to him, he says, and he was good at it: after art school, he had been offered a job in a wax museum. He had avoided portraiture because of his layering technique, which is not suited to the rendering of facial detail. But he knew that the tilt of a person's head, back, or shoulders could be just as distinctive an identifier, and between 2002 and 2004 he tested out these possibilities in a series of busts of family members, friends, and passersby. Among them is the self-portrait *Boaz* (plate 93), complete with striated slate glasses—quite a departure from *The Left Pillar in the Porch of the Temple*.

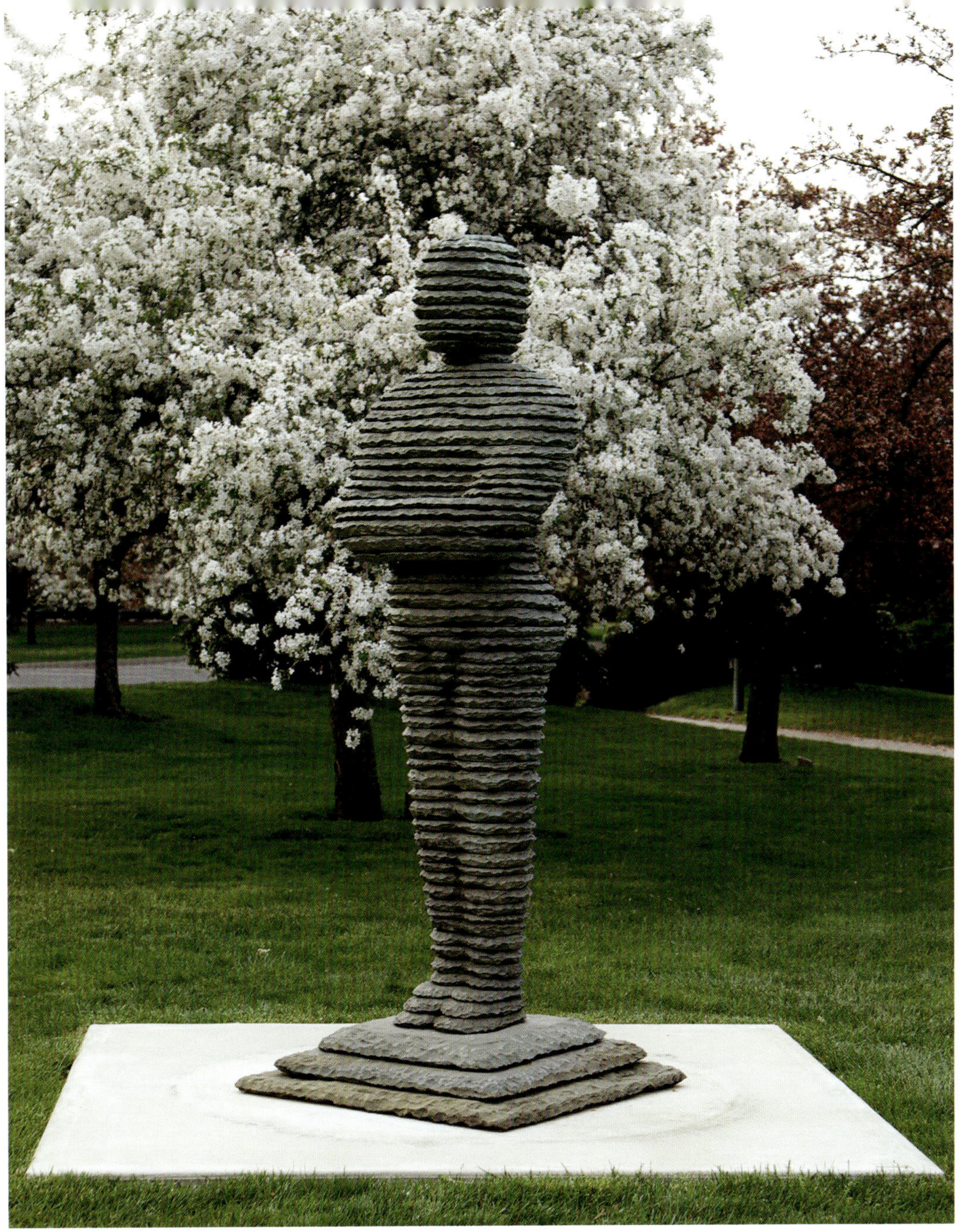

FIG. 13. *David*, 2010.
Bronze and bluestone,
91 x 36 x 36 in. (231.1 x 91.4 x 91.4 cm).
Edition of 5.

In 2004, an accident in the boulder yard put a temporary halt to Vaadia's art making, and when he was able to return to the studio, he went back to his anonymous figures. By adjusting the fit between slabs and applying glue in invisible patches, he found he could create an impression of surprising delicacy and lightness in the tons of stone. The minutest graduation of thickness in a layer would produce a subtle tilt or twist in a figure's orientation. By controlling these deviations from the vertical for emotive effect, Vaadia could suggest affects such as weariness, dependence, or love. Similarly, the angle of his chipping on the edges of each layer could affect the curvature of a back, buttock, or breast, in turn conveying differences in age and attitude. The formal elegance of this mature work is remarkable, as we see in *David* (fig. 13).

Vaadia is proud of his virtuosity with the chisel and savors his interaction with stone. This is a good thing. As his commissions began piling up in the 1980s, he had tried hiring assistants,

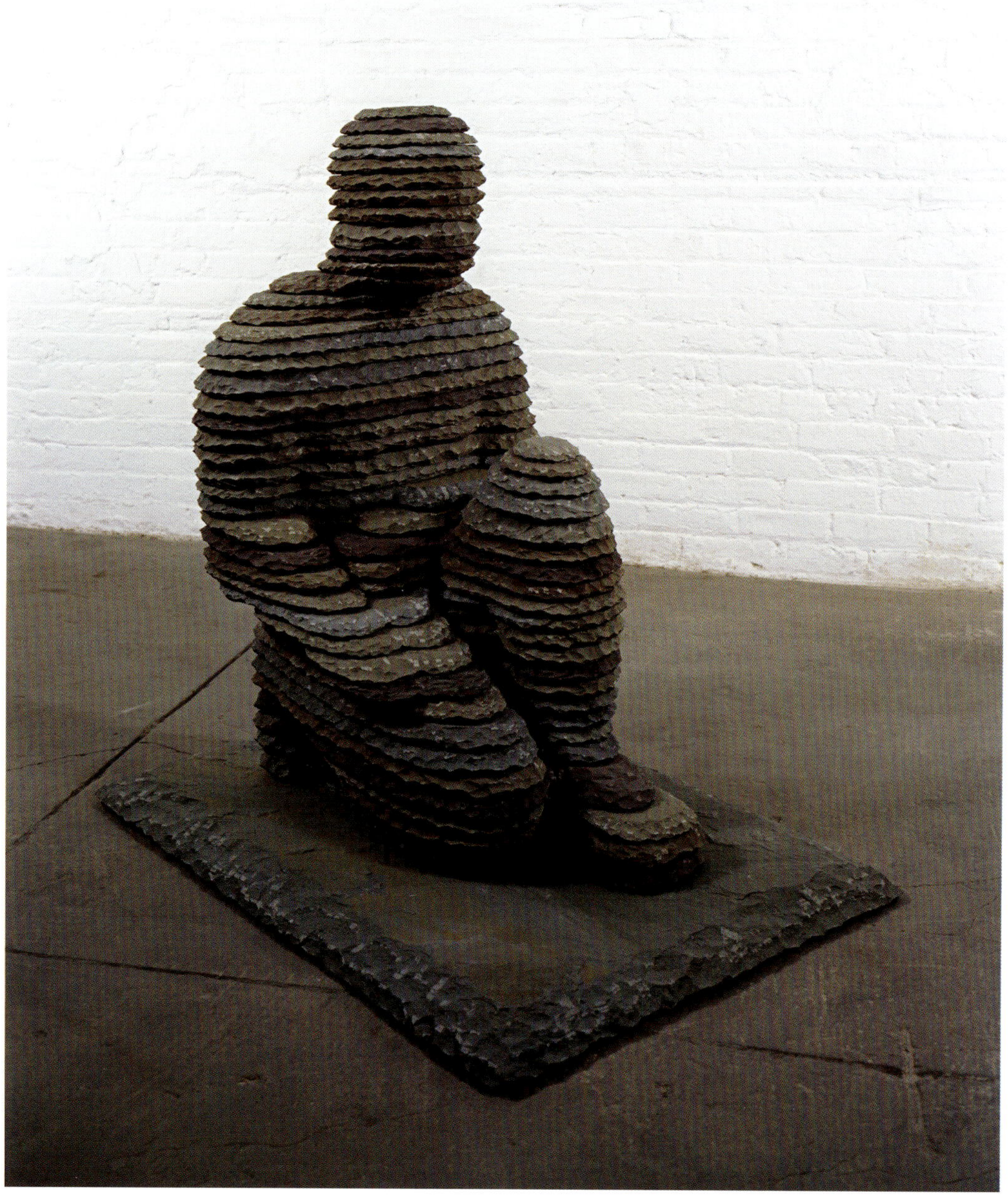

FIG. 14. *Haza'el*, 2010.
Bluestone,
43 x 41 x 29 in. (109 x 104 x 73.5 cm).
Private collection, Long Island, NY.

but even the experienced stone carvers who applied for the job were unable to master his method. He still works each stone layer himself, employing a studio assistant to help with heavy machinery, final assemblage, and correspondence.

In the painstaking ritual and repetition of Vaadia's practice, it takes at least a day to hand-sculpt a single layer. It is a cross section of a figure, an abstract cut, like a transverse slice in a CAT scan. Vaadia treats it as a sculpture in its own right. He is the only one who sees it from every side, and only he understands the complex interplay of horizontality and verticality in

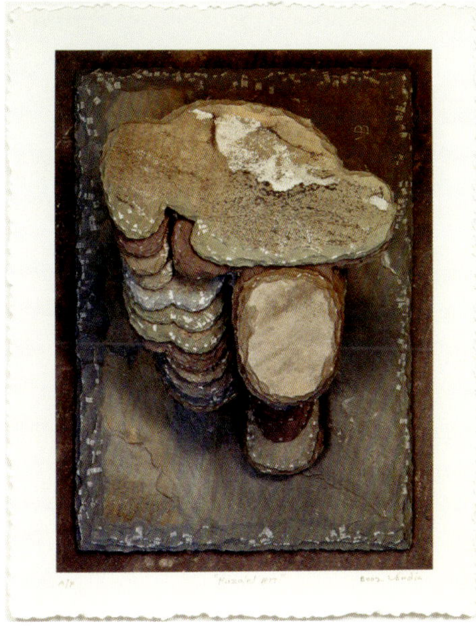

FIG. 15. *Haza'el #17*, 2011.
Archival pigment print on paper,
15¾ x 12 in. (40 x 30.5 cm).
Edition of 9.

which it participates. When Vaadia observes, "No one can see my sculptures the way I do," he is speaking literally, and it concerns him that there is a discrepancy between what he can see and what his viewers see.[24] A standing joke with his dealers is that clients should receive his layers in a box marked "Assembly Required."

In an attempt to provide access to more of what he sees, Vaadia has made a time-lapse video of the assembly of *David*, condensing three weeks of work into three minutes. The video shows Vaadia dressed in coveralls rushing up and down scaffolding to add each layer, drilling through the assembled stack with a gigantic bit, then disassembling the layers, screwing a supporting rod into the base, applying glue to each bluestone layer, and reassembling the layers on the rod. At the end, the artist poses proudly beside the finished product. The pace of the video is cartoonish considering the painstaking process it documents. Viewers gain access to *David* inside and out, but they do not experience its slow growth. As Vaadia says, "Every work is a time lock."[25]

In the process of making *David*, Vaadia photographed each layer as an independent image and had the sequence bound as a book. Then, struck by the multiplicity of artworks within each of his sculptures, in 2011 he developed a new way to make them visible to the viewer. Using his forklift as a camera tripod the year before, he had shot down onto *Haza'el* (fig. 14) after adding each successive layer. The result was forty-two seemingly abstract images, beginning with the bluestone base and ending with the capstone of the head. The base served as the textured background for the accumulating layers, and the shadows deepened as the strata rose, changing the colors of the stone with each shot, as in *Haza'el #17* (fig. 15). Vaadia experimented with the images in 2011 and finally decided they should be hung vertically on a wall, even though they represented downward views. Here, the conventions of photography intervened in the already complicated vertical–horizontal interplay that defines his art.

In this spirit of experiment three years later, Vaadia acted on his longtime desire to make a bas-relief. The great advantage of this form is that it permits poses that in a freestanding sculpture would have fragile, protruding, or unstable elements—"ballerinas," in Vaadia's parlance. A typical relief artist chips, carves, or drills into a solid surface, such as a wall, door, or column, creating negative space around figures that only partially project from the background. They are like Michelangelo's "unfinished" Slave sculptures—much admired by Vaadia—in which the figures writhe as if desperate to break free of their marble background.

Vaadia's reliefs create an utterly different dynamic between figure and ground. Respectful of the limits imposed by slate, he makes each horizontal layer at once background and figure. With a computer he calculates the number of layers required to build the design, but still carves each layer by hand. "It took a while for the reliefs to go to a new place," he explains. "To be in a place like this at my age is great."[26]

The first two in the series, *Family of Four* (Relief) (plate 114) and *Man* (Relief) (plate 115), are based on compositions Vaadia had previously created for sculptures in the round. The arms tightly crossed over the chest in *Man*, for example, form one of his typical, compressed poses in which there are no projecting parts for gravity or weathering to destroy. But this precaution is unnecessary in a relief. With *Mother and 2 Children* (Column Relief) (plate 116), Vaadia took fuller advantage of the new form, curving the figure grouping over the front half of the column to allow viewing from 180 degrees. The mother's delicate arms project outward and back around the column, coming to rest on the heads of the children. Gravity would not have permitted this pose to be rendered in layers in a freestanding sculpture without the use of supports, but here the arms are not a problem. The three figures describe a decorative rhythm over the rounded surface, and their feet melt into the base or "foot" of the column in a visual pun merging figure and architectural ground: the definition of a bas-relief.

The fourth, *Horse* (Relief) (plate 117), shows Vaadia's growing understanding of the possibilities of the bas-relief. We need only compare this work to the freestanding *Grazing Horse* (plate 113) to see the greater delicacy the relief makes possible—though to judge by the horse's pasterns, it would be more at home on a farm than a racetrack. Vaadia would have it no other way. Although the horse's flanks and legs swell voluptuously from their background, the belly is just barely visible, as if it had been worn away by wind and rain over long millennia. Color variations in the slate produce an occasional horizontal stripe, like a vein of stone exposed by weathering. This simple, slightly "blurred" image has an archaic quality, the "barely thereness" of an ancient fossil or a cave drawing. With this work, Vaadia has created yet another site of reverence and wonder.

Barbara Pollack, an arts writer and critic, has written that Vaadia's "sophisticated workmanship forms a bridge from the Stone Age to the digital age."[27] Under the circumstances, his place in the history of art is not easy to specify. His sculpture has been compared to Easter Island moai, Egyptian sphinxes and mummies, African fetishes, Babylonian god-kings and reliefs, and Mesoamerican chac mools. But it would be wrong to think of him as a Neo-Primitive, since Michelangelo, Rodin, Duchamp, Oppenheim, Arte Povera, Giacometti, and Noguchi are

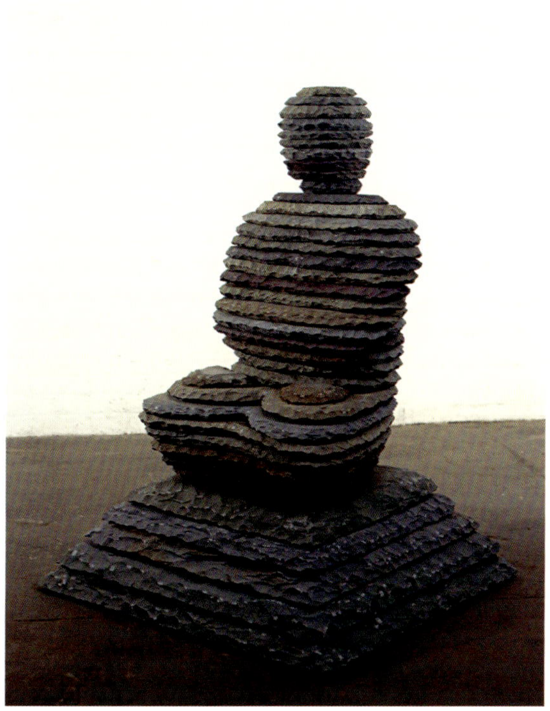

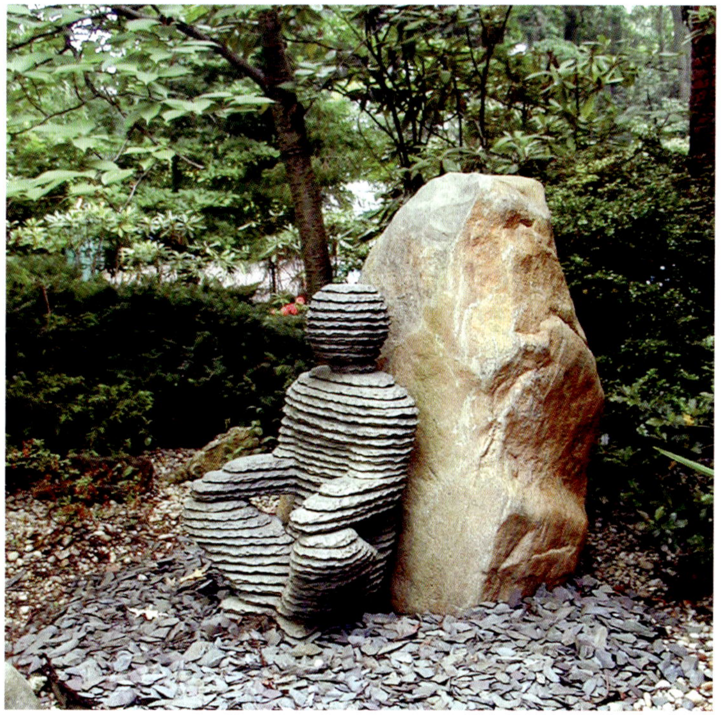

equally discernable in his work. Among his contemporaries, the Ghanaian-Nigerian artist, El Anatsui, is an unexpected kindred spirit. Anatsui's Klimt-like "tapestries" look completely at home beside traditional African weavings—despite the fact that they are made of bottle caps, foil wrappers, and garbage ties. Anatsui and Vaadia achieve this bond between ancient and contemporary sculpture by recycling discarded materials into awe-inspiring works of art.

Asked about his affinities to living artists, Vaadia mentions abstracted figural works of Antony Gormley, such as *Fuse* (2011), with their compact poses and careful workmanship, but he feels no connection to the intellectual theories that drive Gormley's practice. Andy Goldsworthy's rock walls winding through landscapes speak to Vaadia's love of nature and stone, but they are not figurative. Vaadia greatly admires Richard Serra, who "knows what he's doing and does it with great commitment."[28] Still, Serra's huge tilted planes and curves dwarf the viewer, a departure from human scale that Vaadia's principles rule out.

Touching on so many moments in the history of sculpture, Vaadia's pieces have a timeless air. They suggest ancient spiritual practices such as yoga.[29] Vaadia admits that "a lot of my pieces take meditative poses.... Buddha shapes are usually balanced in posture, so I can do the total shape with layers."[30] A Jain figure in lotus position at The Met was the model for *Ba'al-zevuv* (fig. 16) and *Eli'ezer* (fig. 17). Anyone who has sat long in such a pose knows the concentration required to maintain its symmetry, erectness, and equanimity. Peace comes only through sustained attentiveness to the weight of gravity on the body, and of inertia on the mind. When Vaadia praises the Jain pose, he is speaking of its composure as much as its composition.

FIG. 16. *Ba'al-zevuv*, 1999.
Bluestone,
50 x 35½ x 35½ in. (127 x 90.1 x 90.1 cm).
Private collection, Florida.

FIG. 17. *Eli'ezer*, 1999.
Bronze, boulder, and bluestone,
55 x 66 x 66 in. (139.7 x 167.6 x 167.6 cm).
Edition of 5. Private collection of Rebecca Vaadia and Sara Vaadia.

Sitting in the Chinese garden at The Met, Vaadia watches the sunshine streaming through the skylight onto a pool of water, and the luxuriant plants twining among the gnarled scholars' rocks. "I enjoy the energy of this place," he says. "I come here often." He describes himself in terms of the same energy and calm. In the international recognition his art has received, he continues working at the edge, discovering new possibilities in the constantly shifting grounds of his sculpture. Repose for Vaadia is a charged state, something a yogi might describe as full presence in the moment. His figures manifest this presence, and the honesty of his art making honors it.

NOTES

1. Jan Garden Castro, "Balancing Families in Stone: A Conversation with Boaz Vaadia," *Sculpture Magazine*, June 2008, 55.

2. Ibid.

3. From the author's 2016 interview with Vaadia.

4. Ibid.

5. Vaadia's struggles with the written word have given him enormous patience with certain secretarial tasks. Since the age of 18, he has meticulously documented and photographed every work he has made, accumulating hundreds upon hundreds of records that he has filed, boxed, and preserved in his various moves from the farm in Israel to his different apartments in New York City. He describes making art, too, as equal parts obsession and commitment.

6. Richard Friswell, "A Conversation with Boaz Vaadia," *Art of Leadership Series: The Magazine*, November 22, 2010, 8.

7. *Other Gods: Containers of Belief*, Fondo del Sol Arts Center et al, Washington, DC, June, 1986.

8. Julia Keydel, "Boaz Vaadia," in *Boaz Vaadia: Five Years* (New York: Elise Meyer, Inc., 1979); first published in *ARTS Magazine*, November 1979.

9. Grant Moser, "Boaz Vaadia, Sculptor of Coincidence," *11211 Magazine*, May / June 2003, n.p.

10. Friswell, "A Conversation with Boaz Vaadia," 6.

11. Dana Micucci, "Force of Nature," *Art & Antiques Magazine*, April 2008, 50.

12. From the author's 2011 conversation with the artist.

13. Gabi Benzano, *Boaz Vaadia—Outdoor Sculptures* (Raanana, Israel: The Studio Gallery, College of Art Studies, 2001), 34.

14. Friswell, "A Conversation with Boaz Vaadia," 7.

15. Ibid, 6.

16. From the author's 2011 conversation with the artist.

17. Benzano, *Boaz Vaadia—Outdoor Sculptures*, 35.

18. Benzano makes the same association: "The image is always presented in a positive comfortable position expressing presence, stability and tranquility. The work does not pretend to immortalize the struggle between individuals or any other struggle, with each image capturing its own physical space, neither threatening nor overpowering—like the presence of people in a park. Very similar to the images painted by George[s] Seurat, the images are very general and physical—as if the sculptures were aware of their eternal stone structure." *Boaz Vaadia—Outdoor Sculptures*, 34.

19. Michael Fried, *Absorption and Theatricality: Painting and Beholder in the Age of Diderot* (Berkeley: University of California Press, 1980).

20. Stephen Sondheim's lyrics from the song "Sunday in the Park with George," from the musical *Sunday in the Park with George*, 1984: http://lyrics.astraweb.com/display/882/sunday_in_the_park_with_george..musical_ost..sunday_finale.html, accessed June 6, 2016.

21. Kingsley, *Boaz Vaadia: Five Years* (New York, 1979), n.p.

22. In this spirit, the Connaught Brown gallery used *Hanokh* and *Hattush* for the front and back covers of its catalogue for Vaadia's fall 2011 exhibition, *Boaz Vaadia*.

23. Vaadia makes a practice of casting all his work in limited bronze editions: five bronzes for life-size figures and seven for pedestal-size works. The bronzes permit simultaneous exhibitions of his work in different galleries, satisfy the heavy demand among his institutional and individual collectors, and allow him to retain a copy of each work for archival purposes.

24. From the author's 2011 interview with the artist.

25. Ibid.

26. From the author's 2016 interview with the artist.

27. Barbara Pollack, "Boaz Vaadia," *ARTnews*, September 2003, 138.

28. From the author's 2011 interview with the artist.

29. Michael Kimmelman notes the longstanding prejudice against sculpture as an art because of its basis in cult and ritual: "Sculpture…is too literal, too direct, too steeped in religious ceremony and too complex for a historically amnesiac culture," he reports (although he says he does not share this view), "In Art World, Has Sculpture Become Just Another Pretty Face?" *New York Times*, August 10, 2011, C5. Vaadia not only ignores this prejudice, but cultivates the primordial associations of his art.

30. Castro, "Balancing Families in Stone: A Conversation with Boaz Vaadia," 55.

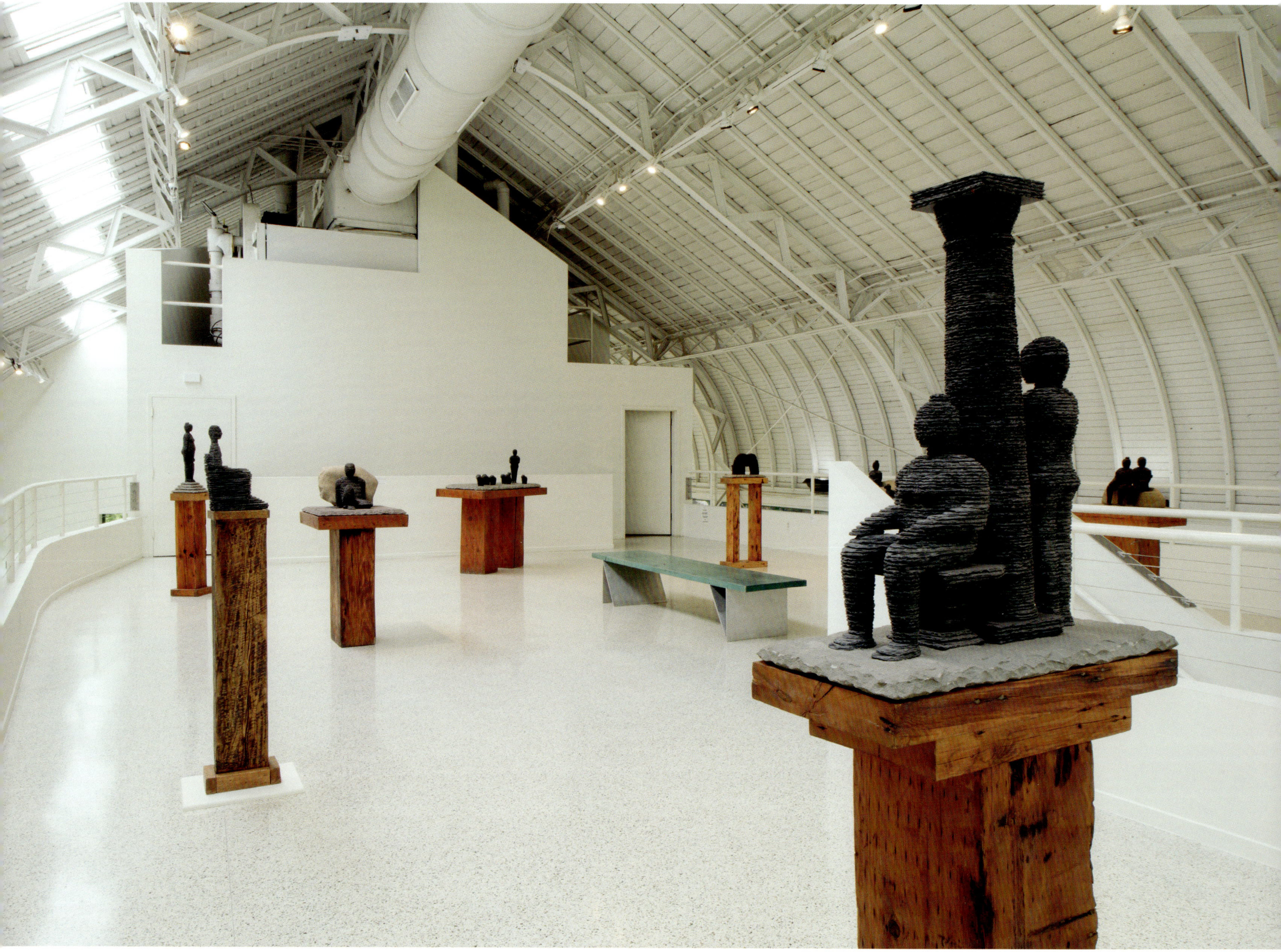

Boaz Vaadia: Sculpture

Director's Acknowledgments

THIS VOLUME IS PUBLISHED on the occasion of the exhibition, *Boaz Vaadia: Sculpture*, an ambitious presentation, spread throughout the 42-acre campus of Grounds For Sculpture. Vaadia's work is displayed in two indoor galleries as well as the outdoor sculpture garden, and also includes featured placement in the community. This exhibition provides the unique opportunity to experience an in-depth look at the signature body of work by Israeli-born, New York artist Boaz Vaadia, which comprises the majority of the work in this exhibition. These works feature Vaadia's exploration of figurative compositions created by stacking layers of bluestone or slate, with some of these works later cast in bronze. Although this exhibition is not organized as a comprehensive retrospective, it contains an entire gallery of Vaadia's rarely seen early sculptures. These early works display Vaadia's interest in the effects of gravity and the inherent qualities of material, all of which continue to inform and influence his later work. The exhibition and publication allow us to follow his artistic evolution and see the threads that carry forth.

We are pleased to acknowledge Quaker Bridge Mall, A Simon Mall, as the presenting sponsor of this exhibition and catalogue. We wish to thank Lynda Benedetto, Christopher Dudley, and the entire Quaker Bridge Mall team for their vision, dedication, and support of the arts in our community. Their support has enabled Grounds For Sculpture to host and present this ambitious exhibition. Their generous contributions have also allowed us to share this important work with our community in a very intimate manner. With their support, we have been given the opportunity to place a series of sculptures in the community as part of our Sculpture Along the Way program.

This exhibition and catalogue have been generously supported by The Office of The Consulate General of Israel in New York. I want to give special thanks to Consul General Ido Aharoni, Consul for Cultural Affairs in North America; Aviad Ivri, The Cultural Attaché; as well as Eran Polishuk, Vick Giasov, Renee Schreiber, and Tal Shoham of the Consulate for their assistance in connecting Grounds For Sculpture with the Israeli arts and cultural community.

Installation at Upper Gallery,
Museum Building,
Grounds For Sculpture,
Hamilton, NJ, 2016.

I would also like to recognize and thank the New Jersey State Council on the Arts, the New Jersey Department of State, the National Endowment for the Arts, the Geraldine R. Dodge Foundation, the Atlantic Foundation, and the Johnson Art and Education Foundation for their generous support of all of our exhibitions.

Throughout his career, Vaadia has had the benefit of working with a number of supportive art dealers including Ivan C. Karp at OK Harris early on, during an influential time in his career. It is important to acknowledge that galleries help to build a base of support as well as a trusted space for artists to focus on their creative practice. For this reason, we are pleased to acknowledge all of the galleries that show his work and Baker Sponder Gallery, Imago Galleries, Jim Kempner Fine Art, and Vered Gallery for their ongoing commitment to Boaz Vaadia and for their generous support of this catalogue.

Without the guidance, expertise, and collaborative partnership of The Artist Book Foundation, this catalogue would not be possible. We graciously thank Leslie Pell, publisher and co-founder, for her enthusiasm and steadfast guidance that has resulted in this important publication. Our team at Grounds For Sculpture has greatly benefited from the opportunity to work with such a well-regarded and accomplished publisher on this project. In addition we are grateful for the expertise of Wendy Steiner, author of the essay on Boaz Vaadia's work featured in this catalogue.

Executing exhibitions of this scale could not be possible without the dedication and close collaboration of the entire staff at Grounds For Sculpture. Our staff has exemplified great leadership and stewardship in shaping this project from an idea to realization. I want to give great thanks to Tom Moran, chief curator, for his intelligent and sensitive curatorial process that always elevates the artist's voice. I want to thank our exhibition team, ably led by Faith McClellan, director of collections & exhibitions management, for the meticulous attention to detail given to this project to actualize the vision for this exhibition on both Grounds For Sculpture's campus and in our community. This exhibition marks a new milestone for our organization in terms of garnering fundraising support. As a result, I want to personally thank Rhonda DiMascio, director of development, and Janis Martin Hughes, manager of corporate engagement, for their tireless, patient, and persistent efforts to raise funds for this great endeavor. Acknowledgment and gratitude go to Coby Green Rifkin, director of marketing communications, who contributed greatly by working to build an audience for this exhibition. Additionally, a heartfelt thank you goes to Keith Pyatt, manager of technology and digital media, who produced a thoughtful and revealing video interview of the artist that accompanies the exhibition.

An ambitious project of this scale would not be possible without the loving support of family. We at Grounds For Sculpture greatly appreciate the contribution of Boaz's wife, Kim Vaadia, his daughters Sara and Rebecca, and his entire extended family for providing their enthusiastic support and vivid memories to this project. From stories of retrieving sculpture long stored in his parents' old chicken coop in Israel; to his stepson from his first marriage Tal's childhood memories of playing among early sculptures in their SoHo loft; and how later his Williamsburg studio became Rebecca and Sara's favorite childhood place to visit and play, and still is today; the essence of the Vaadia family has been woven throughout this exhibition. Most important, we wish to thank Boaz Vaadia for the rewarding experience of working with him. He has generously shared his remarkable body of sculpture with our audience and we thank him for making this exhibition possible.

GARY GARRIDO SCHNEIDER
EXECUTIVE DIRECTOR
GROUNDS FOR SCULPTURE
HAMILTON, NEW JERSEY
MAY 2016

Sculpture

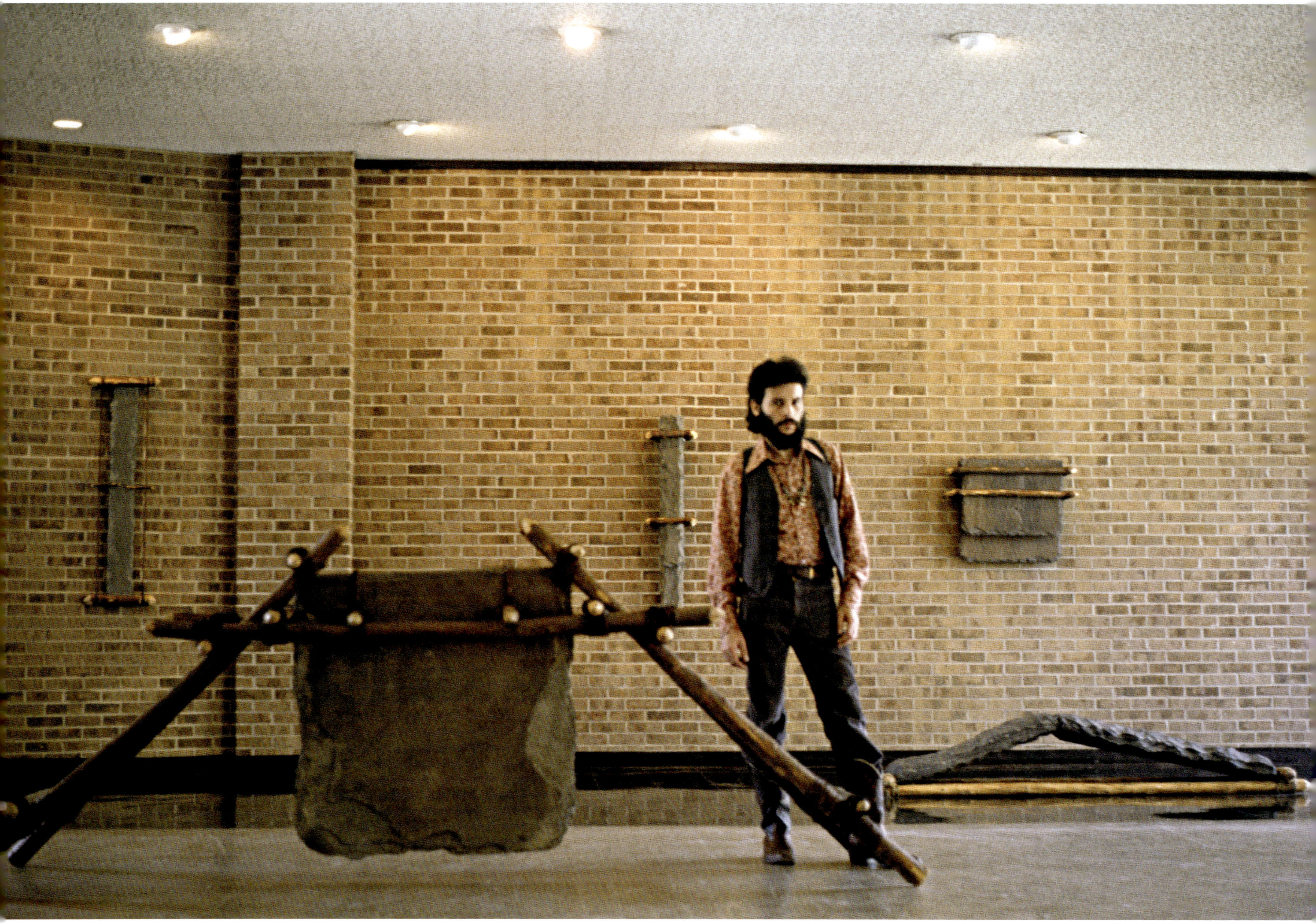

Early Works, 1971–1985

IN 1971, Boaz Vaadia graduated from the Avni Institute of Fine Arts in Tel Aviv. Staying on to teach there and already familiar with welding steel, Vaadia built a foundry from scratch so that he could learn how to cast his works in bronze. Early bronze works from this period, including a work in steel, are represented in this plate section. By 1972, Vaadia introduced stone into his works and eventually added human hair in his exploration of the subject of death. By 1973, he began exploring surrealist influences by creating dripping shapes in metal and stone in addition to using sheep hides, branches, and leather in his work.

When he moved to SoHo in New York City in 1975, Vaadia met Ivan Karp, the legendary gallerist who would later become his dealer. His first major solo show of his early works produced in New York took place at Hundred Acres Gallery. Ritualistic in nature and inspired by African fetishes, altars, and ancient tools, Vaadia created the works in the exhibition from material he had found around SoHo.

By 1976, Vaadia began his work with sedimentary stone such as bluestone and slate, which he had found discarded in SoHo. With these works, he began important explorations using the natural force of gravity. Binding cedar poles together in various structures that held large stones, Vaadia found ways to use gravity in the creation of compelling sculptures that would inform and preoccupy him in his future explorations in sculpture.

Boaz Vaadia with *Untitled*, 1977.

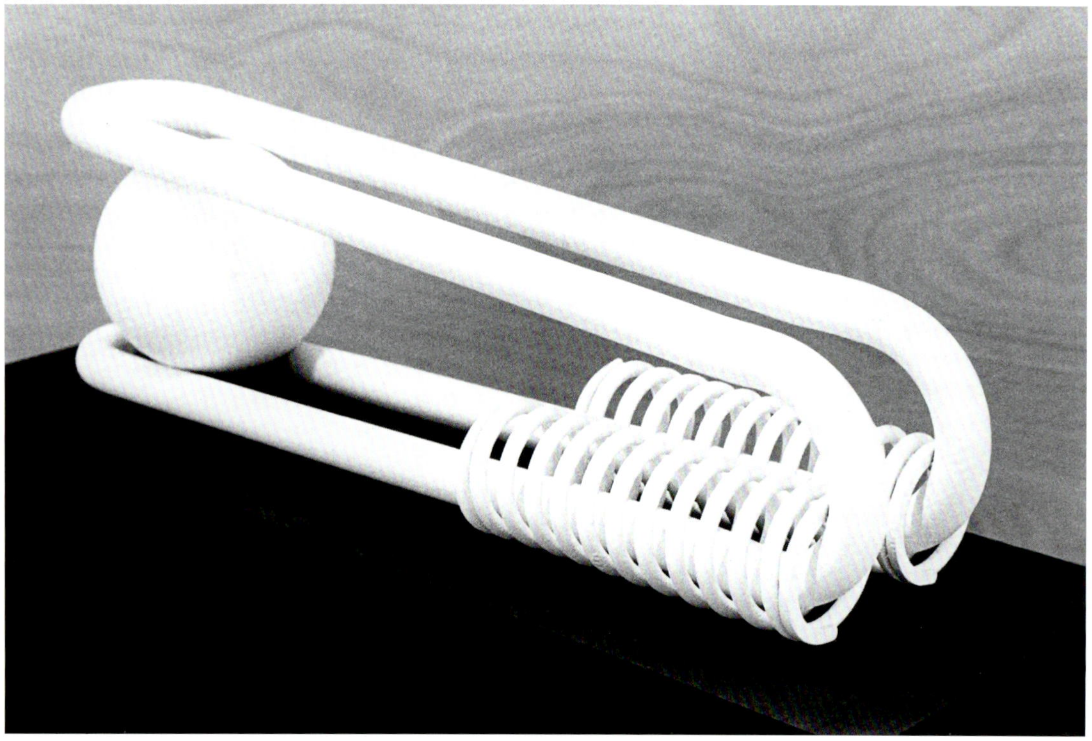

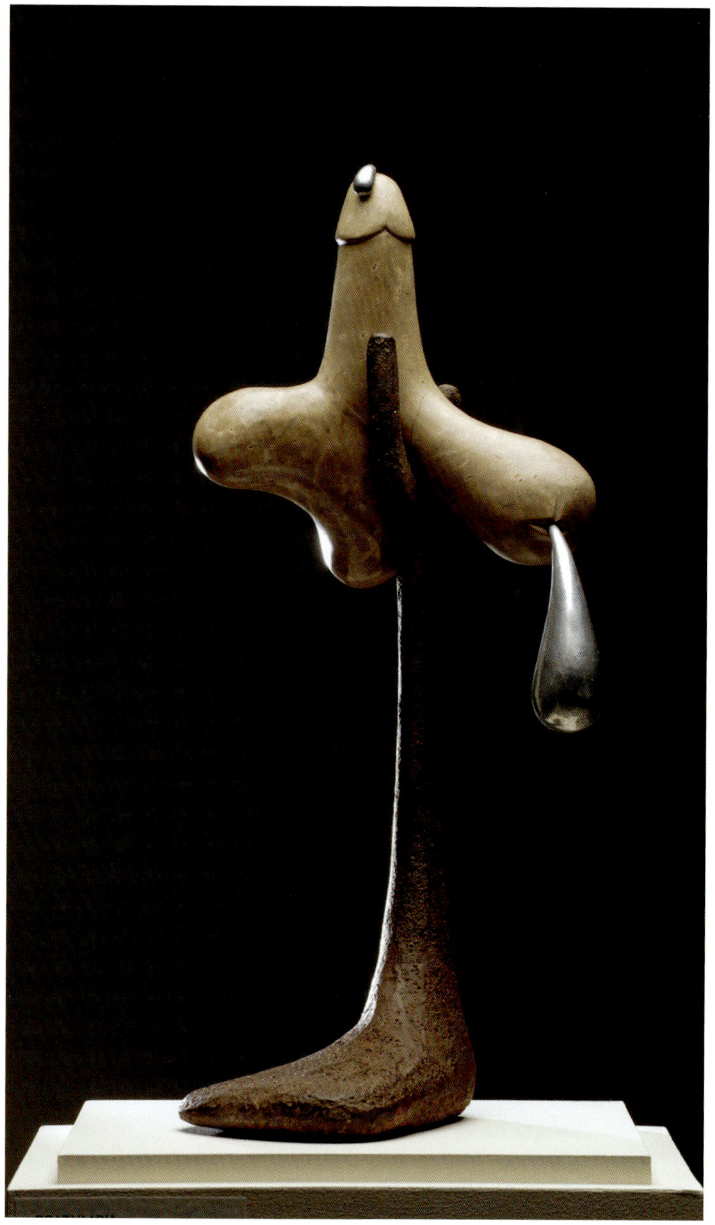

LEFT TO RIGHT

PLATE 1. *Untitled*, 1971.
Painted steel,
14 x 12½ x 48 in. (35.6 x 31.7 x 121.9 cm).

PLATE 2. *Untitled*, 1973.
Stone, aluminum, and iron,
28½ x 10 x 13 in. (72.4 x 25.4 x 33 cm).

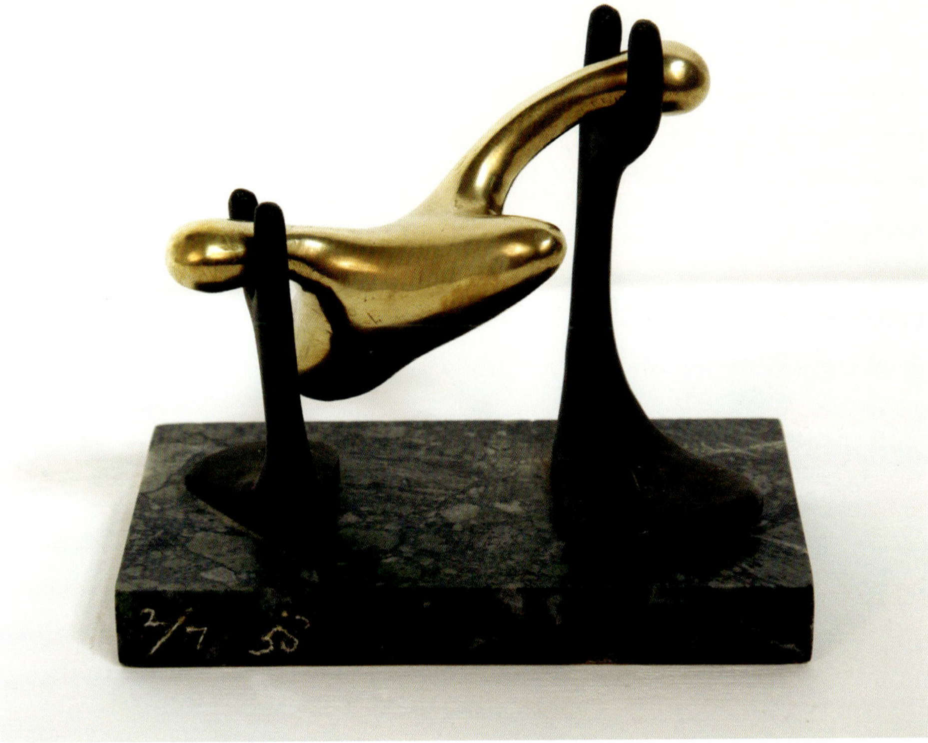

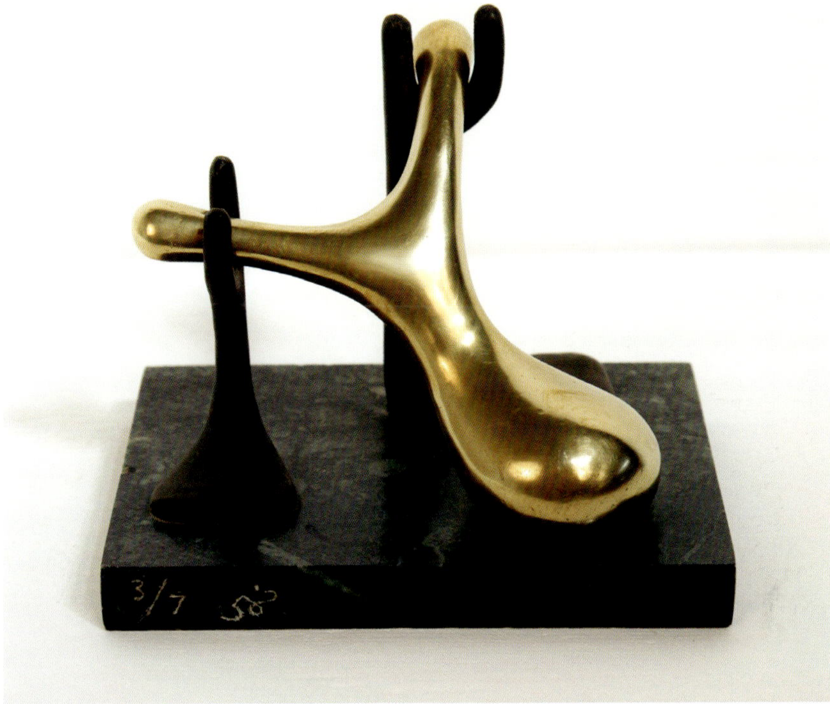

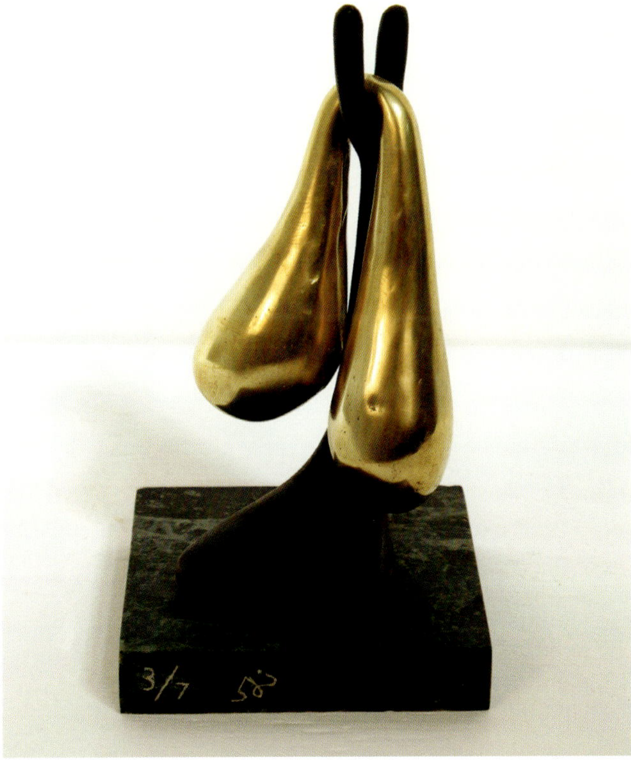

CLOCKWISE FROM TOP LEFT

PLATE 3. *Untitled*, 1973.
Bronze and stone,
$5\frac{3}{4} \times 6\frac{3}{4} \times 4$ in. (14.6 x 17.1 x 10.2 cm).
Edition of 7.

PLATE 4. *Untitled*, 1973.
Bronze and stone,
$5\frac{1}{2} \times 6\frac{1}{2} \times 5$ in. (14 x 16.5 x 12.7 cm).
Edition of 7.

PLATE 5. *Untitled*, 1973.
Bronze and stone,
$7\frac{1}{2} \times 4\frac{1}{4} \times 4\frac{1}{4}$ in. (19.1 x 36.2 x 36.2 cm).
Edition of 7.

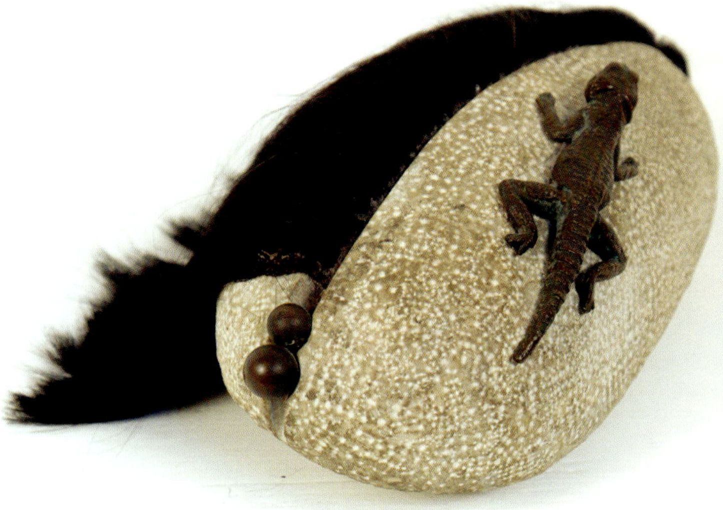

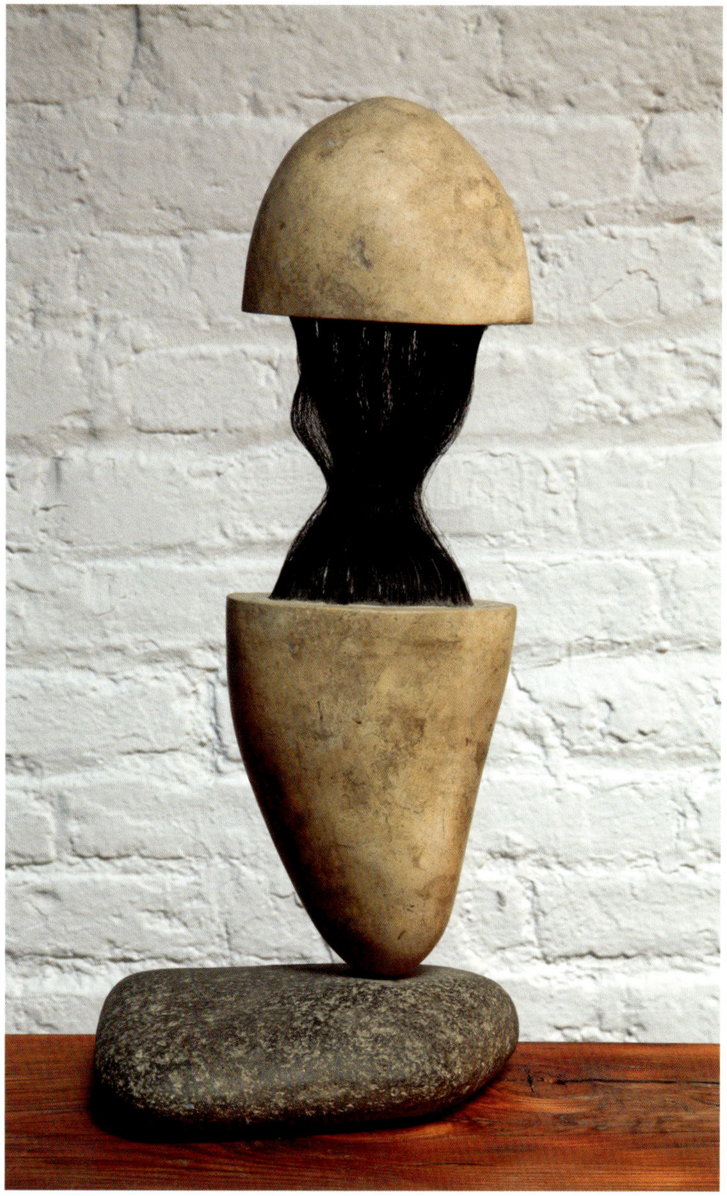

LEFT TO RIGHT

PLATE 6. *Untitled*, 1973.
Stone, bronze, and human hair,
4¾ x 15 x 8½ in. (12.1 x 38.1 x 21.6 cm).

PLATE 7. *Untitled*, 1973.
Stone and human hair,
16 x 7 x 6 in. (40.6 x 17.8 x 15.2 cm).

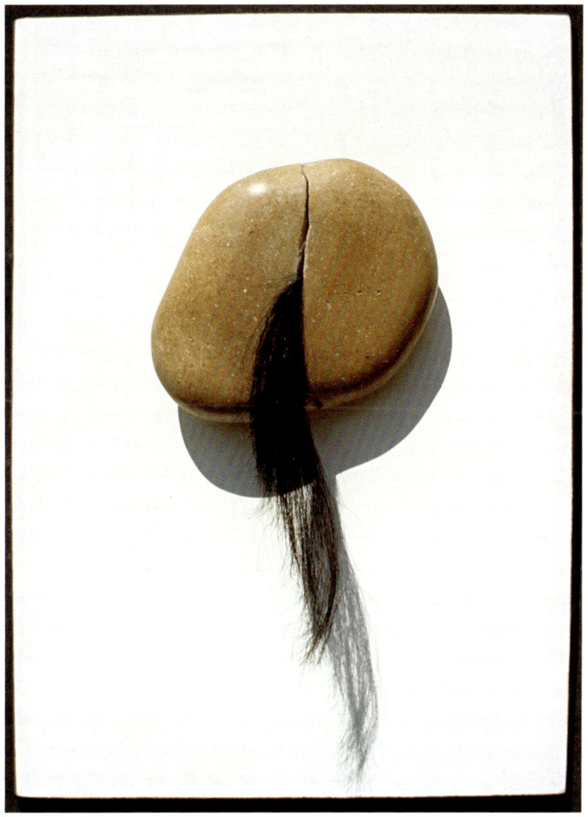

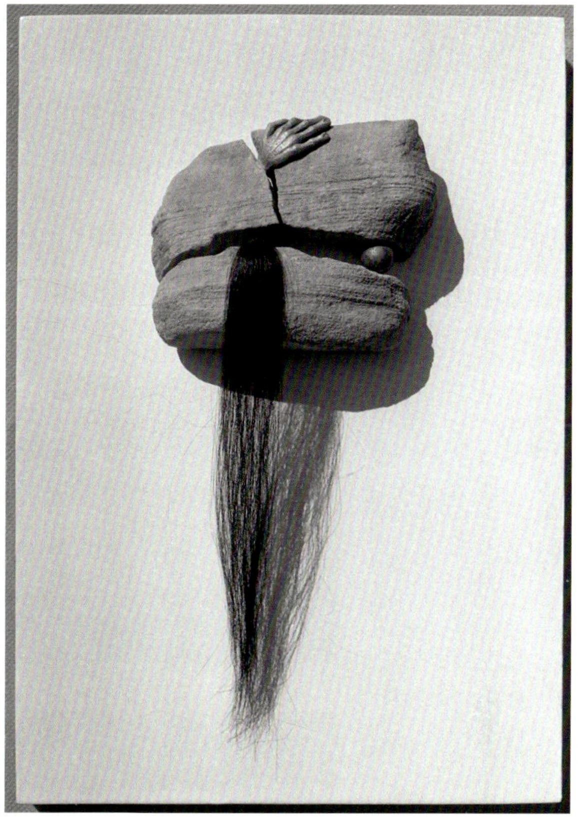

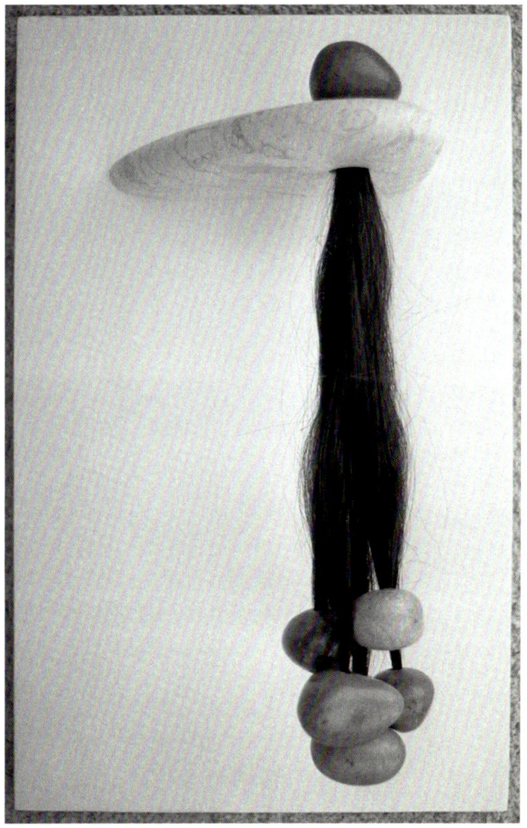

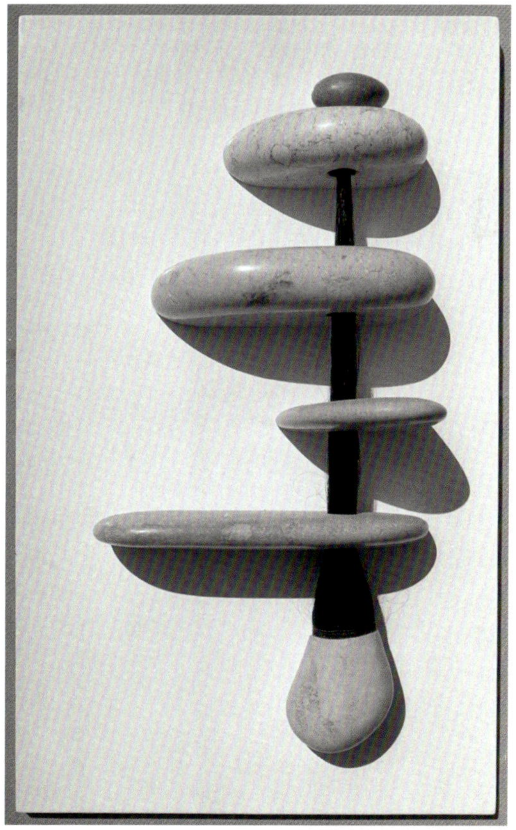

LEFT TO RIGHT

PLATE 8. *Untitled*, 1973.
Stone, human hair, and wood,
15¾ x 11 x 3 in. (40 x 27.9 x 7.6 cm).

PLATE 9. *Untitled*, 1973.
Stone, human hair, bronze, and wood,
17½ x 11¾ x 3 in. (44.4 x 29.8 x 7.6 cm).

PLATE 10. *Untitled*, 1973.
Stone, human hair, and wood,
16¾ x 10 x 6 in. (42.5 x 25.4 x 15.2 cm).

PLATE 11. *Untitled*, 1973.
Stone, human hair, and wood,
19¾ x 11¾ x 3¾ in. (50.2 x 29.8 x 9.5 cm).

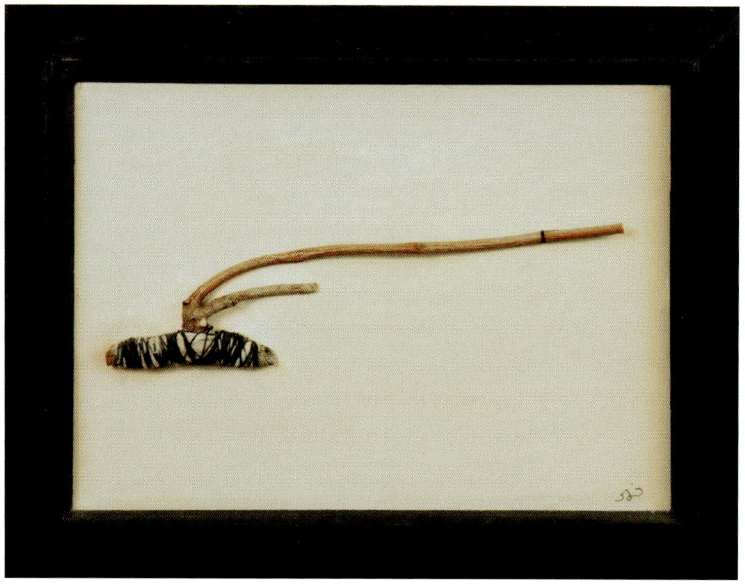

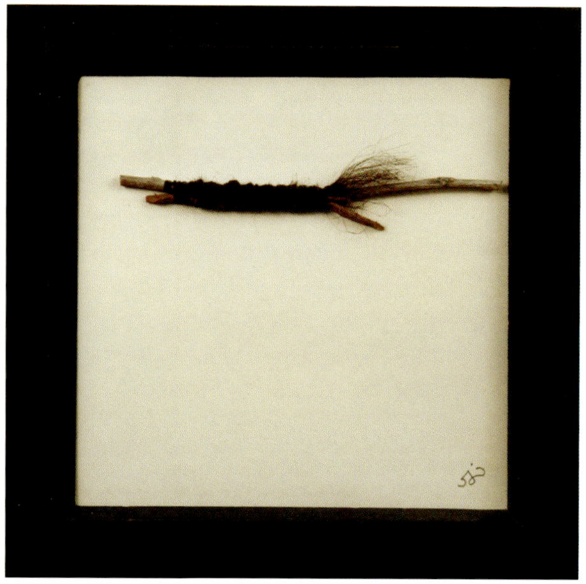

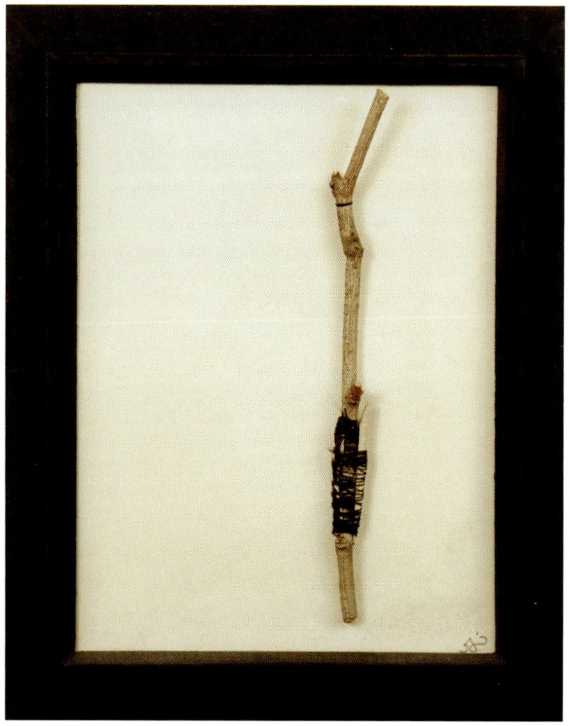

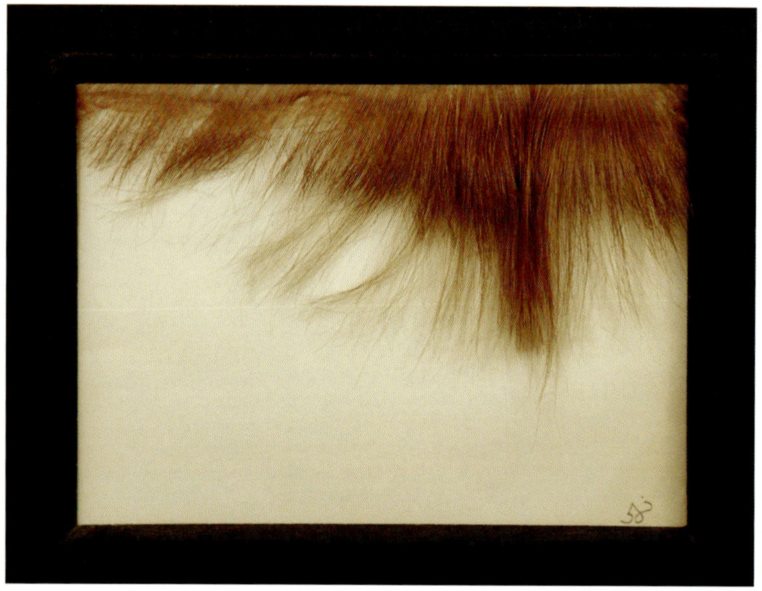

LEFT TO RIGHT

PLATE 12. *Untitled*, 1974.
Wood, string, fur, and paper,
8¼ x 10½ x 1 in. (21 x 26.7 x 2.54 cm).

PLATE 13. *Untitled*, 1974.
Wood, string, leather, human hair, and paper,
8¼ x 8¼ x 1 in. (20.9 x 20.9 x 2.54 cm).

PLATE 14. *Untitled*, 1974.
Wood, string, fur, and paper,
10½ x 8¼ x 1 in. (26.7 x 20.9 x 2.54 cm).

PLATE 15. *Untitled*, 1974.
Fur and paper,
8¼ x 10½ x 1 in. (20.9 x 26.7 x 2.54 cm).

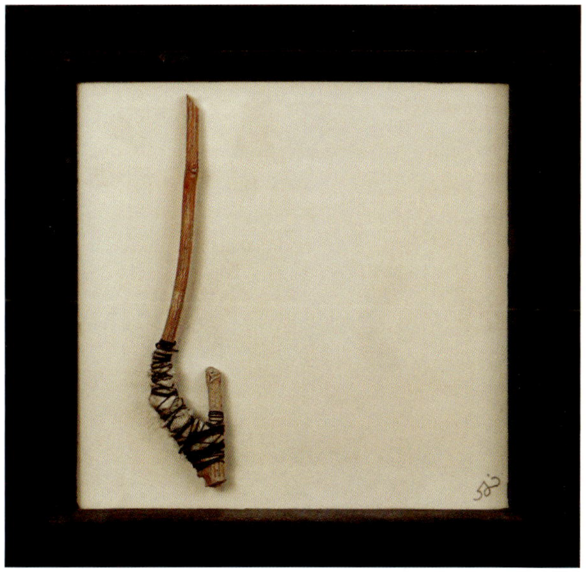
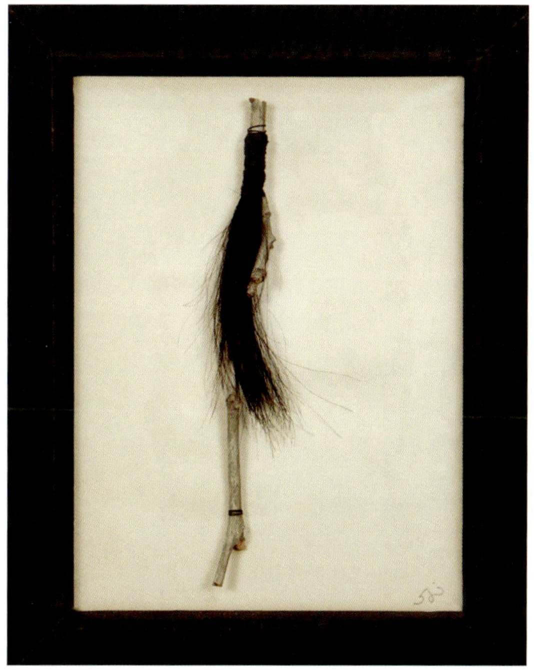
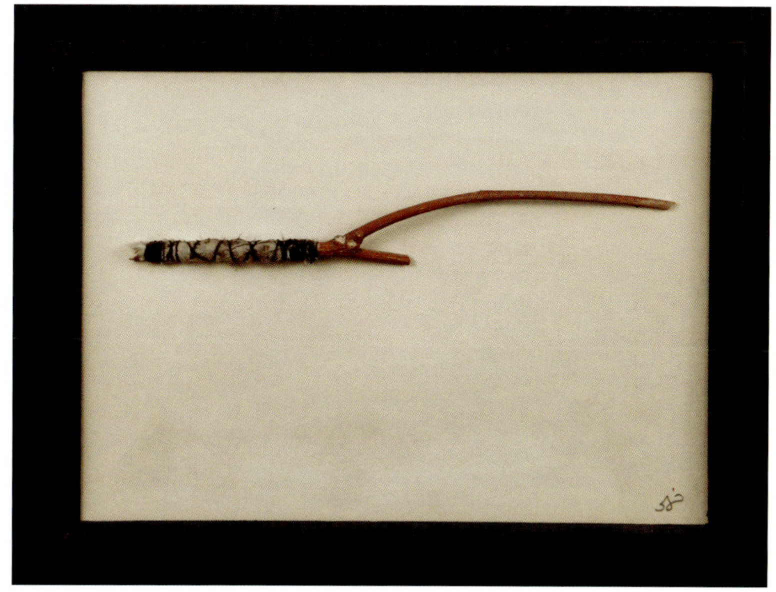
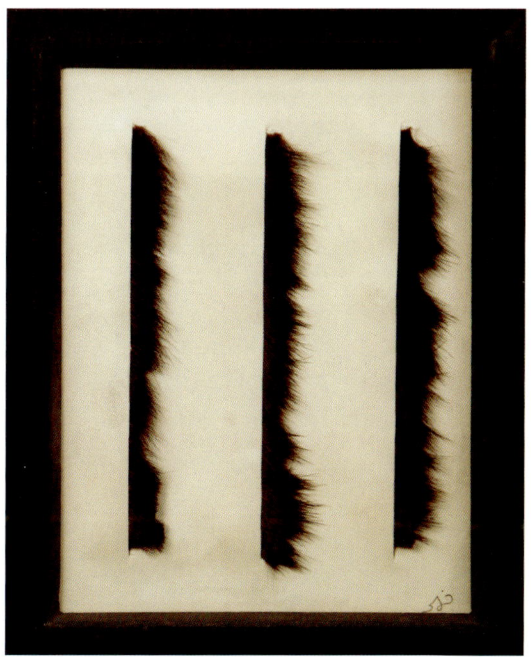
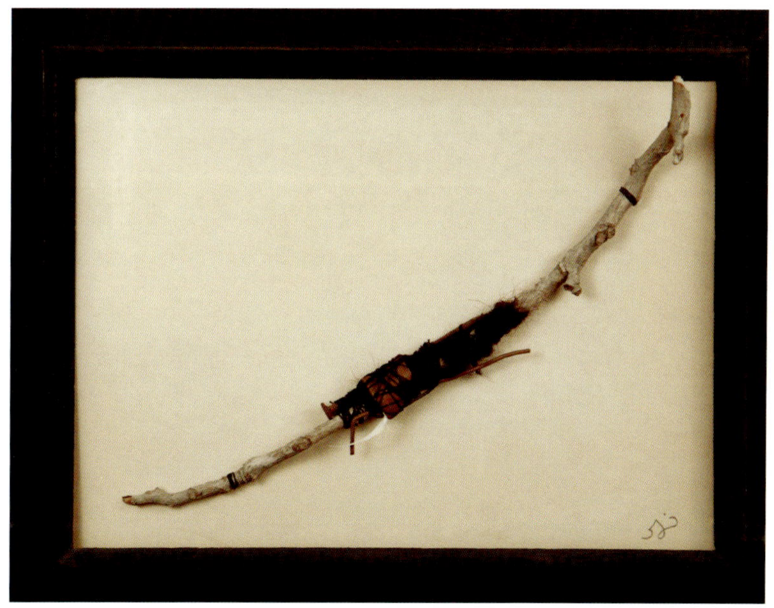

LEFT TO RIGHT

PLATE 16. *Untitled*, 1974.
Wood, string, fur, and paper,
8¼ x 8¼ x 1 in. (20.9 x 20.9 x 2.54 cm).

PLATE 17. *Untitled*, 1974.
Wood, string, human hair, and paper,
10½ x 8¼ x 1 in. (26.7 x 20.9 x 2.54 cm).

PLATE 18. *Untitled*, 1974.
Wood, string, fur, and paper,
10½ x 8¼ x 1 in. (26.7 x 20.9 x 2.54 cm).

PLATE 19. *Untitled*, 1974.
Fur and paper,
8¼ x 10½ x 1 in. (20.9 x 26.7 x 2.54 cm).

PLATE 20. *Untitled*, 1974.
Wood, string, nail, copper, feather, and paper,
8¼ x 10½ x 1½ in. (20.9 x 26.7 x 3.8 cm).

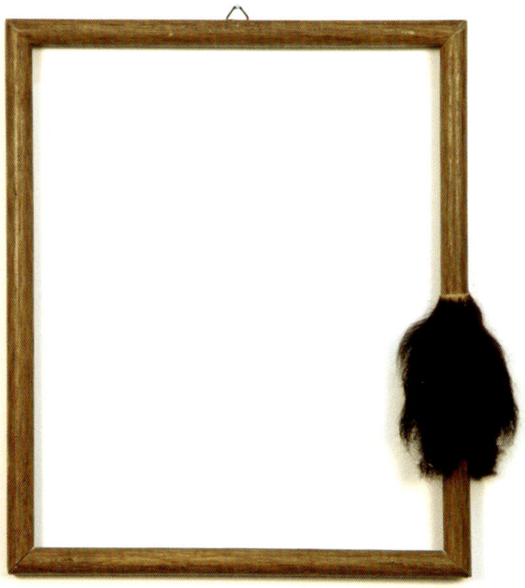

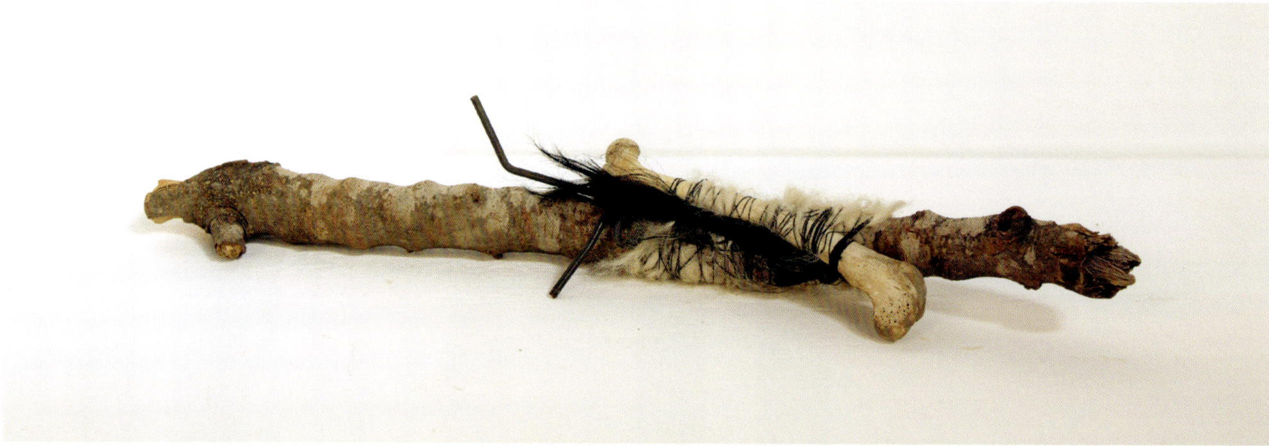

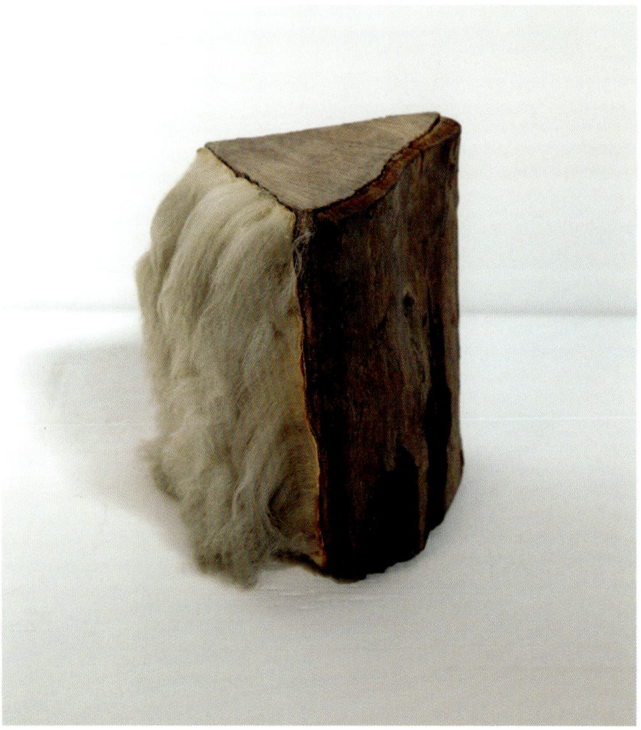

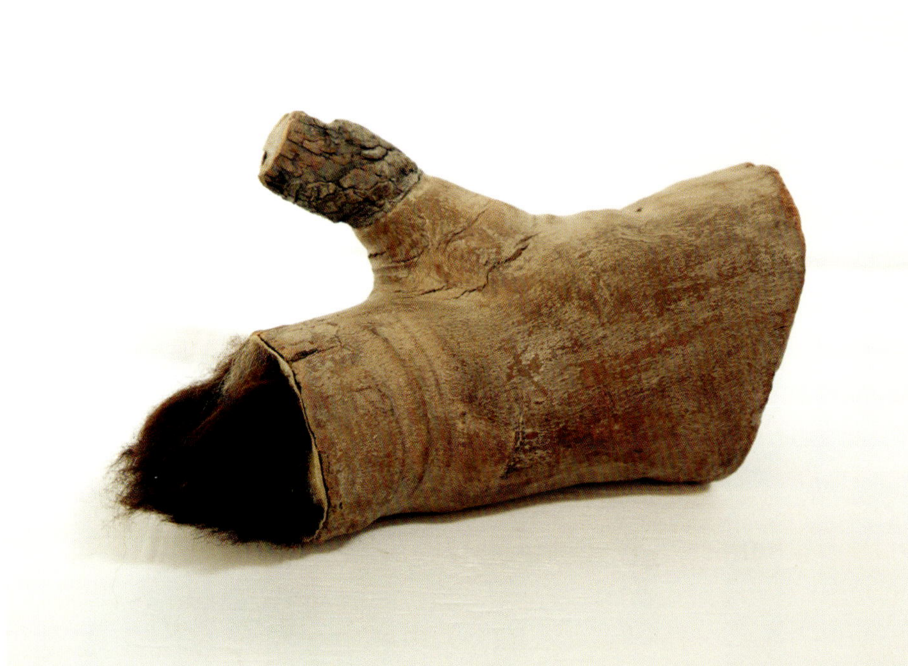

LEFT TO RIGHT

PLATE 21. *Untitled*, 1974.
Wood and fur,
11¾ x 11 x 1½ in. (29.8 x 27.9 x 3.8 cm).

PLATE 22. *Untitled*, 1974.
Wood, bone, fur, string, and wire,
3½ x 18 x 3½ in. (8.9 x 45.7 x 8.9 cm).

PLATE 23. *Untitled*, 1974.
Wood and fur,
6¼ x 5½ x 4 in. (15.9 x 14 x 10.2 cm).

PLATE 24. *Untitled*, 1974.
Wood and fur,
5 x 9 x 5 in. (12.7 x 22.9 x 12.7 cm).

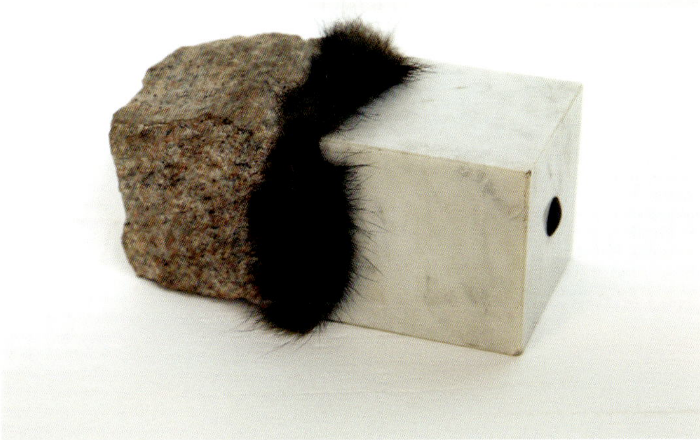

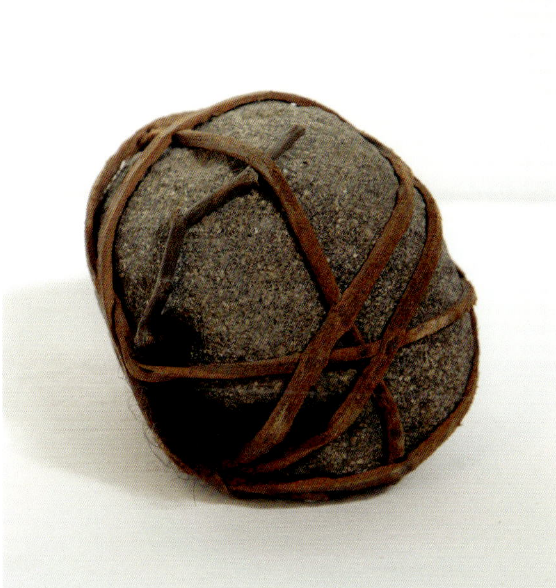

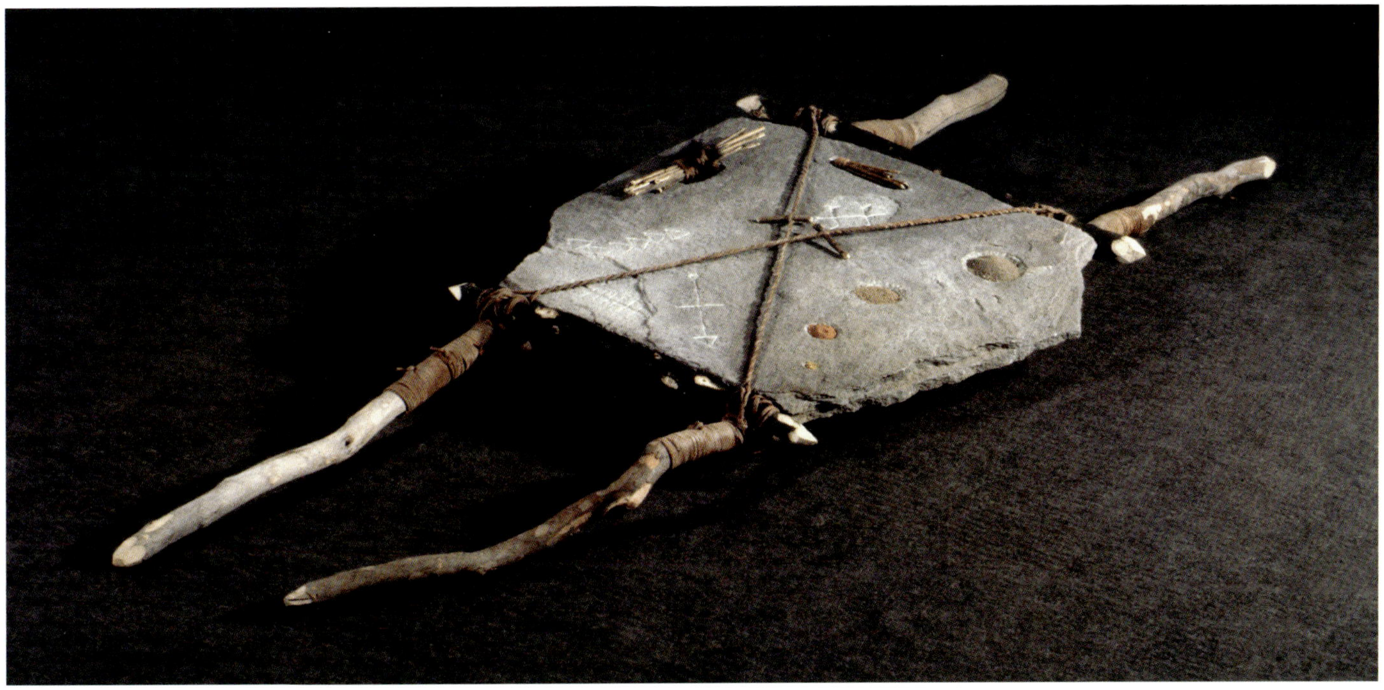

CLOCKWISE FROM TOP LEFT

PLATE 25. *Untitled*, 1975.
Stone, fur, and steel,
3¾ x 6 x 4 in. (9.5 x 15.2 x 10.2 cm).

PLATE 26. *Untitled*, 1976.
Stone, fur, leather, and wood,
4½ x 5 x 4½ in. (11.4 x 12.7 x 11.4 cm).

PLATE 27. *Untitled*, 1976.
Stone, wood, feathers, leather, fur, and sand,
5½ x 70 x 25 in. (14 x 177.8 x 63.5 cm).

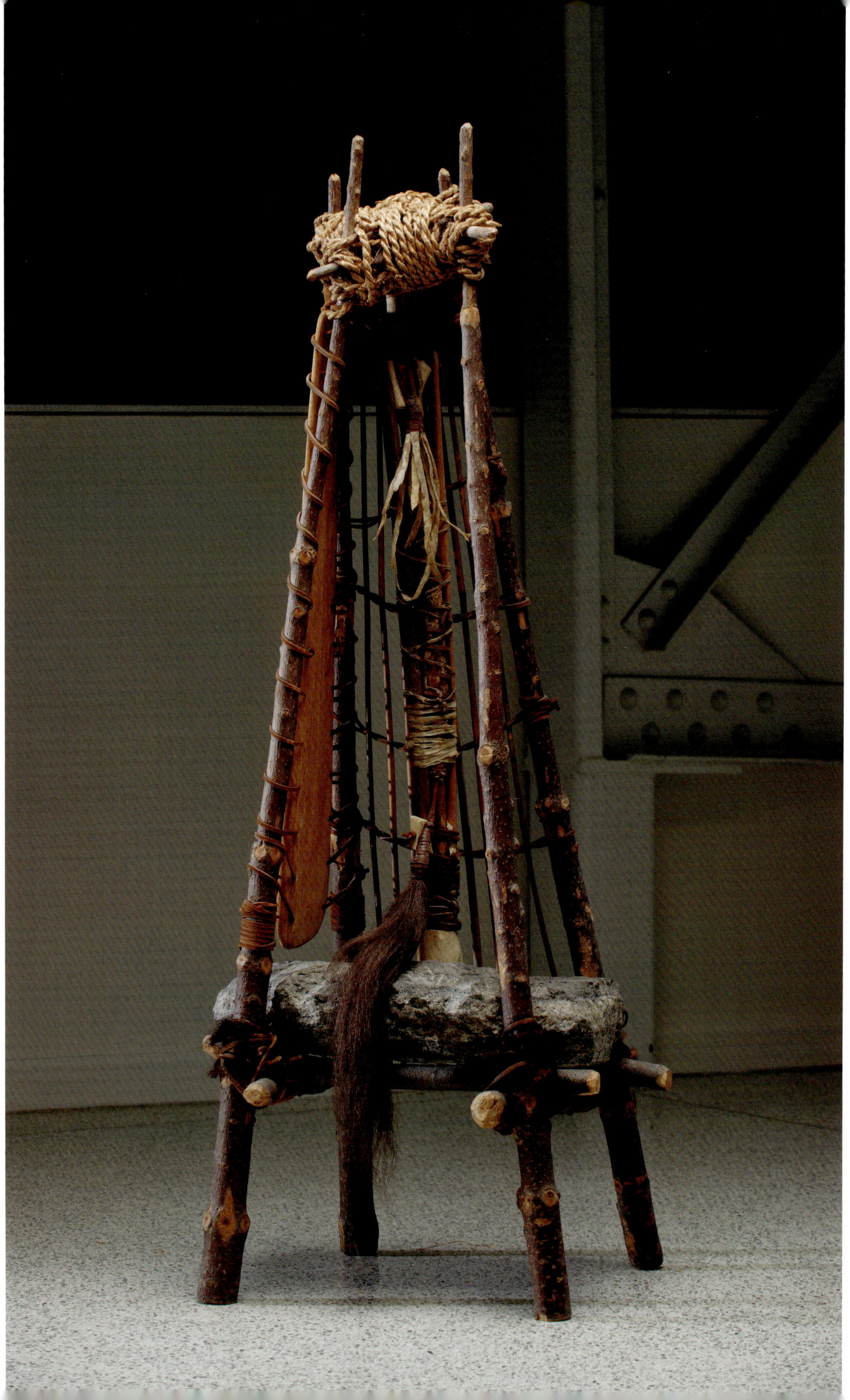

PLATE 28. *Untitled*, 1976.
Wood, stone, leather, human hair, fur, and bone,
$50\frac{1}{2}$ x 20 x 17 in. (128.3 x 50.8 x 43.2 cm).

OPPOSITE

PLATE 29. *Untitled*, 1976.
Stone, wood, feathers, leather, and fur,
51 x 15 x 13 in. (129.5 x 38.1 x 33 cm).

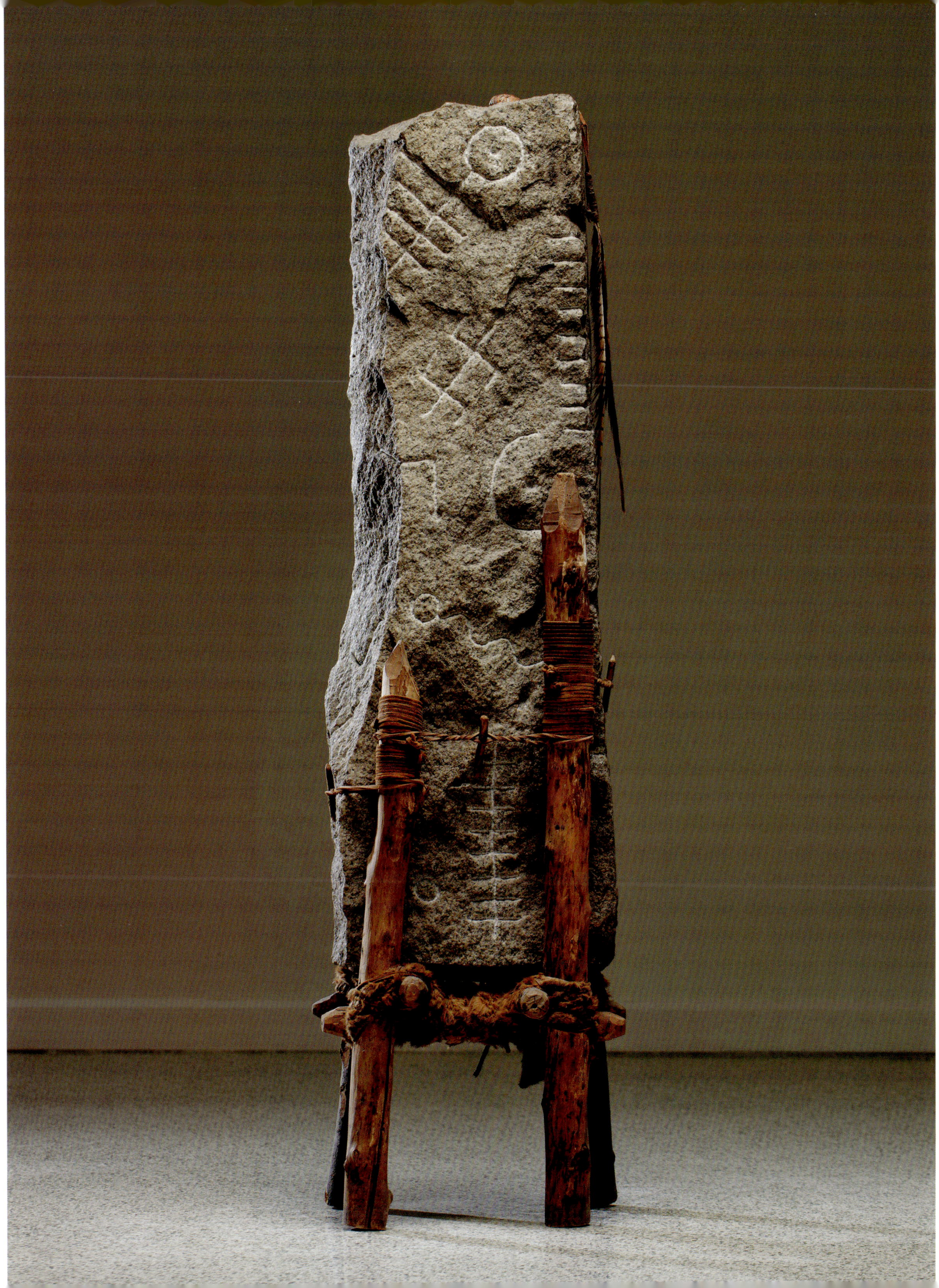

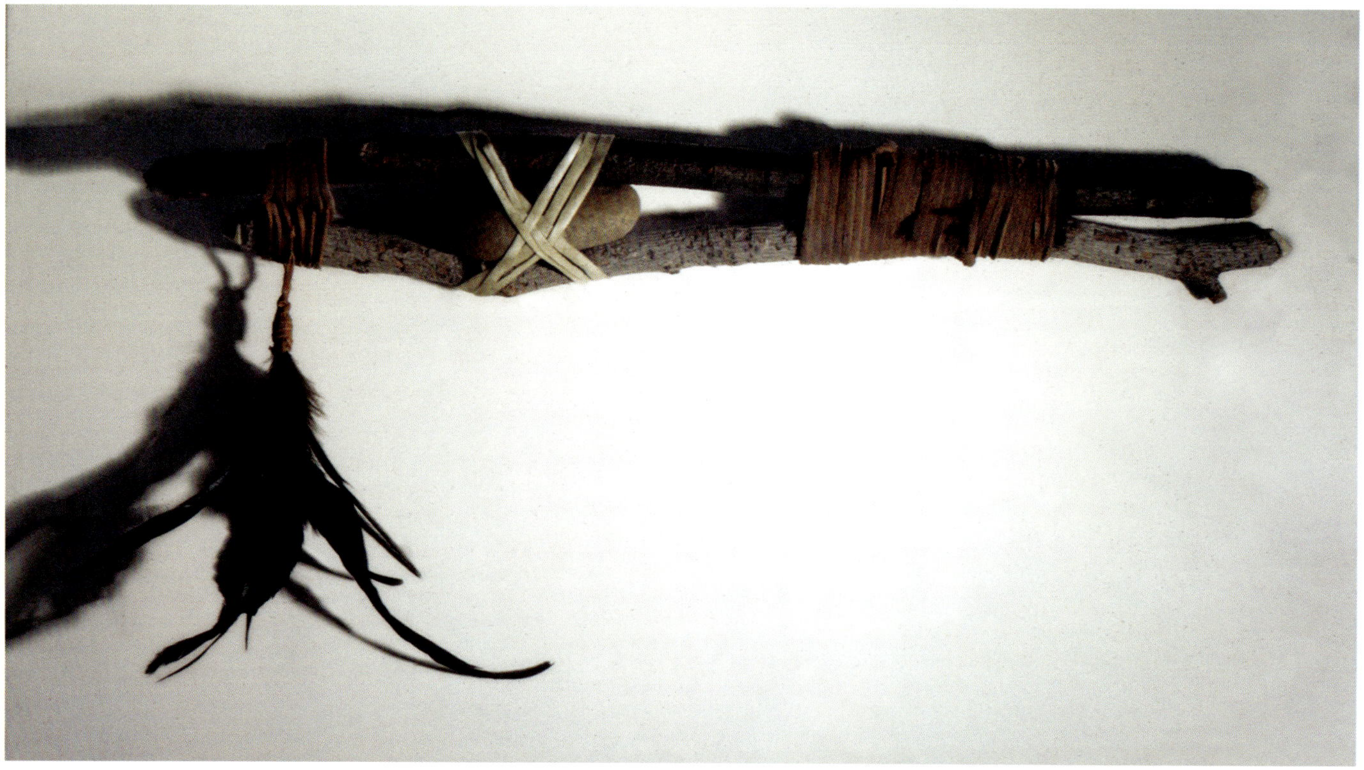

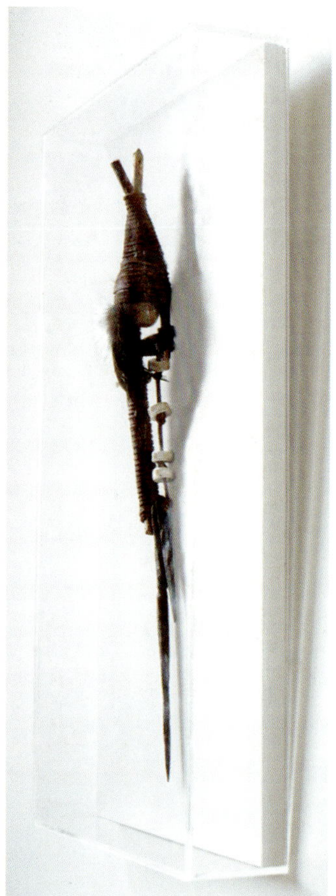

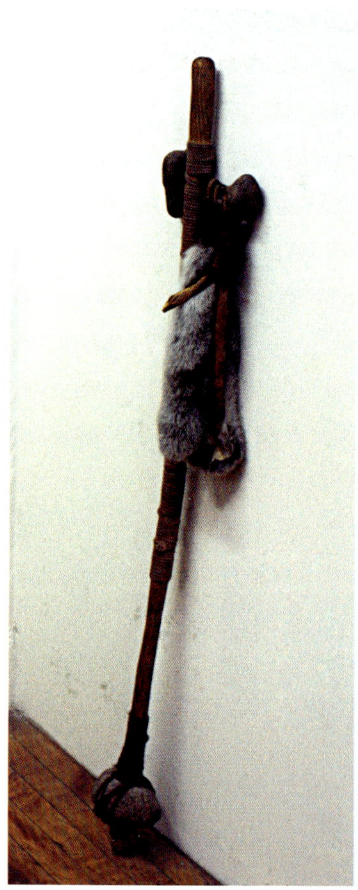

CLOCKWISE FROM TOP

PLATE 30. *Untitled*, 1976.
Wood, leather, stone, and feather,
$16^{1}/_{4}$ x $25^{1}/_{2}$ x $3^{3}/_{4}$ in. (41.3 x 64.8 x 9.5 cm).

PLATE 31. *Untitled*, 1976.
Wood, leather, stone, fur, and antler,
54 x $8^{1}/_{2}$ x 5 in. (137.2 x 21.6 x 12.7 cm).

PLATE 32. *Untitled*, 1976.
Wood, leather, stone, bone, feather, and steel,
$24^{1}/_{4}$ x $12^{1}/_{2}$ x $3^{1}/_{4}$ in. (61.6 x 31.7 x 8.2 cm).

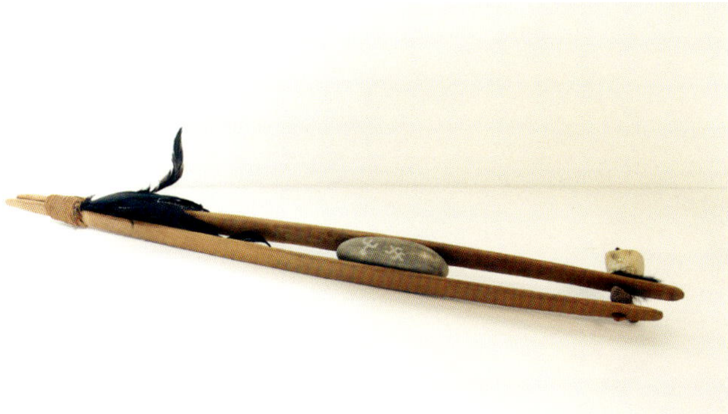

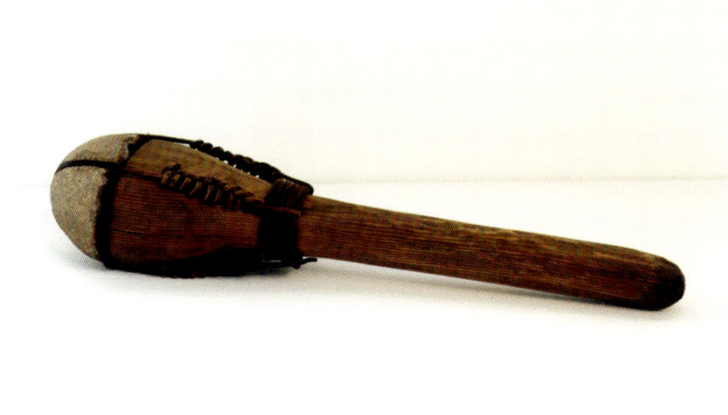

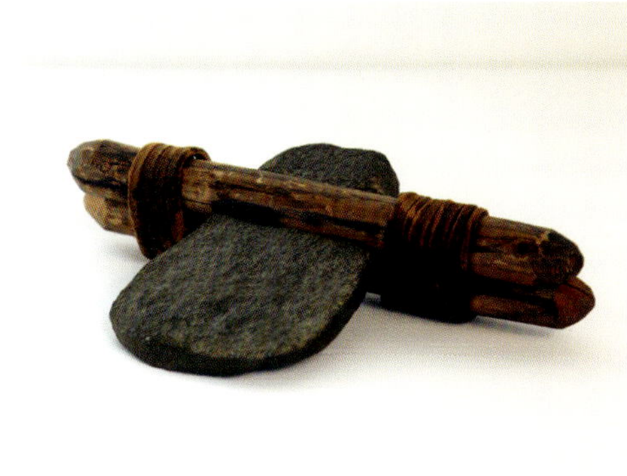

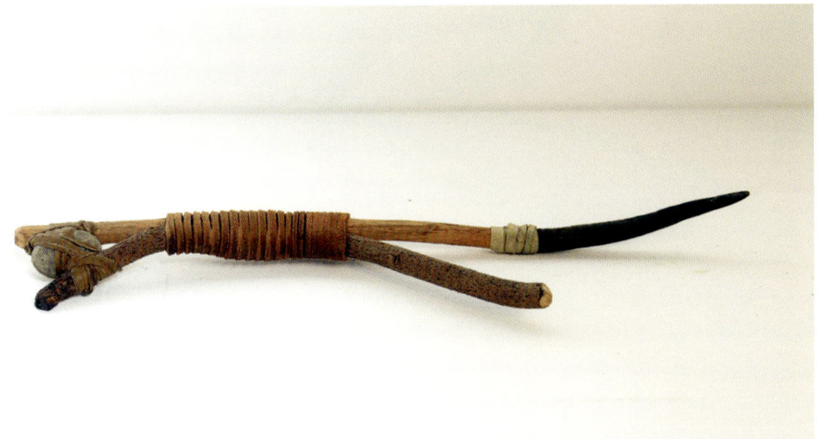

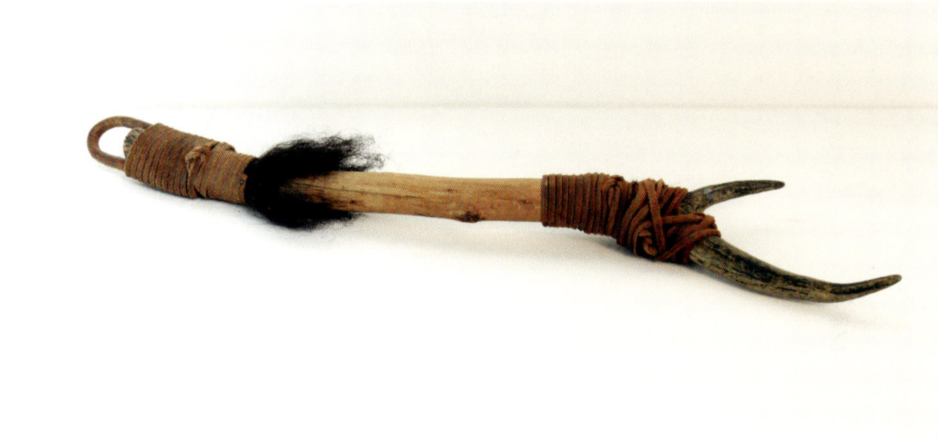

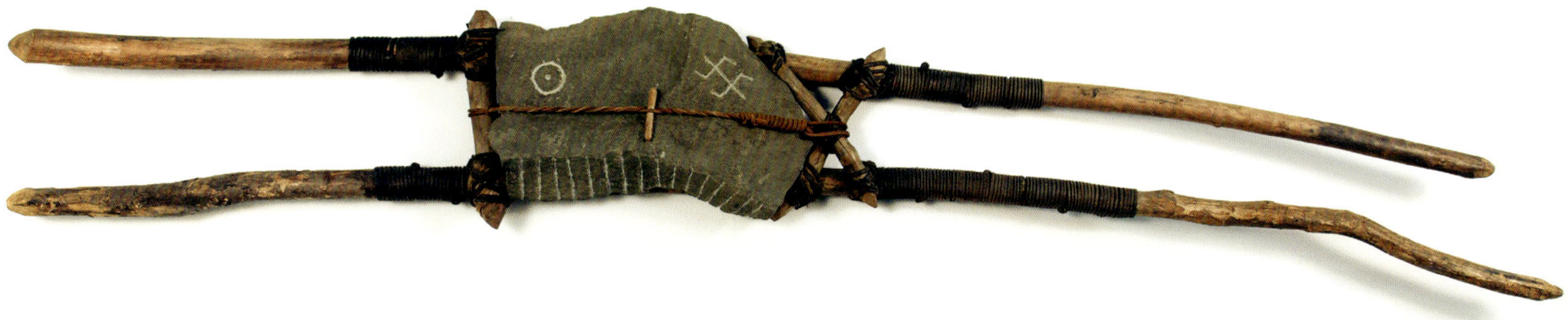

LEFT TO RIGHT

PLATE 33. *Untitled*, 1976.
Wood, leather, stone, feather, and bone,
2½ x 29 x 3 in. (6.3 x 73.7 x 7.6 cm).

PLATE 34. *Untitled*, 1976.
Wood, leather, fur, and stone,
3 x 16 x 4 in. (7.6 x 40.6 x 10.2 cm).

PLATE 35. *Untitled*, 1976.
Wood, leather, and stone,
1¾ x 8 x 4½ in. (4.4 x 20.3 x 11.4 cm).

PLATE 36. *Untitled*, 1976.
Wood, leather, stone, and antler,
1¾ x 16 x 4½ in. (4.4 x 40.6 x 11.4 cm).

PLATE 37. *Untitled*, 1976.
Wood, leather, antler, and human hair,
1¾ x 21 x 4½ in. (4.4 x 53.3 x 11.4 cm).

PLATE 38. *Untitled*, 1976.
Stone, wood, and leather,
10 x 70 x 4½ in. (25.4 x 177.8 x 11.4 cm).

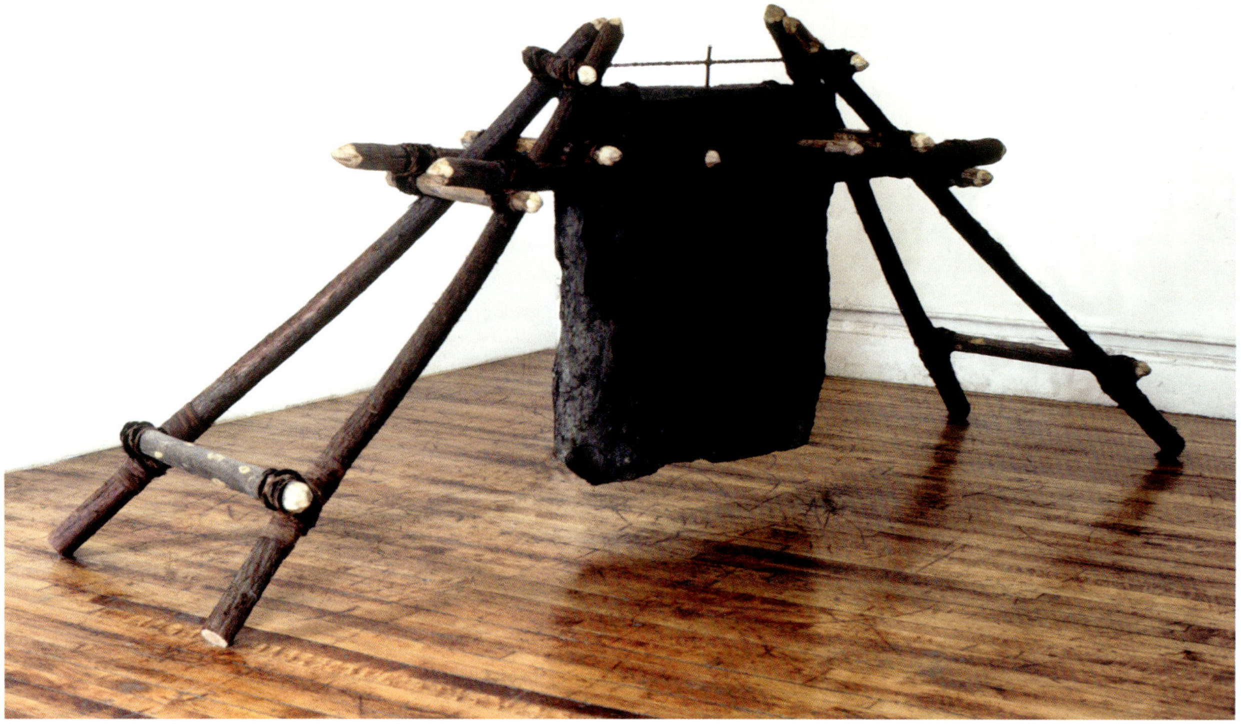

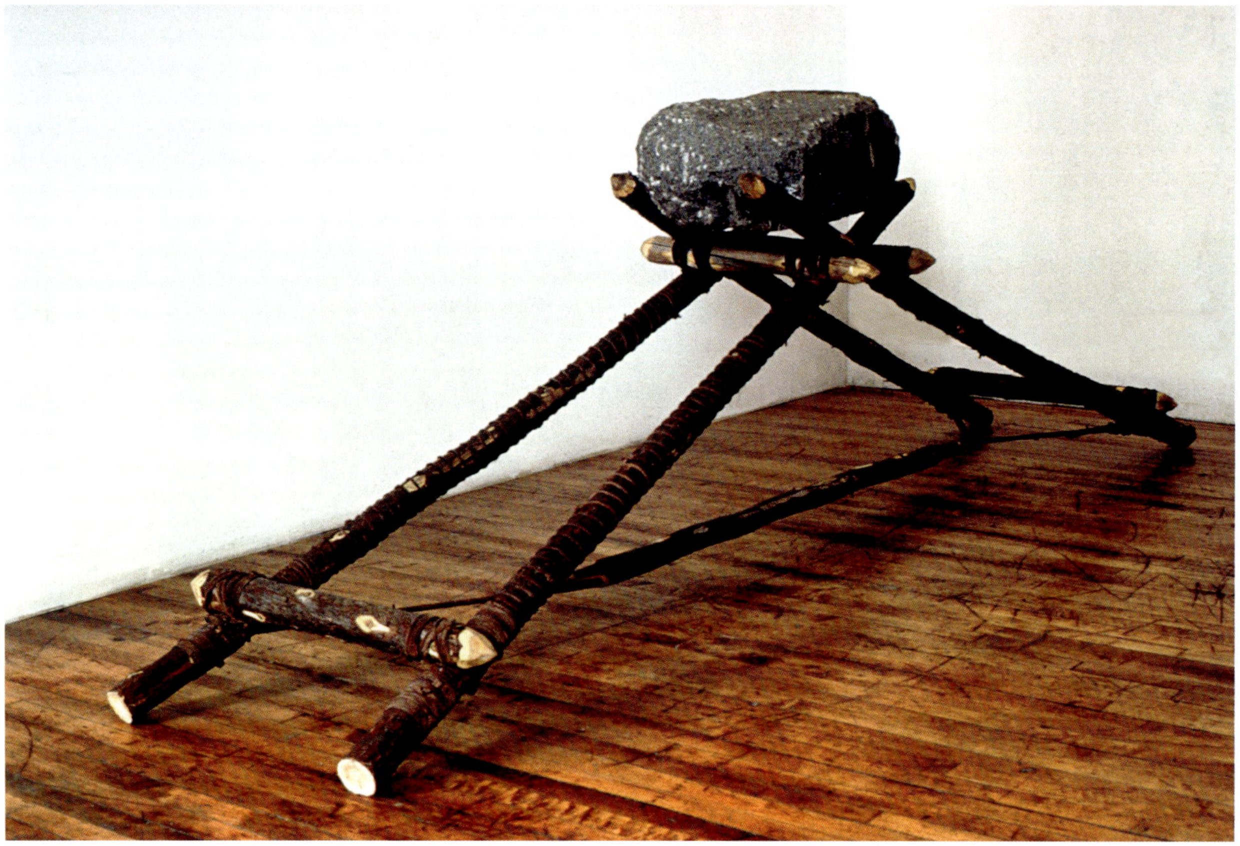

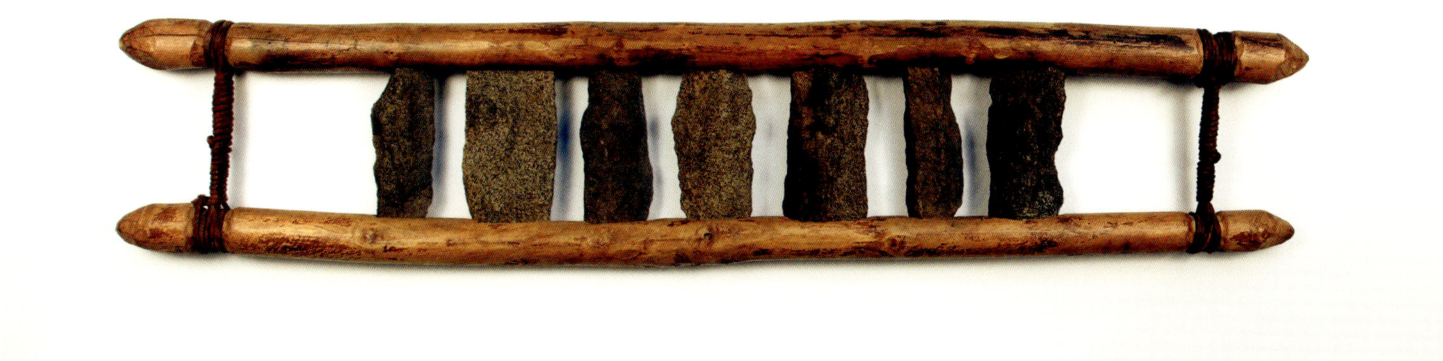

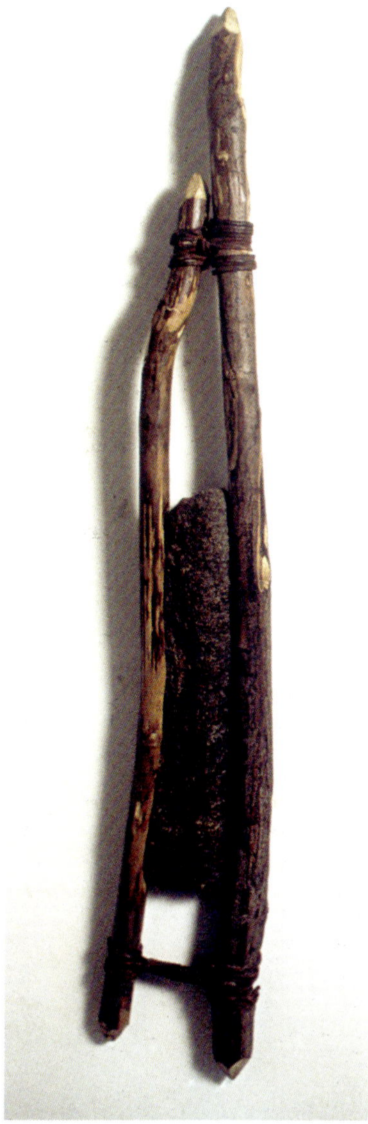

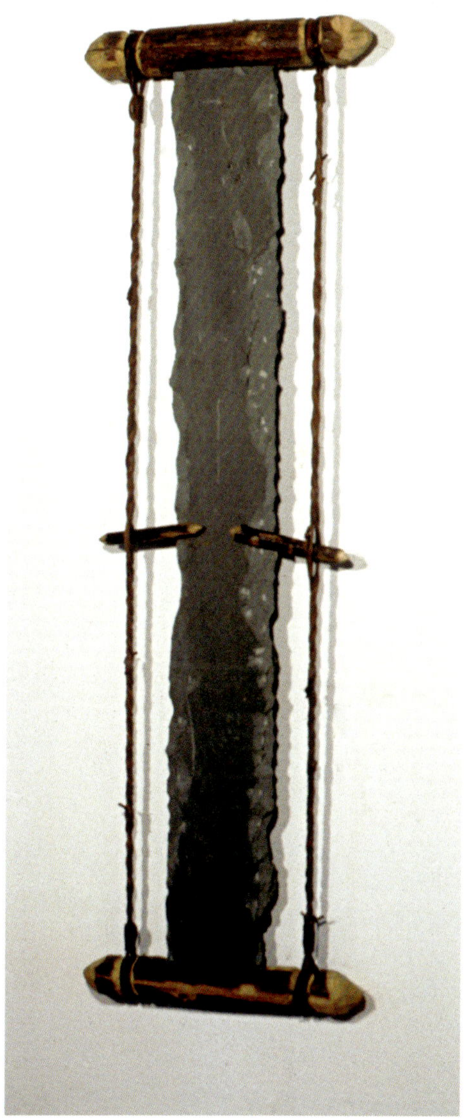

OPPOSITE

PLATE 39. *Untitled*, 1977.
Stone, wood, leather and fur,
46 x 115 x 32 in. (99.1 x 305 x 73.7 cm).

PLATE 40. *Untitled*, 1977.
Stone, wood, and leather,
39 x 120 x 29 in. (99.1 x 305 x 73.7 cm).

CLOCKWISE FROM TOP

PLATE 41. *Untitled*, 1977.
Stone, wood, and leather,
8 x 28 x 2 in. (20.3 x 71.1 x 5.1 cm).

PLATE 42. *Untitled*, 1977.
Stone, wood, and leather,
51 x 14½ x 2½ in. (129.5 x 36.8 x 6.3 cm).

PLATE 43. *Untitled*, 1977.
Stone, wood, and leather,
41 x 6½ x 2 in. (104.1 x 16.5 x 5.1 cm).

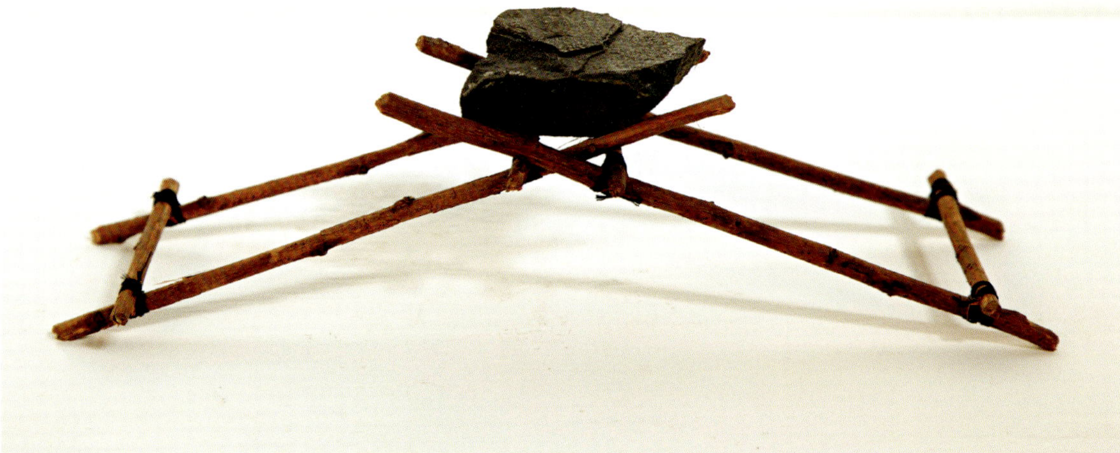

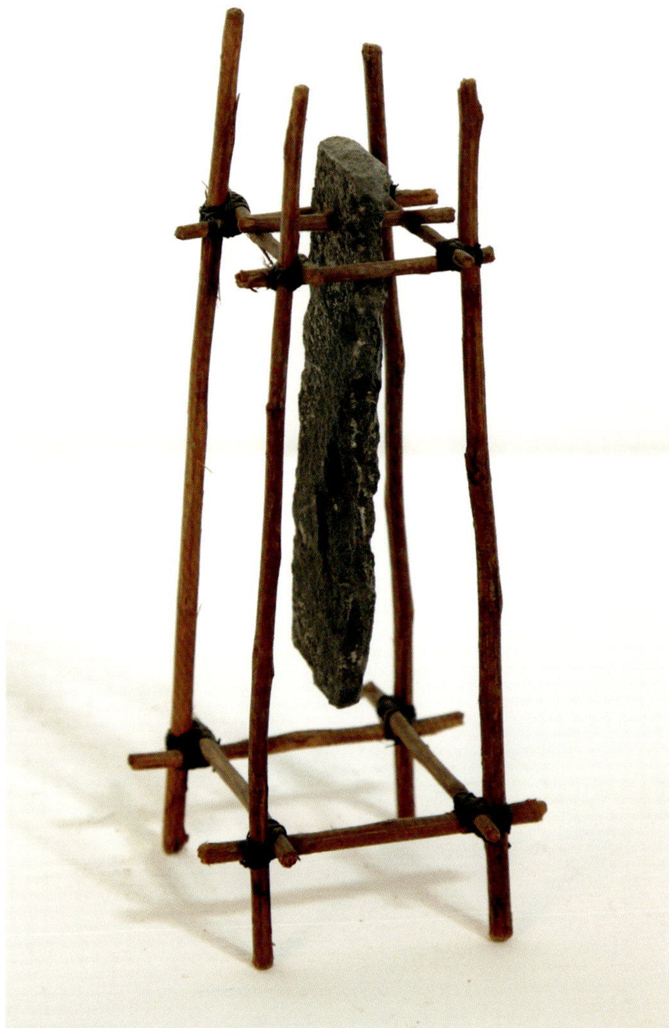

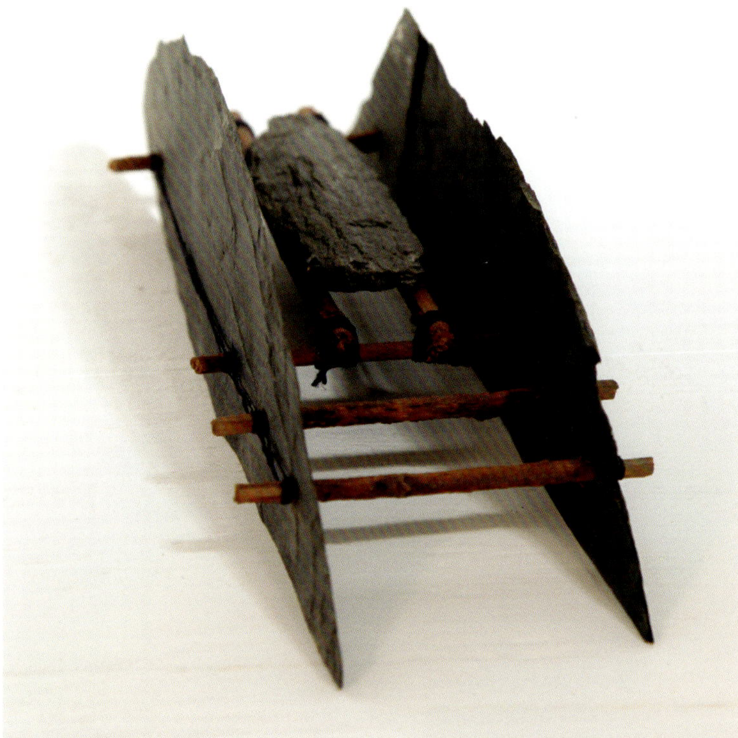

CLOCKWISE FROM TOP LEFT

PLATE 44. *Untitled* (maquette), 1977.
Stone, wood, and string,
3¼ x 10 x 3 in. (8.2 x 25.4 x 7.6 cm).

PLATE 45. *Untitled* (maquette), 1977.
Stone, wood, and string,
7 x 3¼ x 2½ in. (17.8 x 8.2 x 6.3 cm).

PLATE 46. *Untitled* (maquette), 1977.
Slate, wood, and string,
2½ x 8¾ x 3¼ in. (6.3 x 22.2 x 8.2 cm).

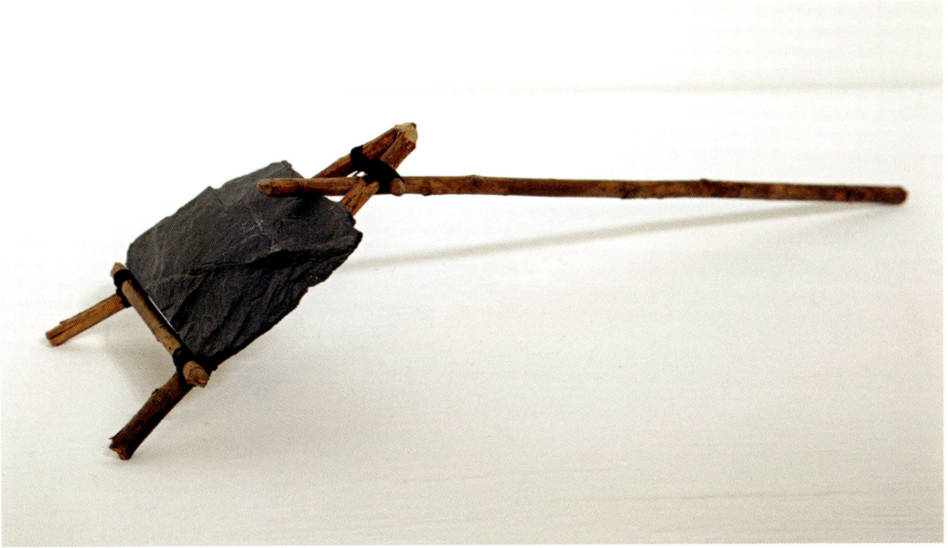

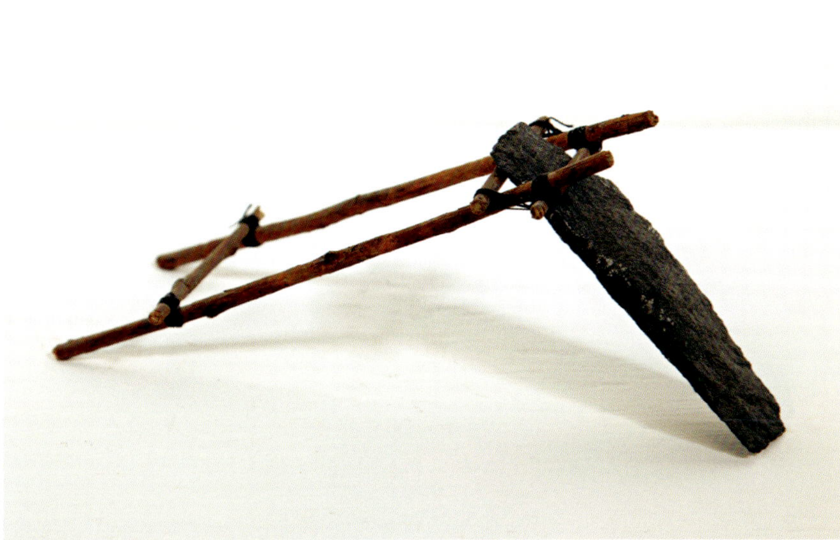

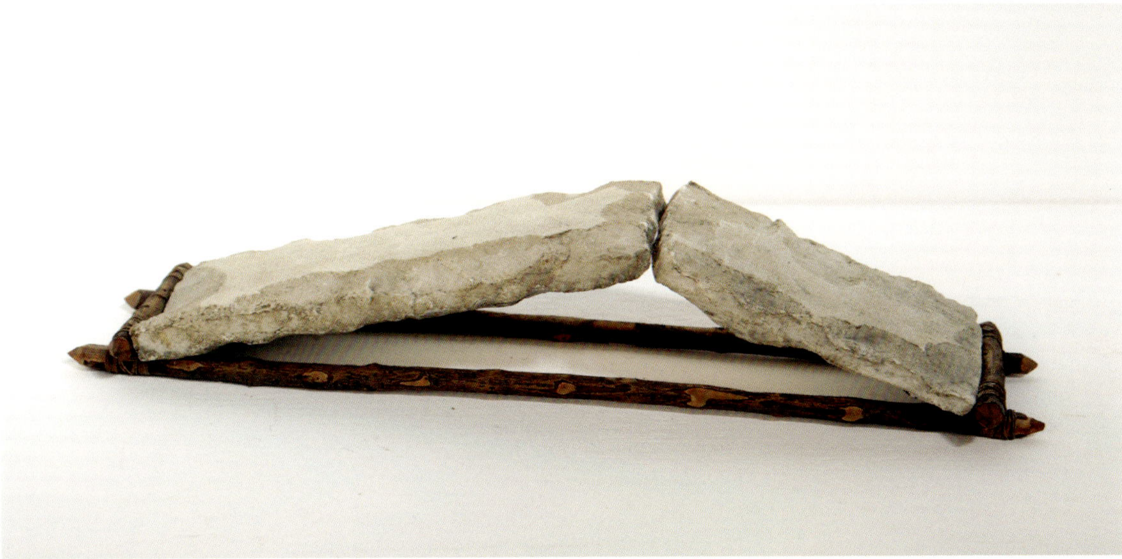

CLOCKWISE FROM TOP LEFT

PLATE 47. *Untitled* (maquette), 1977.
Slate, wood, and string,
3 x $14\frac{1}{2}$ x $3\frac{3}{4}$ in. (7.6 x 36.8 x 9.5 cm).

PLATE 48. *Untitled* (maquette), 1977.
Stone, wood, and string,
$3\frac{3}{4}$ x $7\frac{1}{2}$ x 3 in. (9.5 x 19 x 7.6 cm).

PLATE 49. *Untitled* (maquette), 1978.
Stone, wood, and string,
3 x $16\frac{1}{4}$ x $3\frac{3}{4}$ in. (7.6 x 41.3 x 9.5 cm).

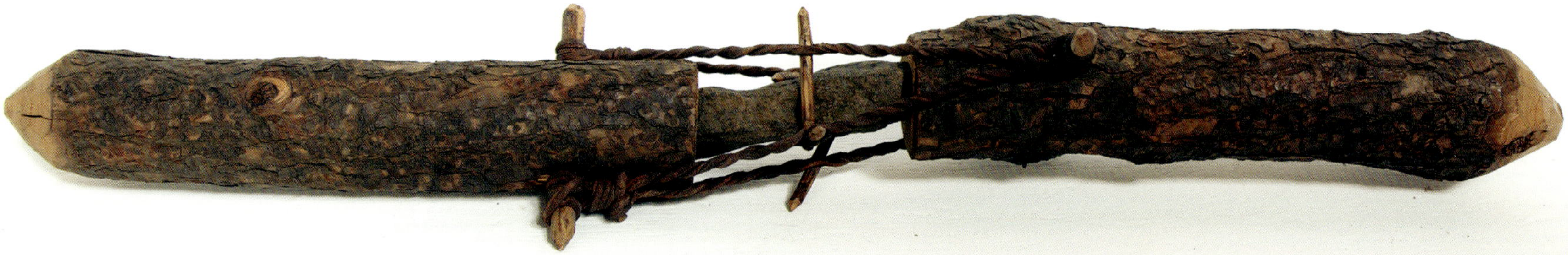

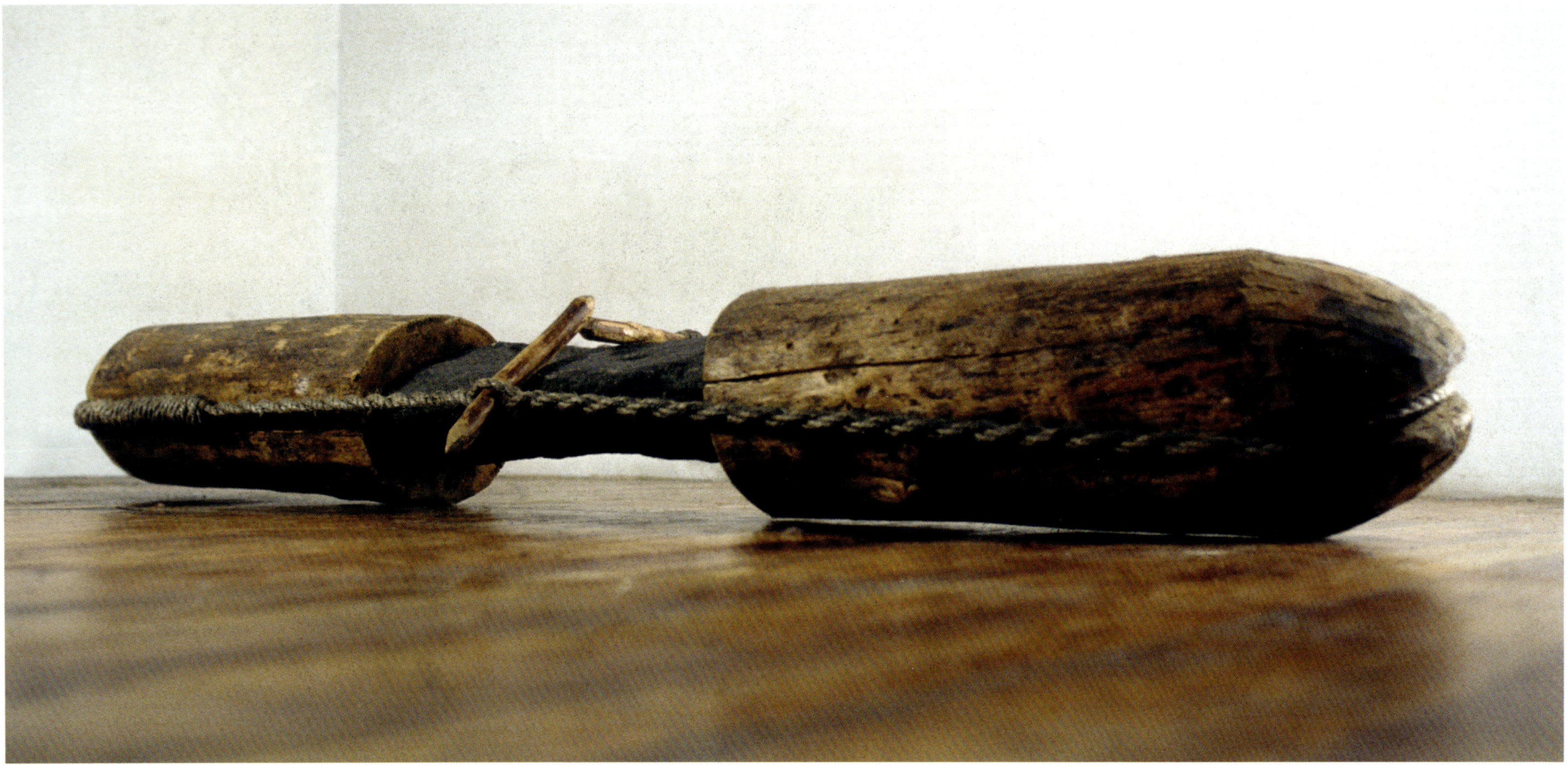

PLATE 50. *Untitled*, 1978.
Stone, wood, and leather,
4 x 30 x 5 in. (10.2 x 76.2 x 12.7 cm).

PLATE 51. *Untitled*, 1978.
Wood, stone, and rope,
11$^{1}/_{2}$ x 87 x 26 in. (29.2 x 221 x 66 cm).

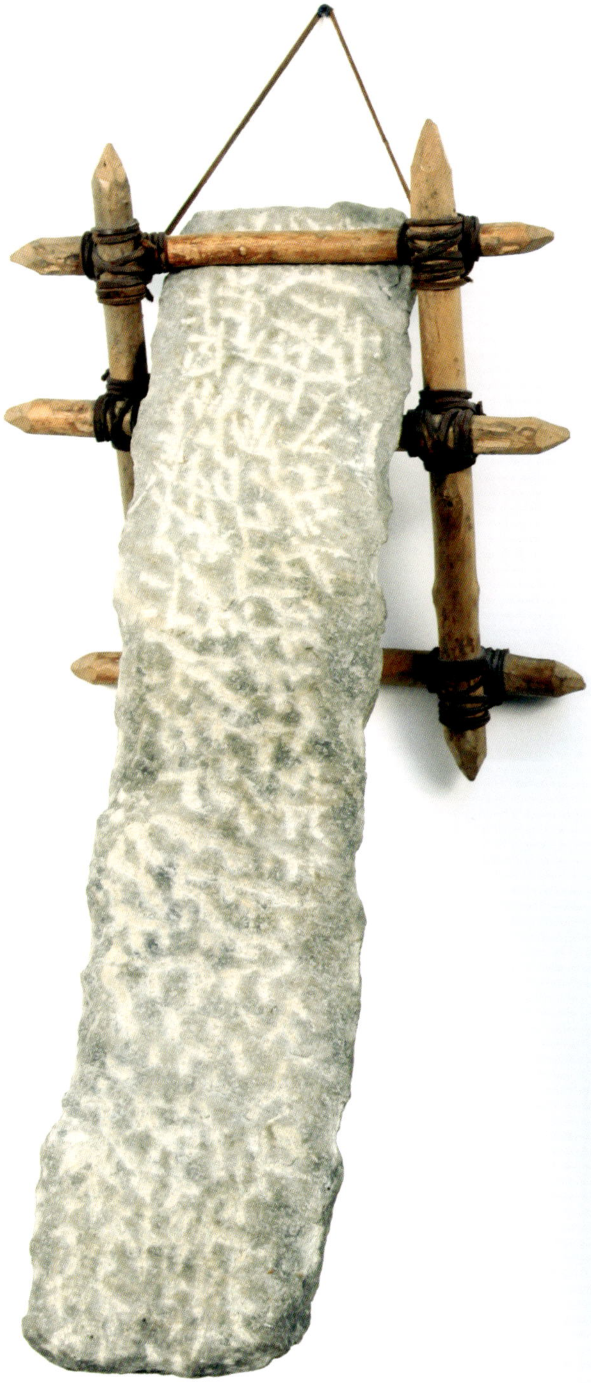

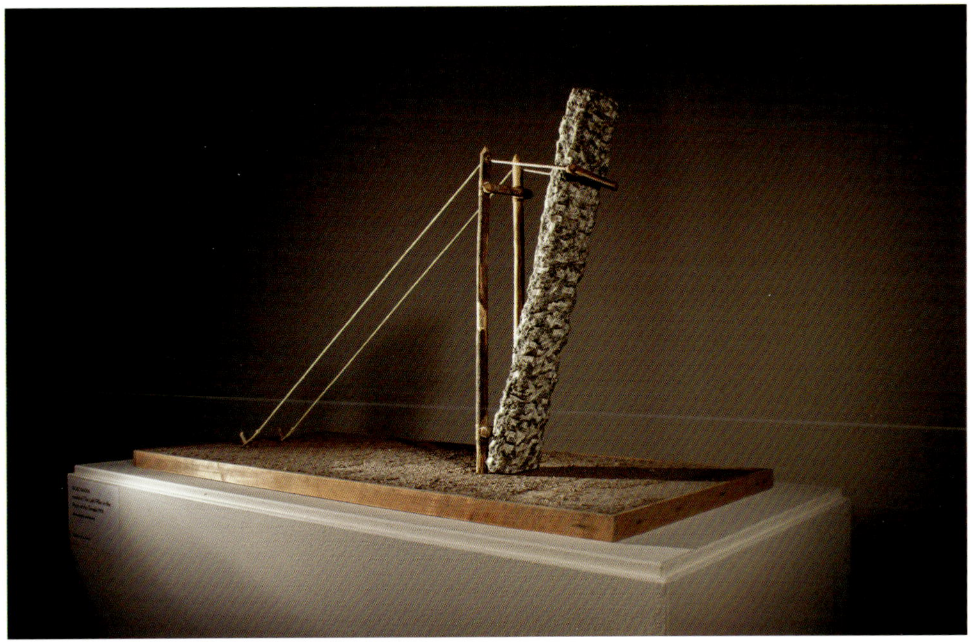

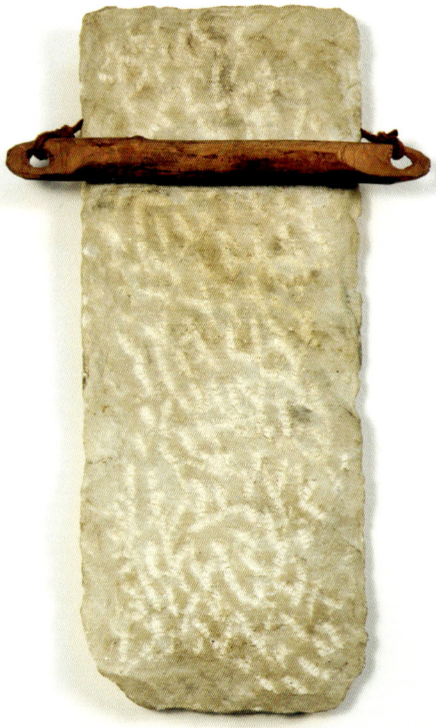

CLOCKWISE FROM TOP LEFT

PLATE 52. *Untitled*, 1978.
Stone, wood, and leather,
23 x 13 x 17 in. (58.4 x 33 x 43.2 cm).

PLATE 53. Model for *The Left Pillar in the Porch of the Temple*, 1978.
Stone, wood, and twine,
20 x 33 x 15¾ in. (50.8 x 83.8 x 40 cm).

PLATE 54. *Untitled*, 1978.
Stone, wood, and leather,
14 x 8 x 2 in. (35.6 x 20.3 x 5 cm).

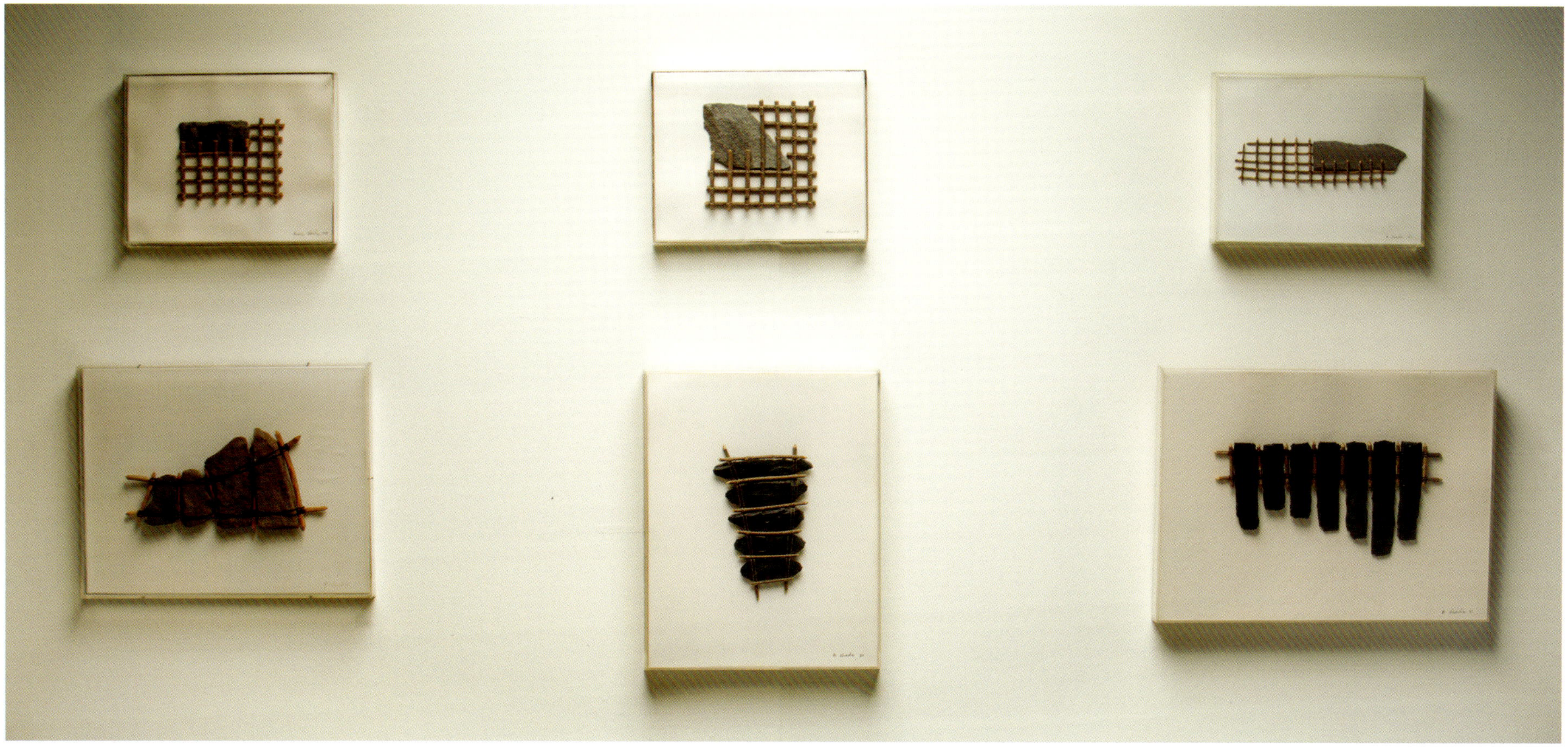

Wall installation at Mezzanine Gallery, Domestic Arts Building, Grounds For Sculpture, Hamilton, NJ, 2016.

LEFT TO RIGHT

PLATE 55. *Untitled*, 1979.
Stone, wood, string, and paper,
8 x 10 x 1 in. (20.3 x 25.4 x 2.54 cm).

PLATE 56. *Untitled*, 1979.
Stone, wood, string, and paper,
8 x 10 x 1 in. (20.3 x 25.4 x 2.54 cm).

PLATE 57. *Untitled*, 1982.
Stone, wood, string, and paper,
8 x 10 x 1 in. (20.3 x 25.4 x 2.54 cm).

PLATE 58. *Untitled*, 1977.
Stone, wood, string, and paper,
11 x 14 x 1 in. (27.9 x 35.6 x 2.54 cm).

PLATE 59. *Untitled*, 1981.
Stone, wood, string, and paper,
14 x 11 x 1 in. (35.6 x 27.9 x 2.54 cm).

PLATE 60. *Untitled*, 1981.
Stone, wood, string, and paper,
12 x 16 x 1 in. (30.5 x 40.6 x 2.54 cm).

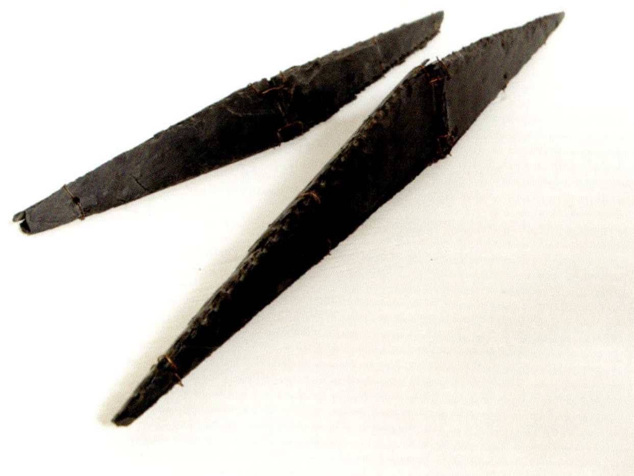

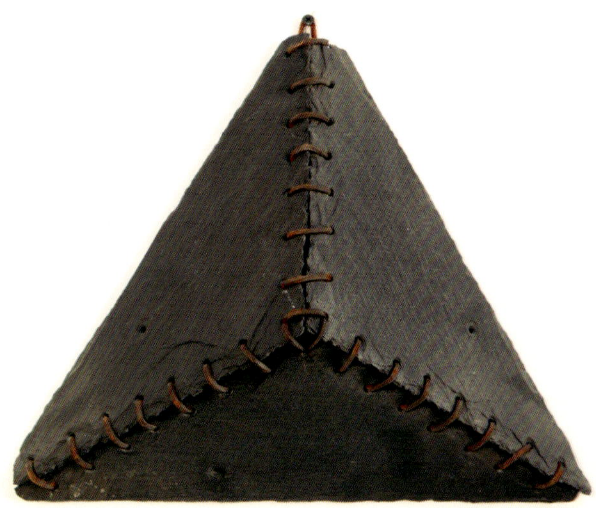

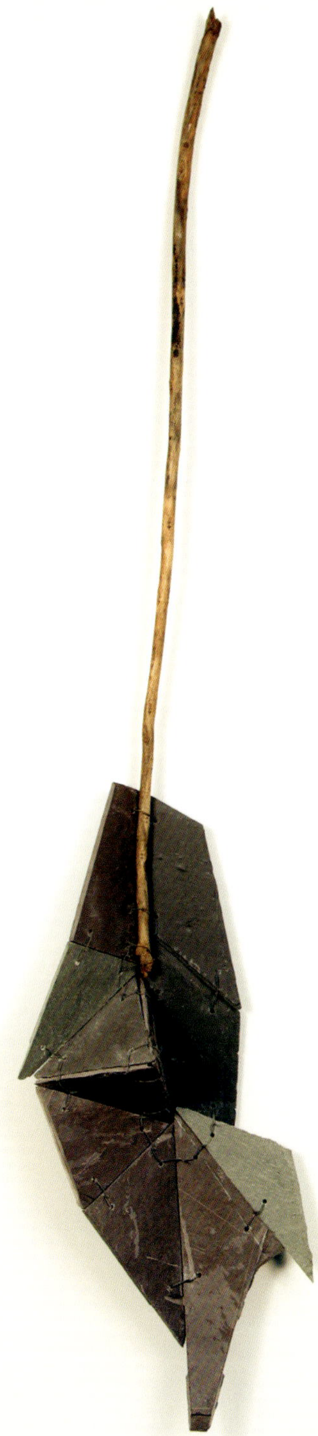

CLOCKWISE FROM TOP LEFT

PLATE 61. *Untitled*, 1982.
Slate and wire,
3 x 28 x 7 in. (7.6 x 71.1 x 17.8 cm).

PLATE 62. *Untitled*, 1982.
Slate, wood, and wire,
43 x 9 x 4 in. (109.2 x 22.9 x 10.2 cm).

PLATE 63. *Untitled*, 1982.
Slate and leather,
12 x 15 x 4 in. (30.5 x 38.1 x 10.2 cm).

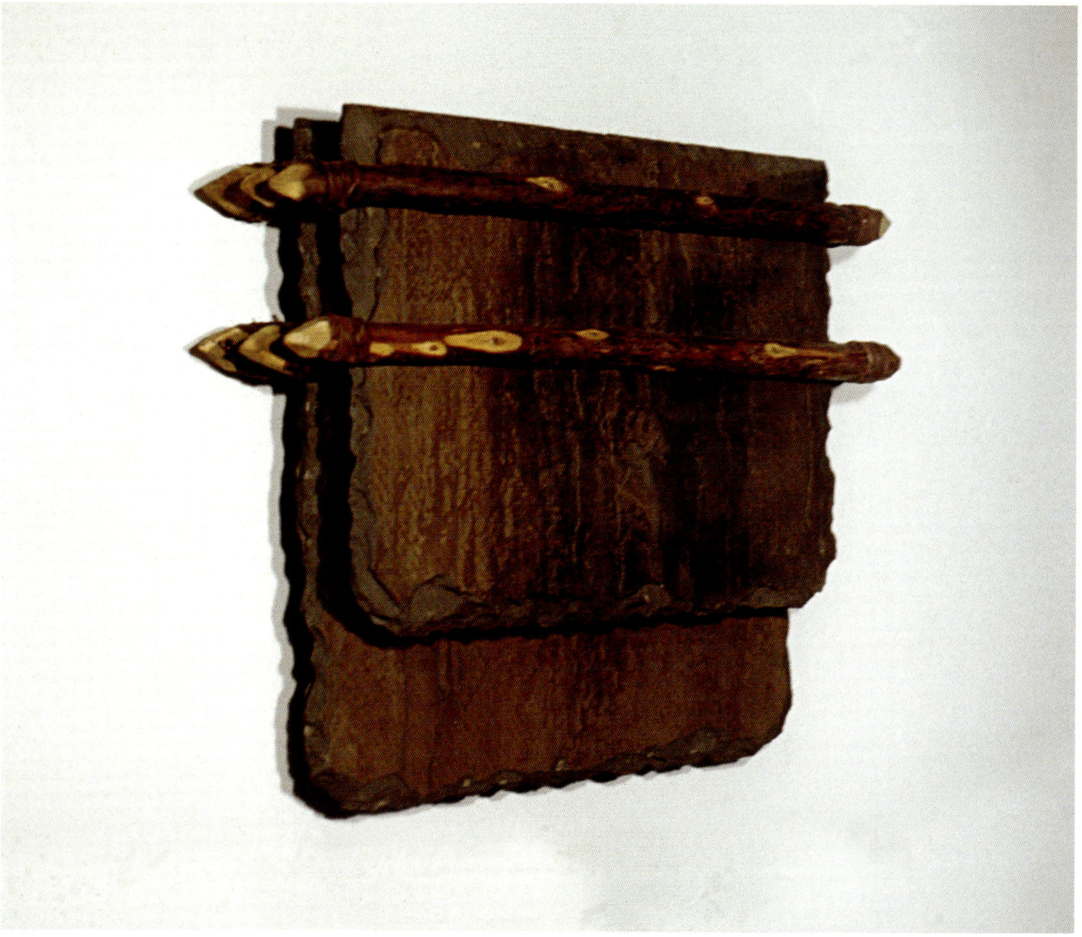

PLATE 64. *Untitled*, 1982.
Stone, wood, and leather,
24 x 30 x 7 in. (61 x 76.2 x 17.8 cm).

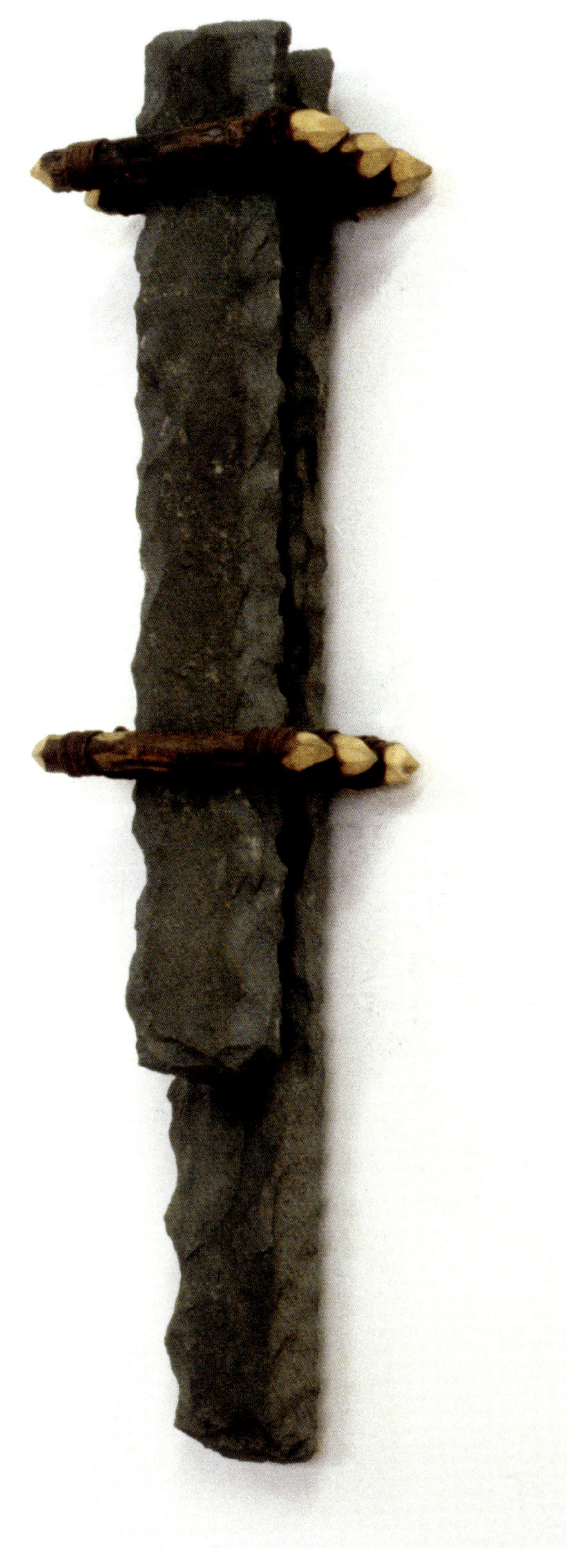

PLATE 65. *Untitled*, 1982.
Stone, wood, and leather,
48 x 12 x 7½ in. (121.9 x 30.5 x 19 cm).

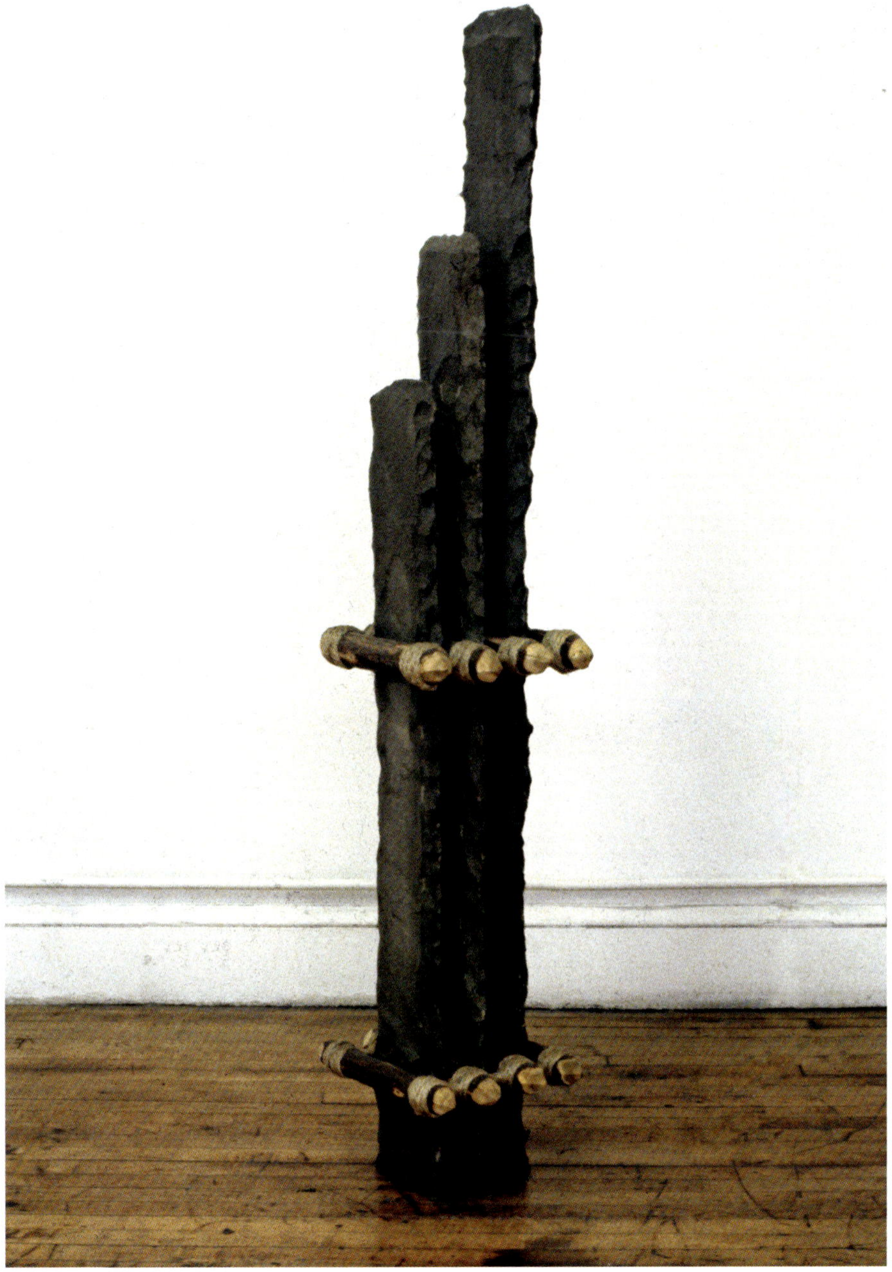

PLATE 66. *Untitled*, 1982.
Stone, wood, and rope,
66½ x 11½ x13 in. (169.9 x 29.2 x 33 cm).

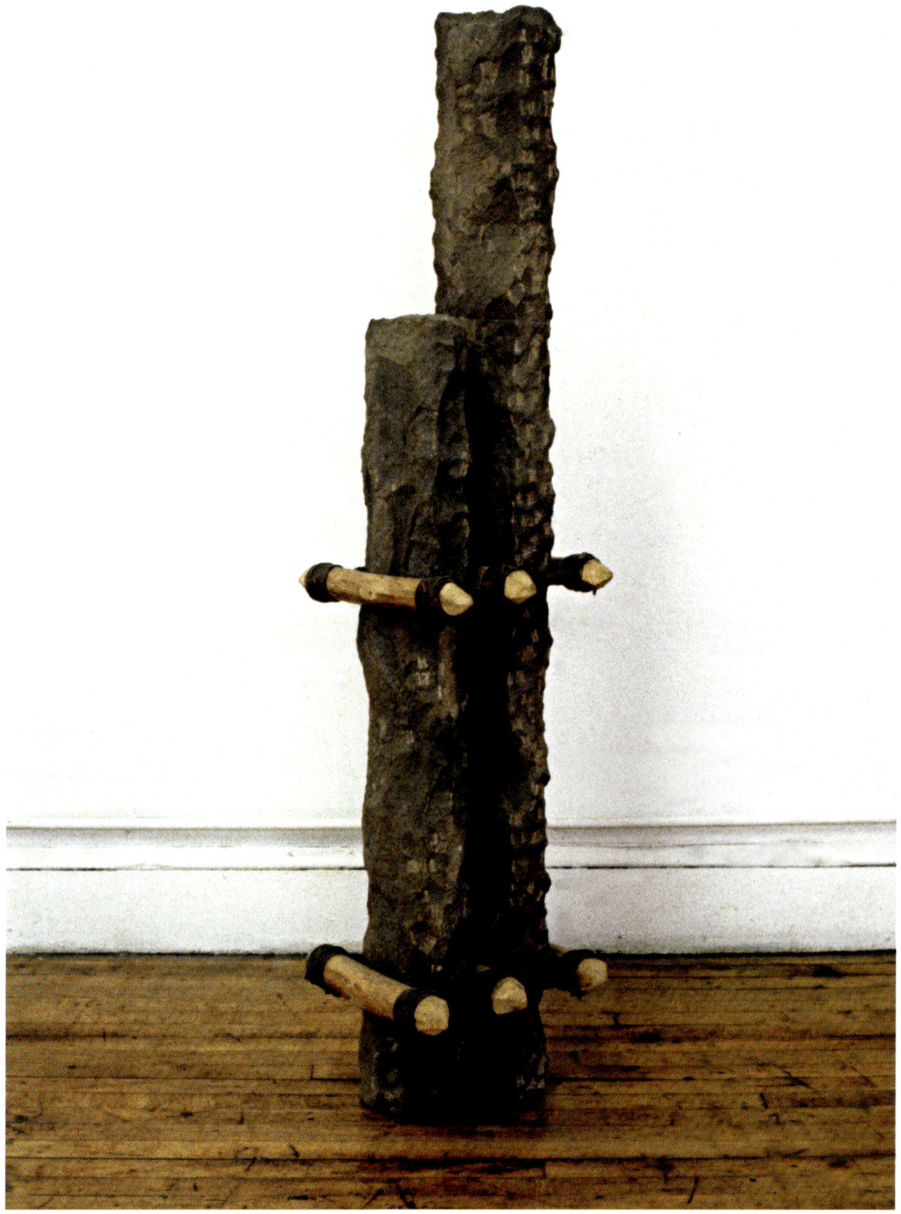

PLATE 67. *Untitled*, 1982.
Stone, wood, and leather,
60½ x 13 x 13 in. (153.7 x 33 x 33 cm).

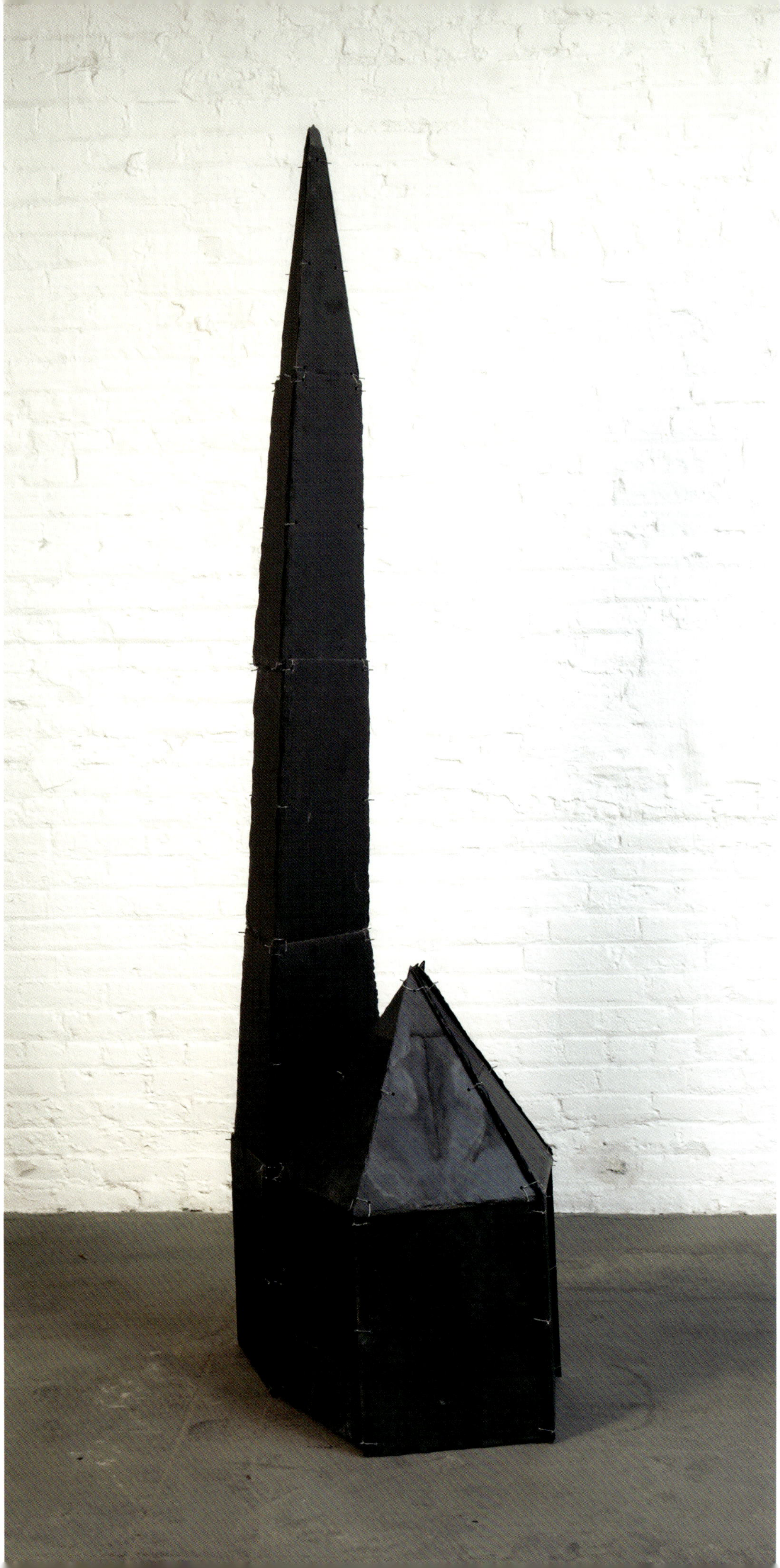

PLATE 68. *Untitled*, 1983.
Slate and wire,
89 x 21 x 30 in. (226.1 x 53.3 x 76.2 cm).

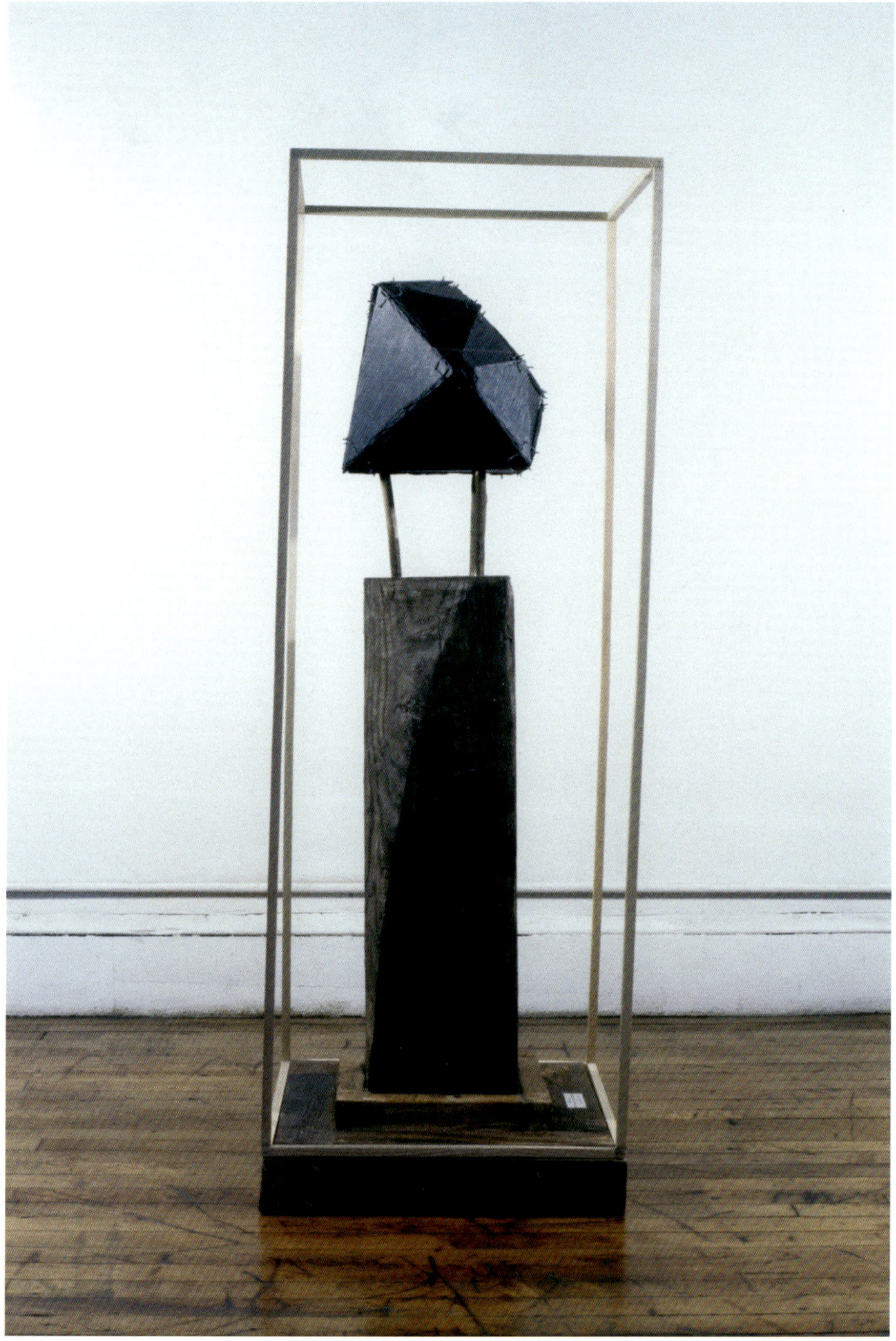

PLATE 69. *My Precious Stones Series No. 2, Star of David Cut*, 1983.
Slate, wood, and wire,
52 x 18 x 18 in. (132.1 x 45.7 x 45.7 cm).

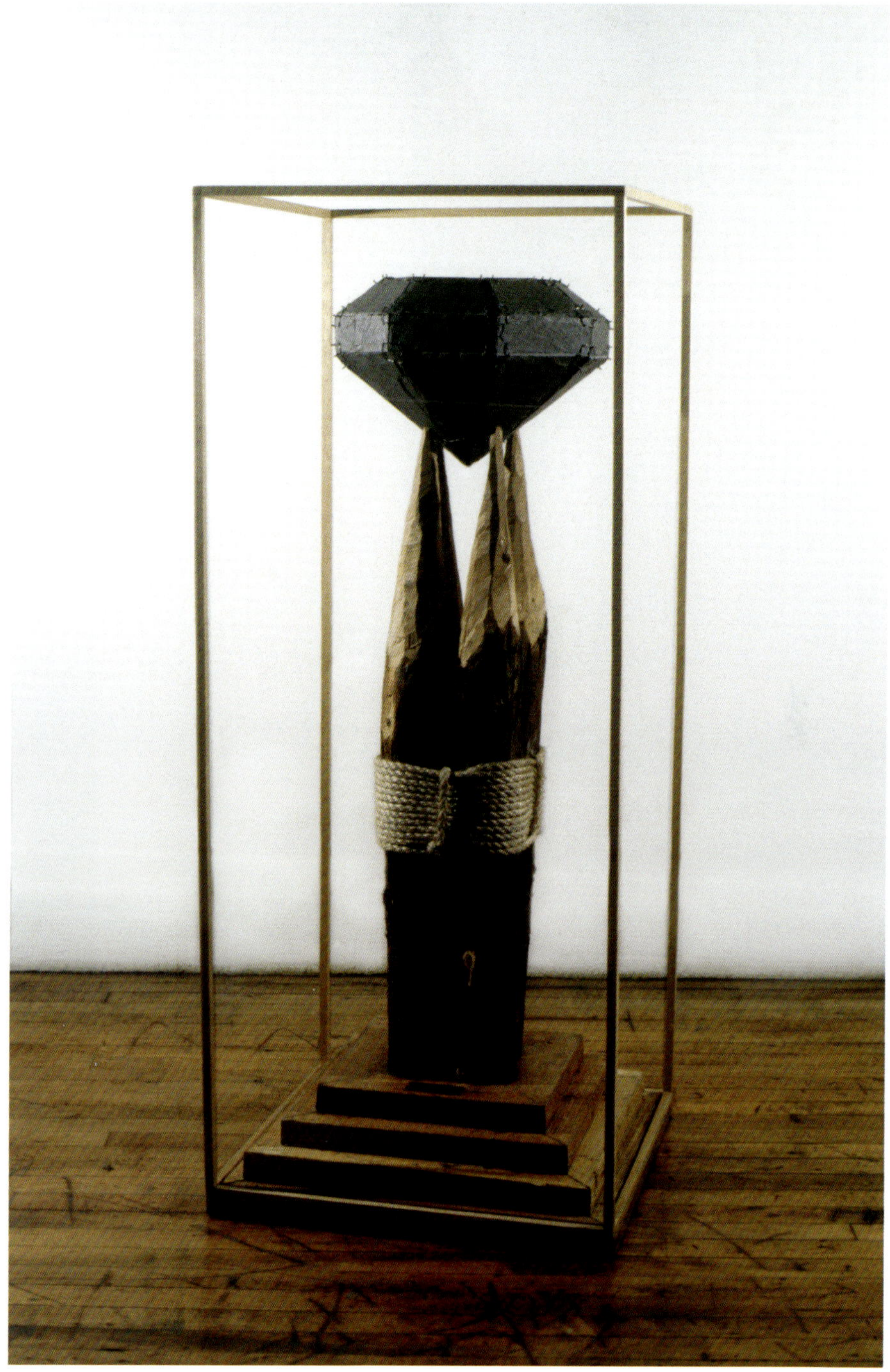

PLATE 70. *My Precious Stones Series No. 5, Octagon Cut*, 1983.
Green slate, wood, rope, and wire,
52 x 21 x 21 in. (132 x 53 x 53 cm).

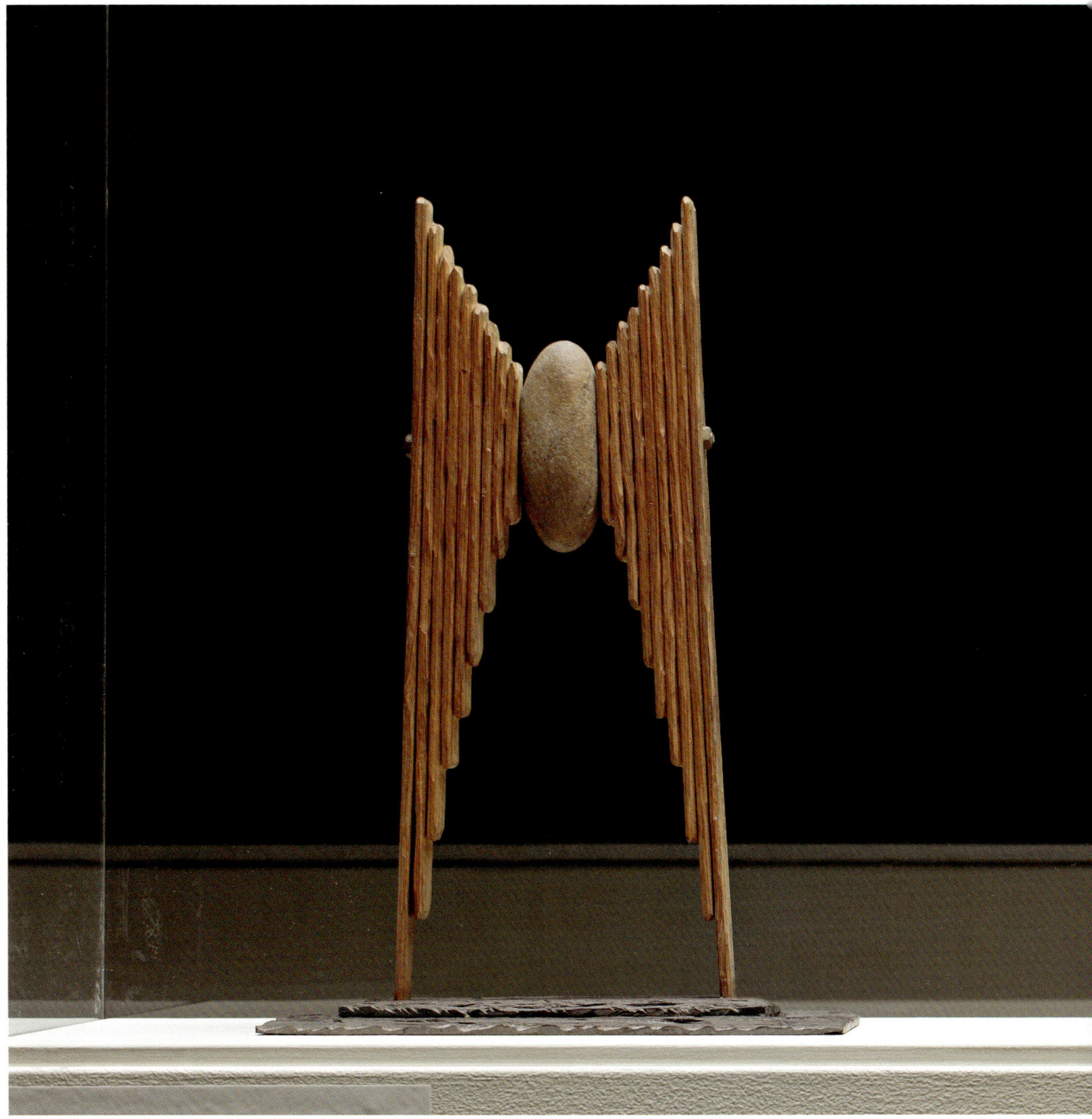

Installation showcase at Mezzanine Gallery,
Domestic Arts Building,
Grounds For Sculpture, Hamilton, NJ, 2016.

LEFT TO RIGHT

PLATE 71. *Untitled*, 1984.
Wood, slate, stone, and metal,
17 x 13 1/2 x 7 in. (43.2 x 34.3 x 17.8 cm).

PLATE 72. *Untitled*, 1984.
Slate, stone, and metal,
17 1/4 x 7 1/4 x 4 in. (43.8 x 18.4 x 10.2 cm).

PLATE 73. *Untitled*, 1984.
Slate, stone, and metal,
13 1/2 x 12 x 8 in. (34.3 x 30.5 x 20.3 cm).

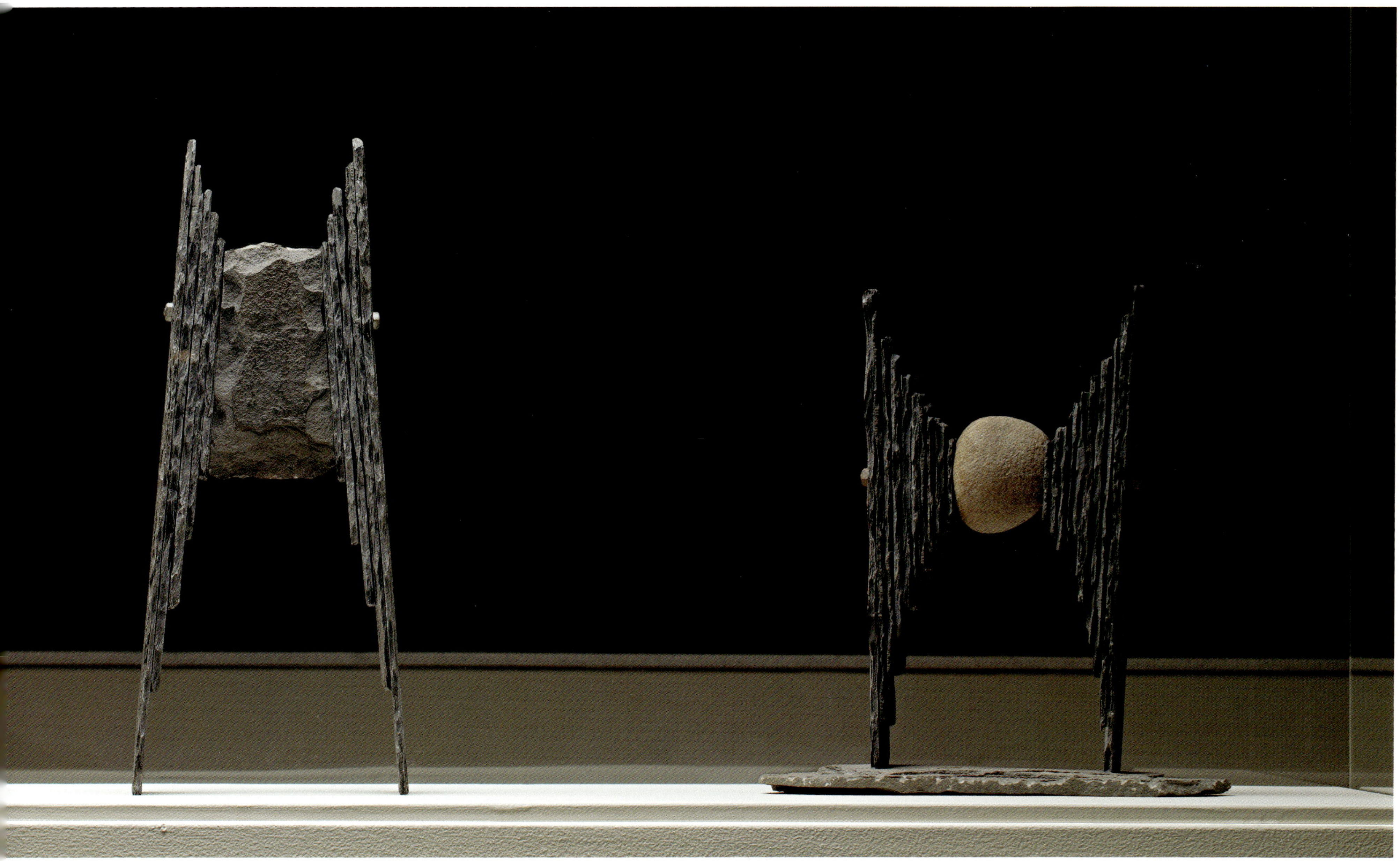

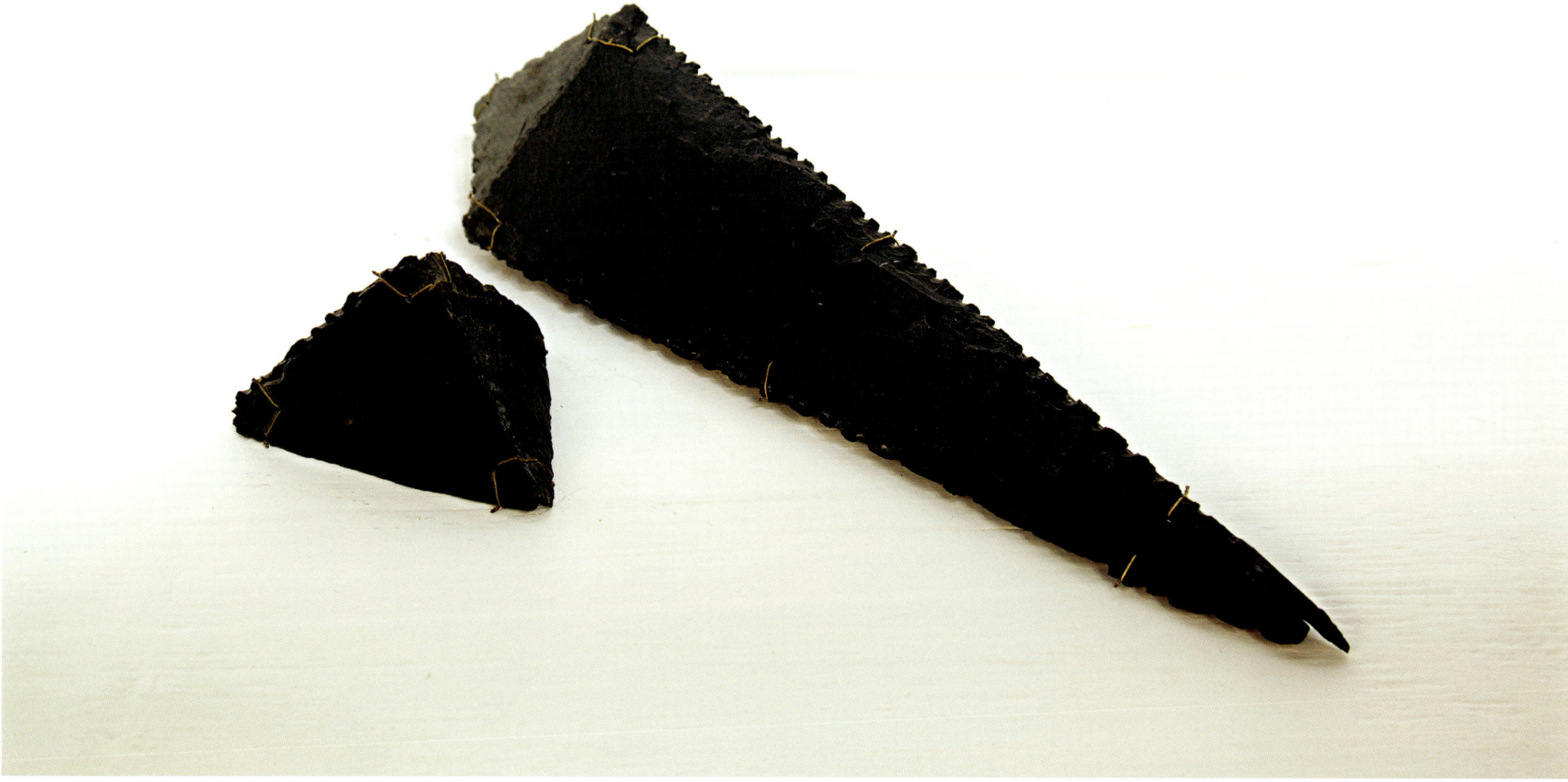

PLATE 74. *Untitled*, 1983.
Slate and wire,
3½ x 17 x 7 in. (8.9 x 43.2 x 17.8 cm).

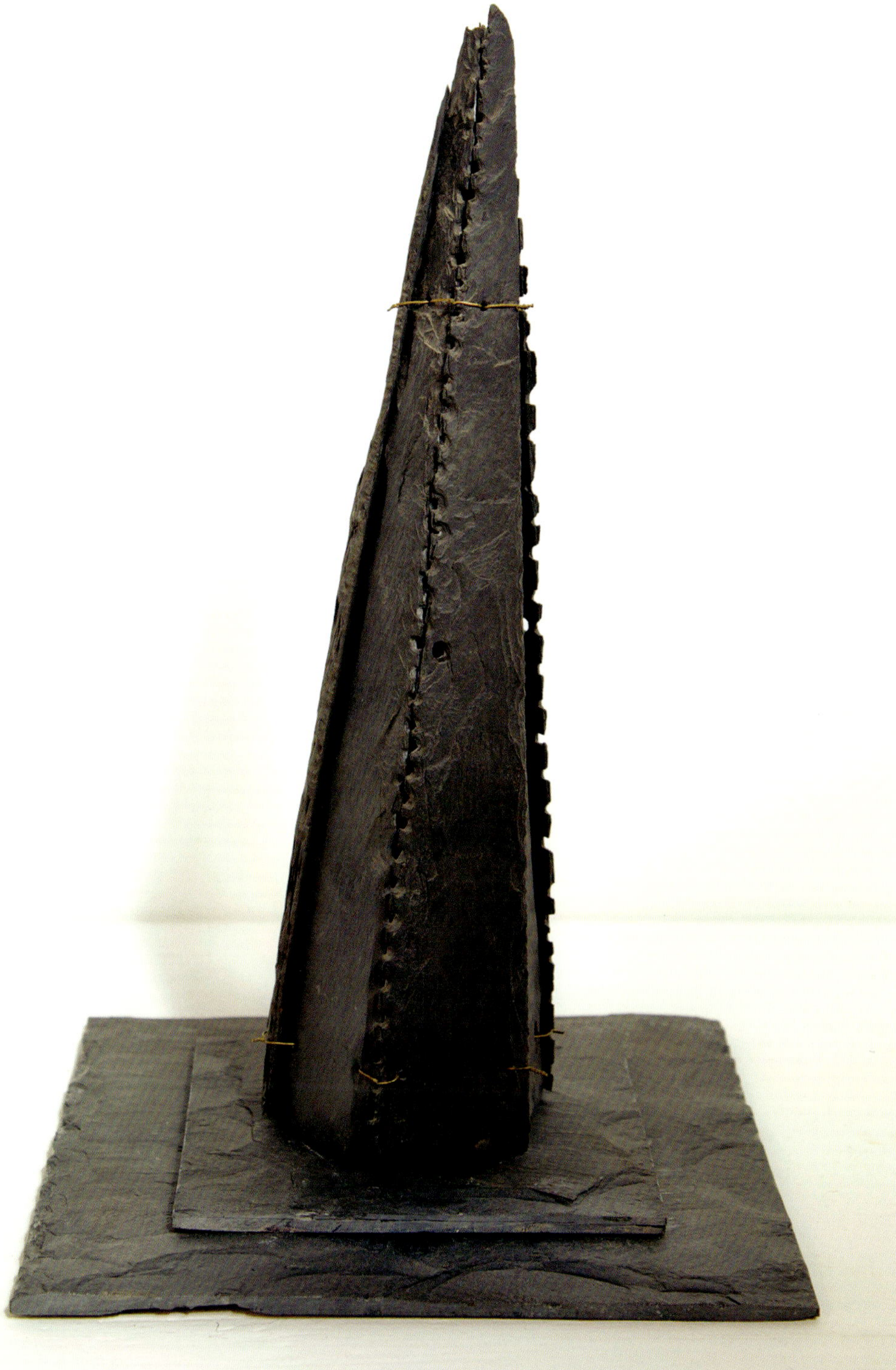

PLATE 75. *Untitled*, 1984.
Slate and wire,
$13^1/_2$ x $8^1/_2$ x $8^1/_2$ in. (34.3 x 21.6 x 21.6 cm).

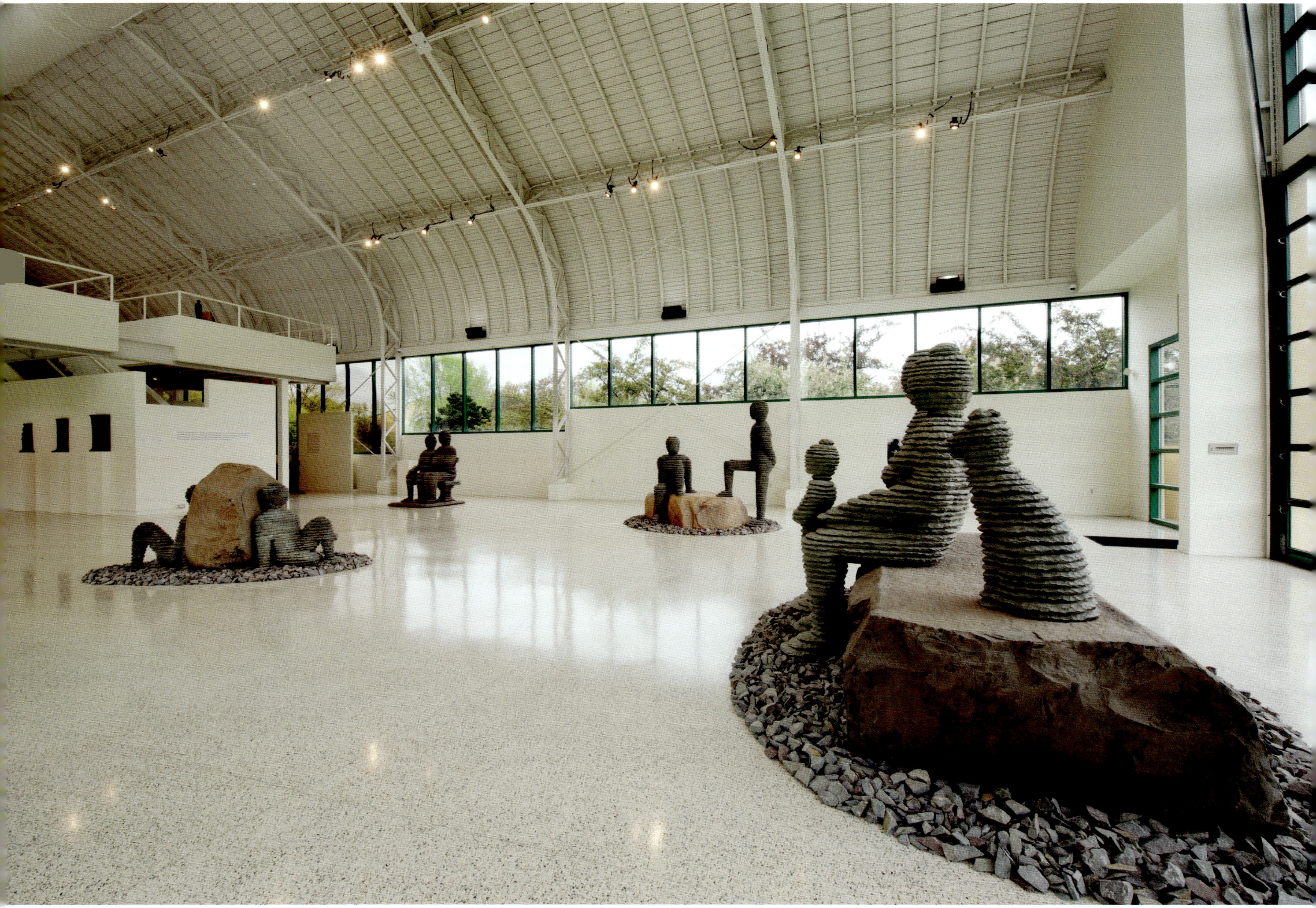

Works in Stone, Slate, and Bronze, 1985–2015

IN 1985, Boaz Vaadia began producing figurative works with stacked layers of slate and bluestone. This work began a long period of great creative success and recognition for him. He marshaled his extensive technical skills of stone carving, fabrication, and bronze casting to create works that resonated all of the creative concerns he had explored in his early works. These later works, created from the stacked layers of sedimentary stone, reveal Vaadia's focus on natural materials and natural physical forces such as gravity as central elements in the composition and construction of his sculptures.

His first exhibition of these works took place at OK Harris Works of Art with Ivan Karp in SoHo. The entire exhibition sold out and marked the beginning of a long and meaningful relationship between Vaadia and Karp. Numerous public and private collectors from around the world have purchased or commissioned Vaadia's works for their collections. They include The Hakone Open-Air Museum, Hakone, Japan; The Jewish Museum, New York City; and The Metropolitan Museum of Art, New York City, among many others.

Installation at
Main Museum Gallery,
Grounds For Sculpture,
Hamilton, NJ, 2016.

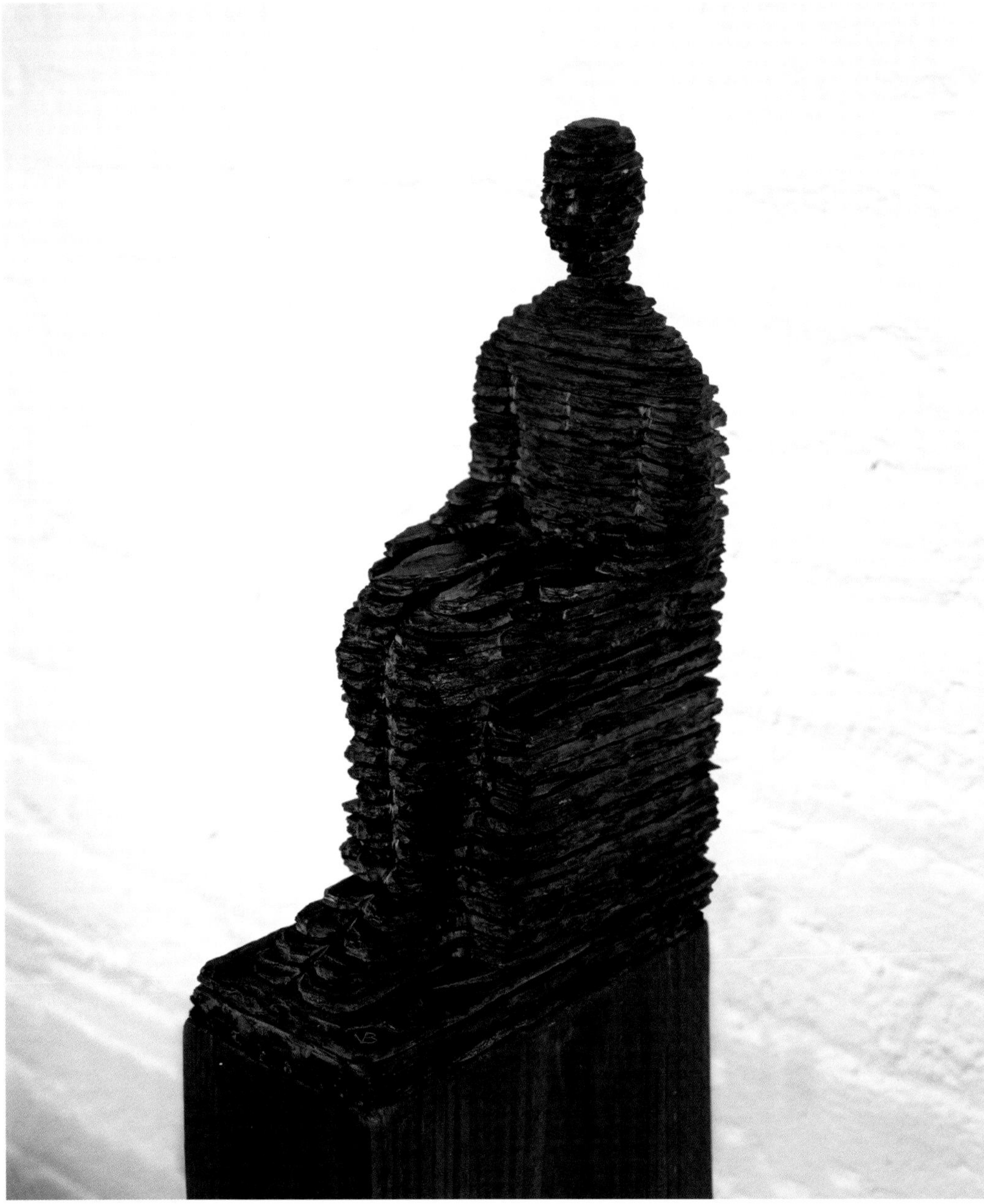

PLATE 76. *Solomon*, 1985.
Slate,
13 x 8¼ x 4 in. (33 x 20.9 x 10.2 cm).
Private collection of Rebecca Vaadia and Sara Vaadia.

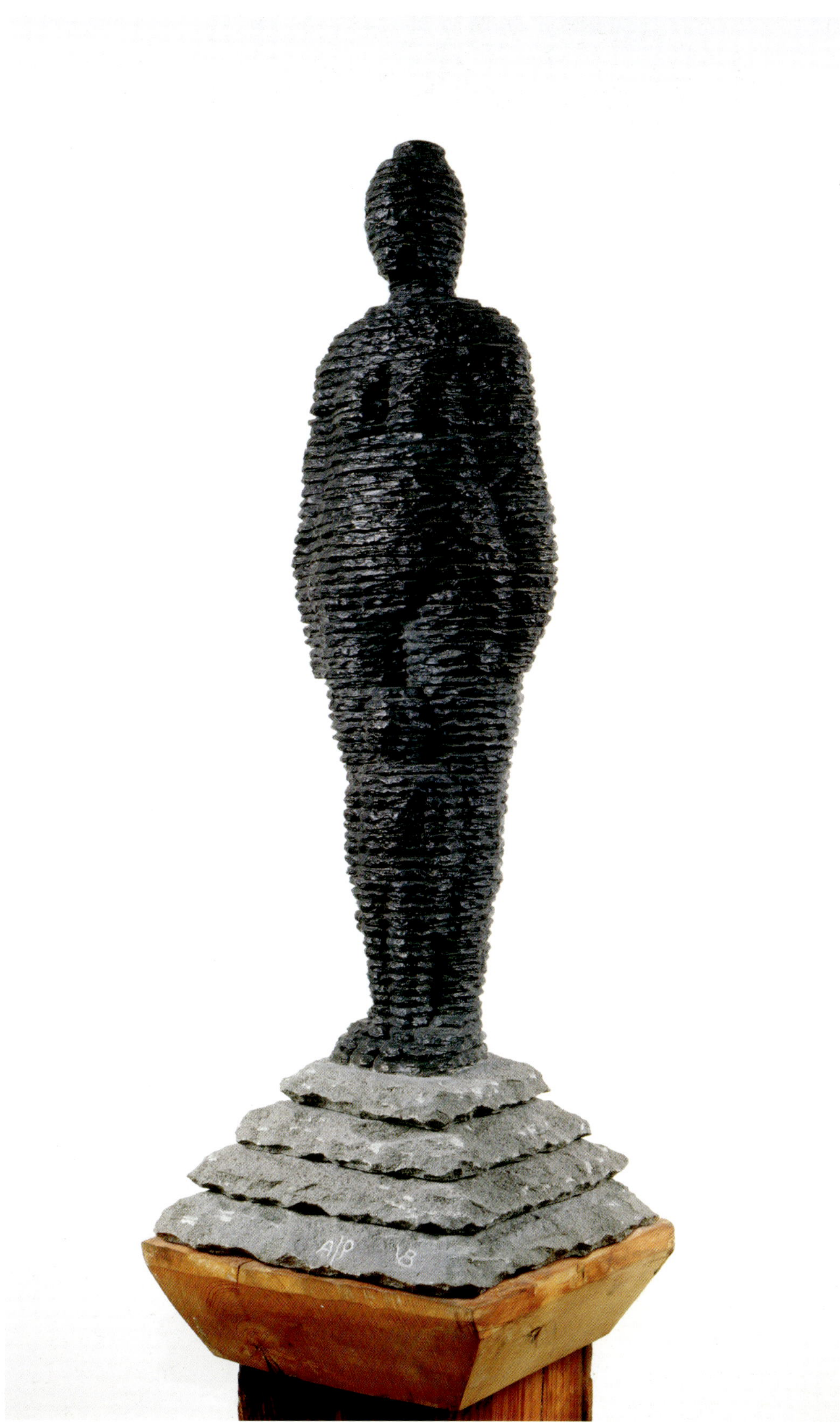

PLATE 77. *Hanna & Shemu'el*, 1988.
Bronze and bluestone,
26 x 9½ x 9½ in. (66 x 24.1 x 24.1 cm).
Edition of 7.

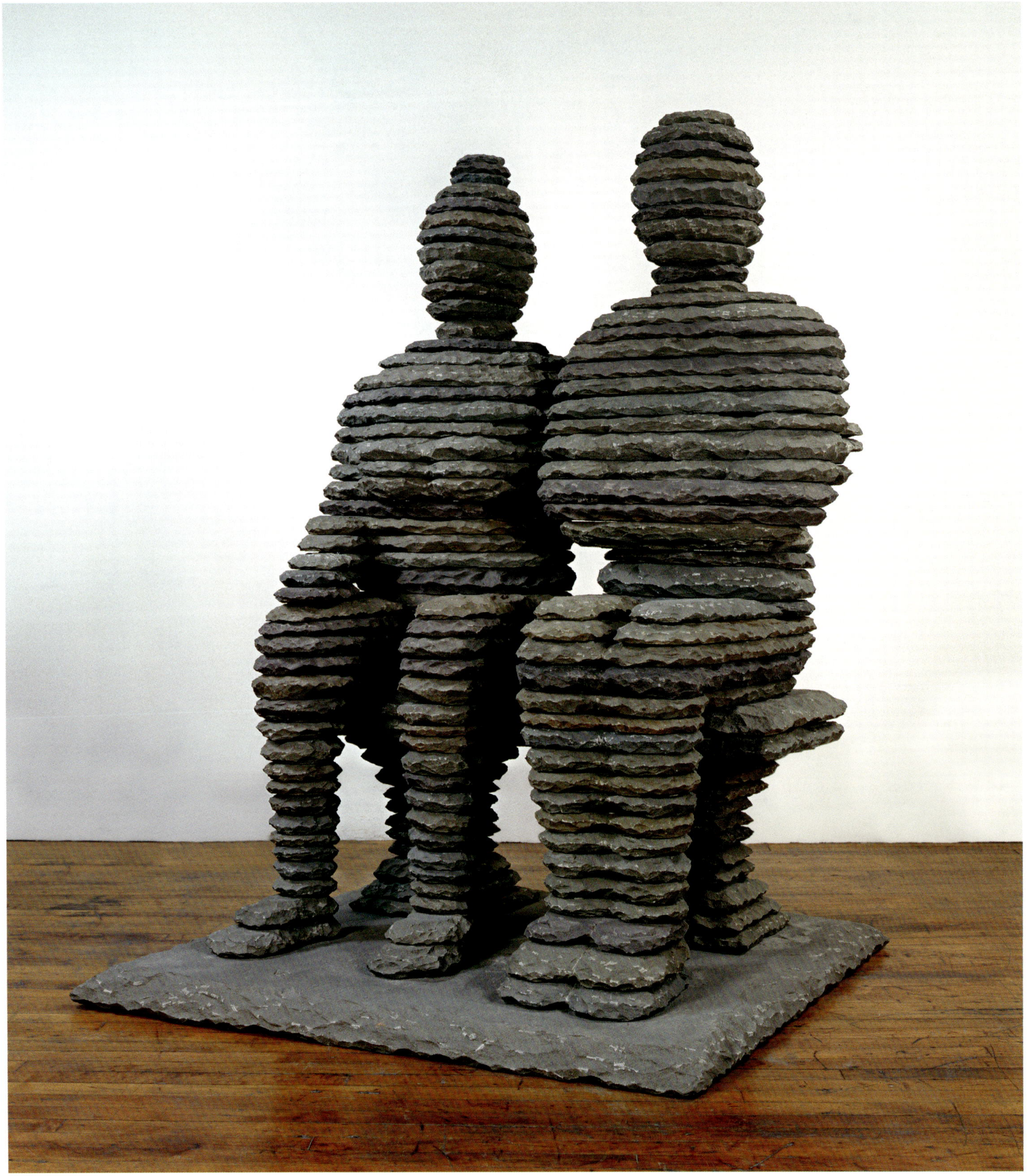

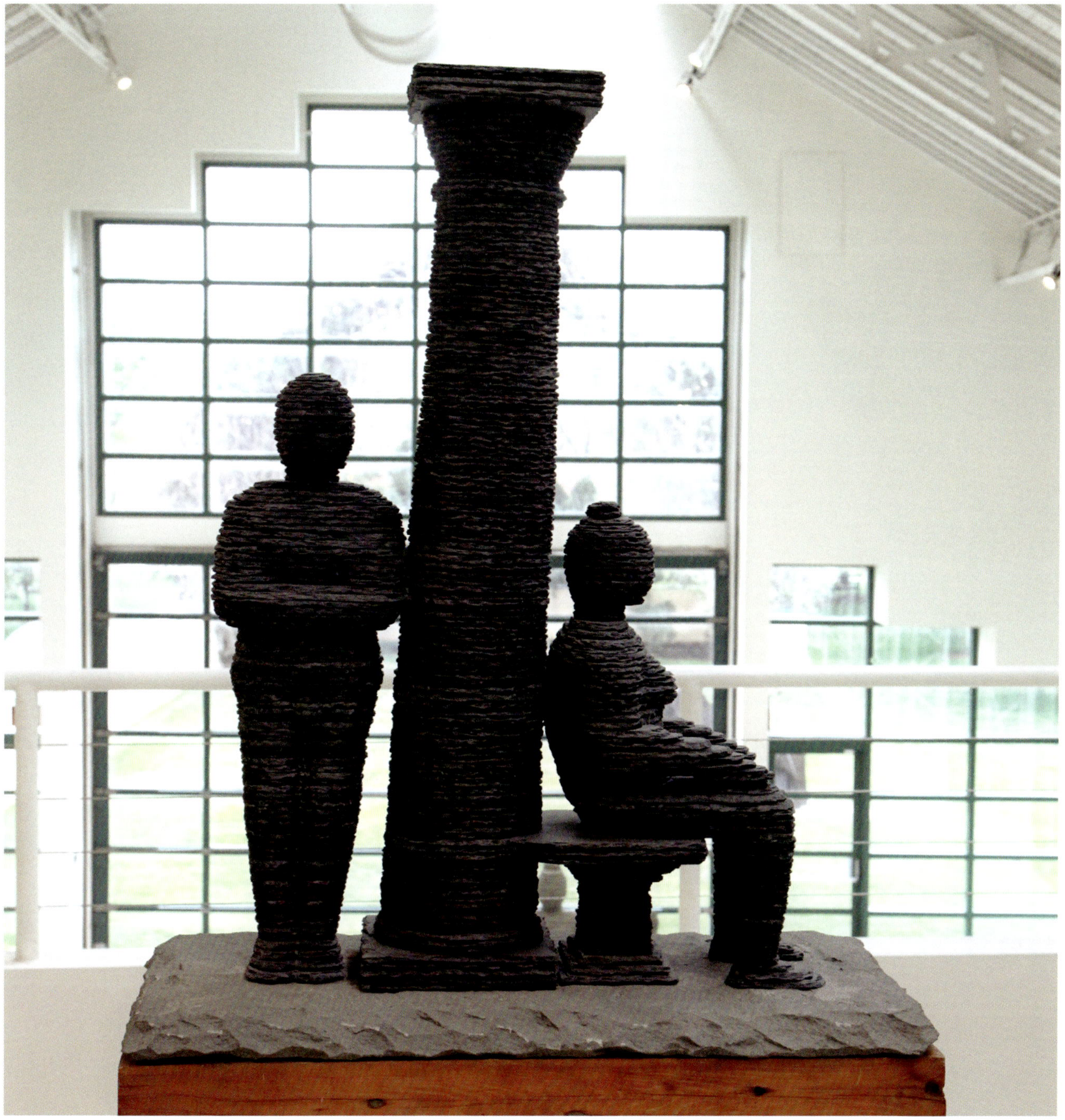

PLATE 79. *Shimshon and Delila*, 1989.
Slate and bluestone,
33½ x 28 x 14 in. (85.1 x 71.1 x 35.6 cm).
Private collection of Rebecca Vaadia and Sara Vaadia.

OPPOSITE

PLATE 78. *Maakha and Rehavam*, 1988.
Bluestone,
66 x 47 x 45 in. (167.5 x 119.5 x 114.5 cm).
Private collection of Rebecca Vaadia and Sara Vaadia.

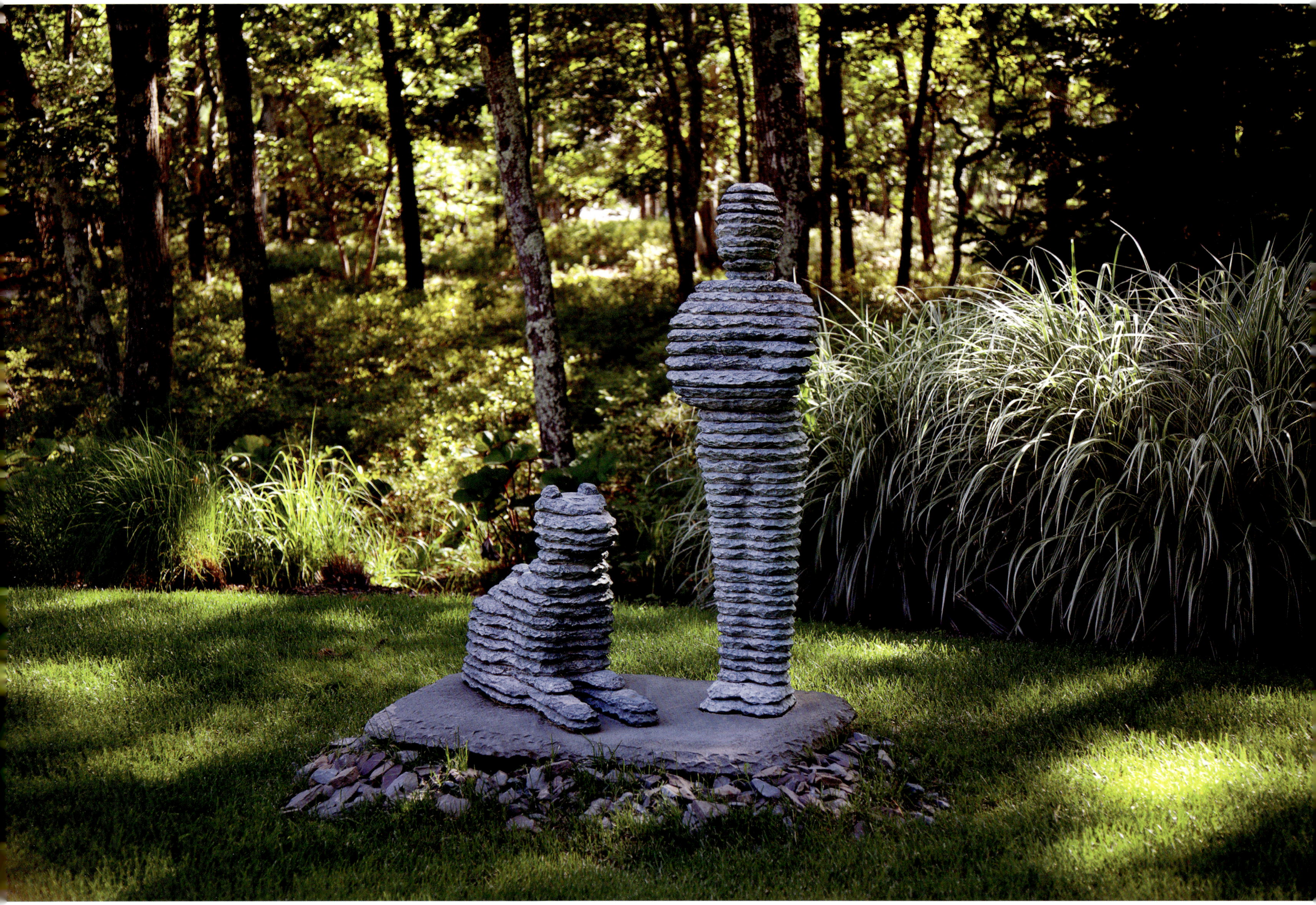

PLATE 80. *Zur with Dog*, 1989.
Bronze and bluestone,
49 x 41 x 29 in. (124.5 x 104.1 x 73.7 cm).
Edition of 5. Private collection of Rebecca Vaadia and Sara Vaadia.

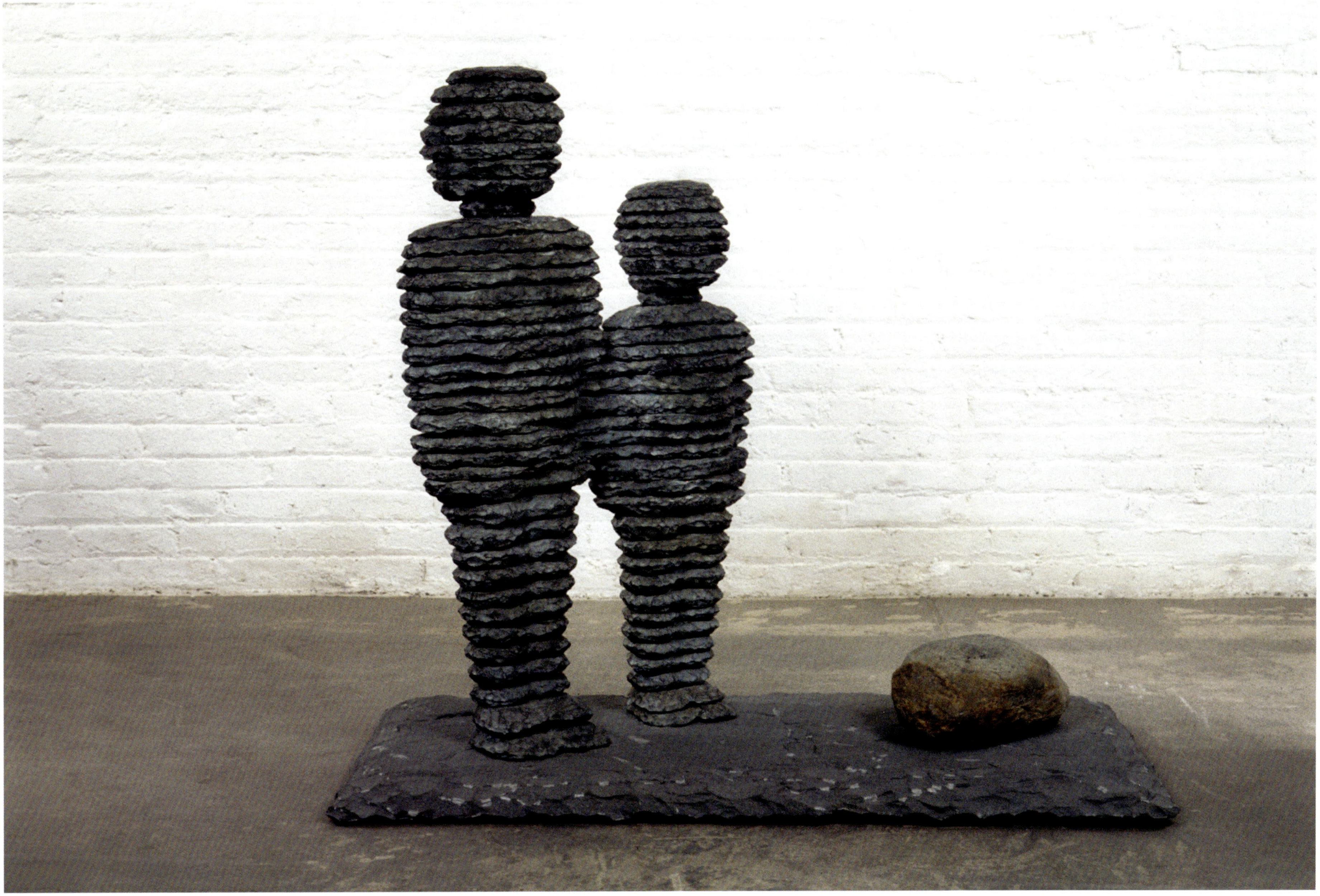

PLATE 81. *Milka & Tirza*, 1990.
Bronze, boulder, and bluestone,
41 x 47 x 24 in. (104.1 x 119.4 x 61 cm).
Edition of 5. Private collection of Rebecca Vaadia and Sara Vaadia.

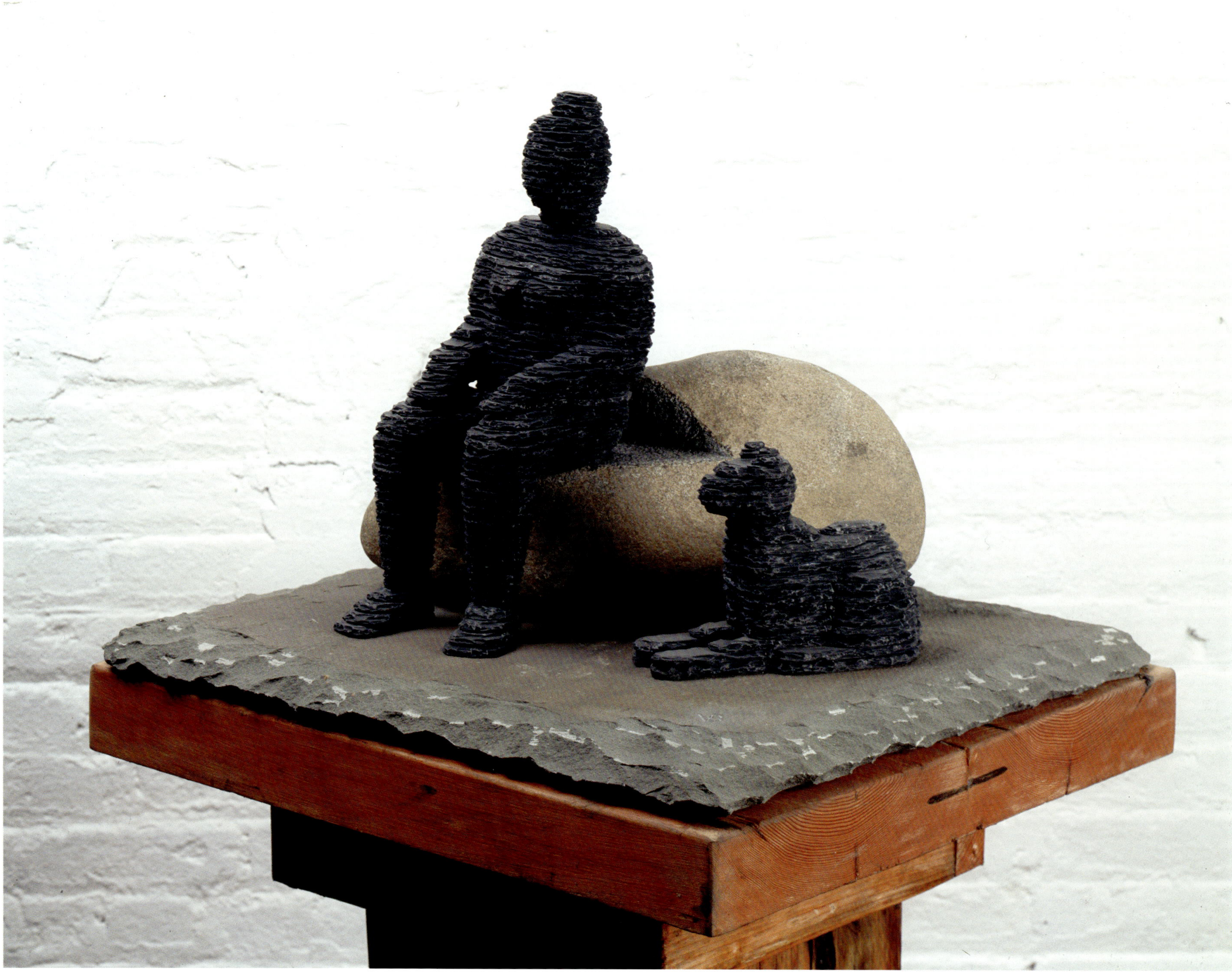

PLATE 82. *Ahino'am with Dog*, 1990.
Slate, boulder, and bluestone,
16 x 23 x 21 in. (40.6 x 58.4 x 53.3 cm).
Private collection of Rebecca Vaadia and Sara Vaadia.

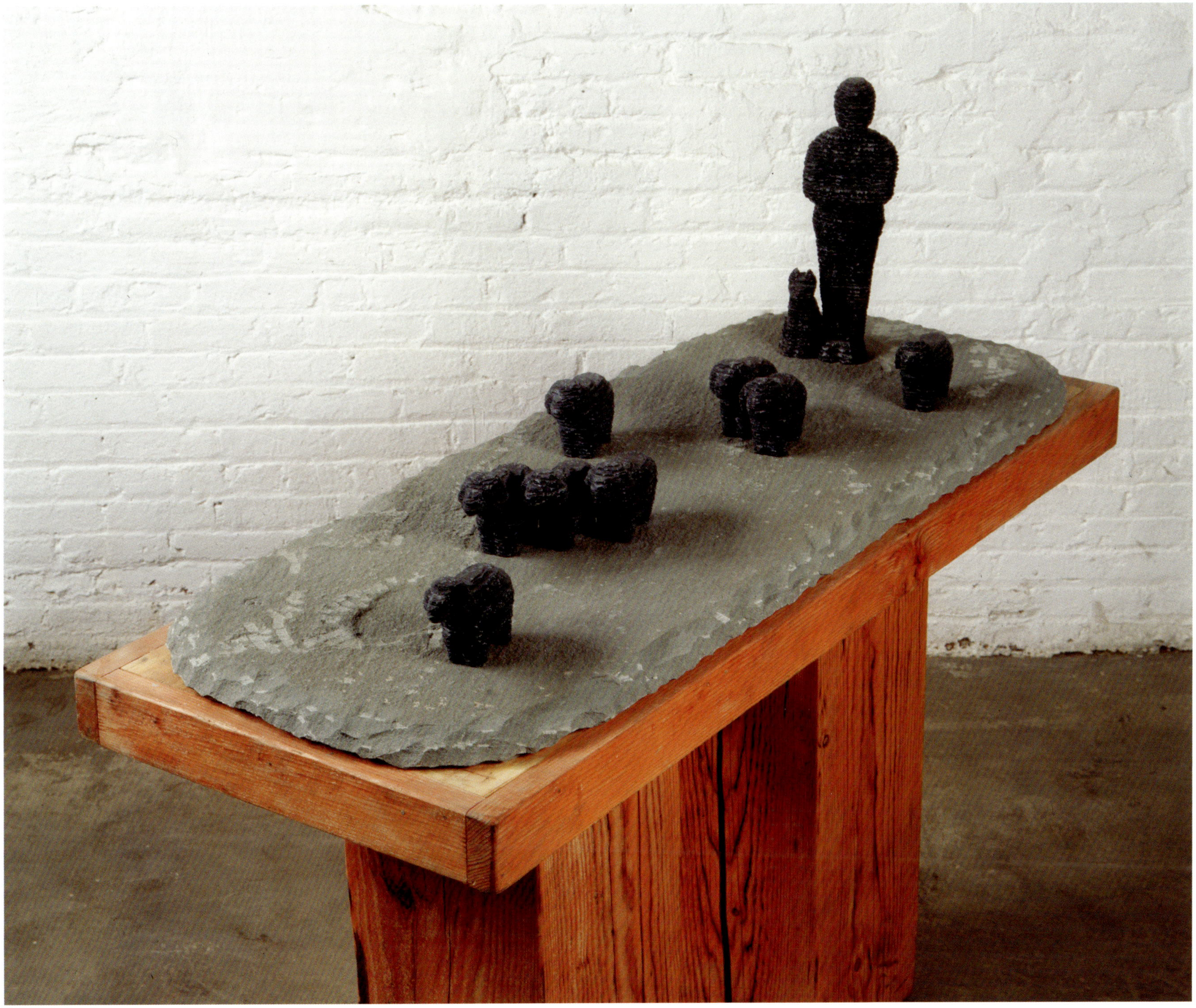

PLATE 83. *Avimelekh with Dog and 8 Lambs*, 1991.
Slate and bluestone,
18 x 59 x 24 in. (45.7 x 149.9 x 61 cm).
Private collection of Rebecca Vaadia and Sara Vaadia.

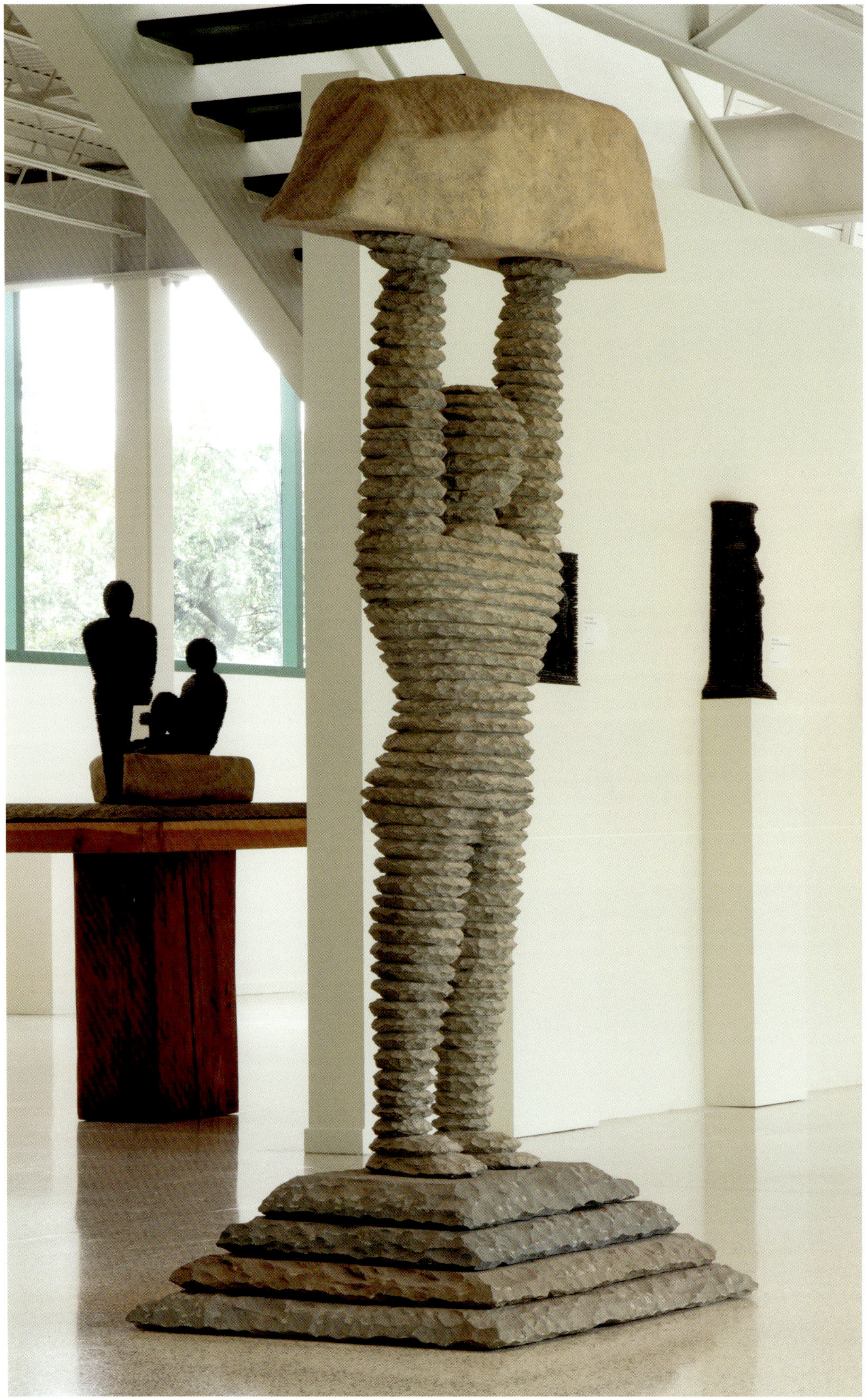

PLATE 84. *Shimshon*, 1998.
Bronze, boulder, and bluestone,
80 x 34 x 29 in. (203.2 x 86.4 x 73.7 cm).
Edition of 5. Private collection of
Rebecca Vaadia and Sara Vaadia.

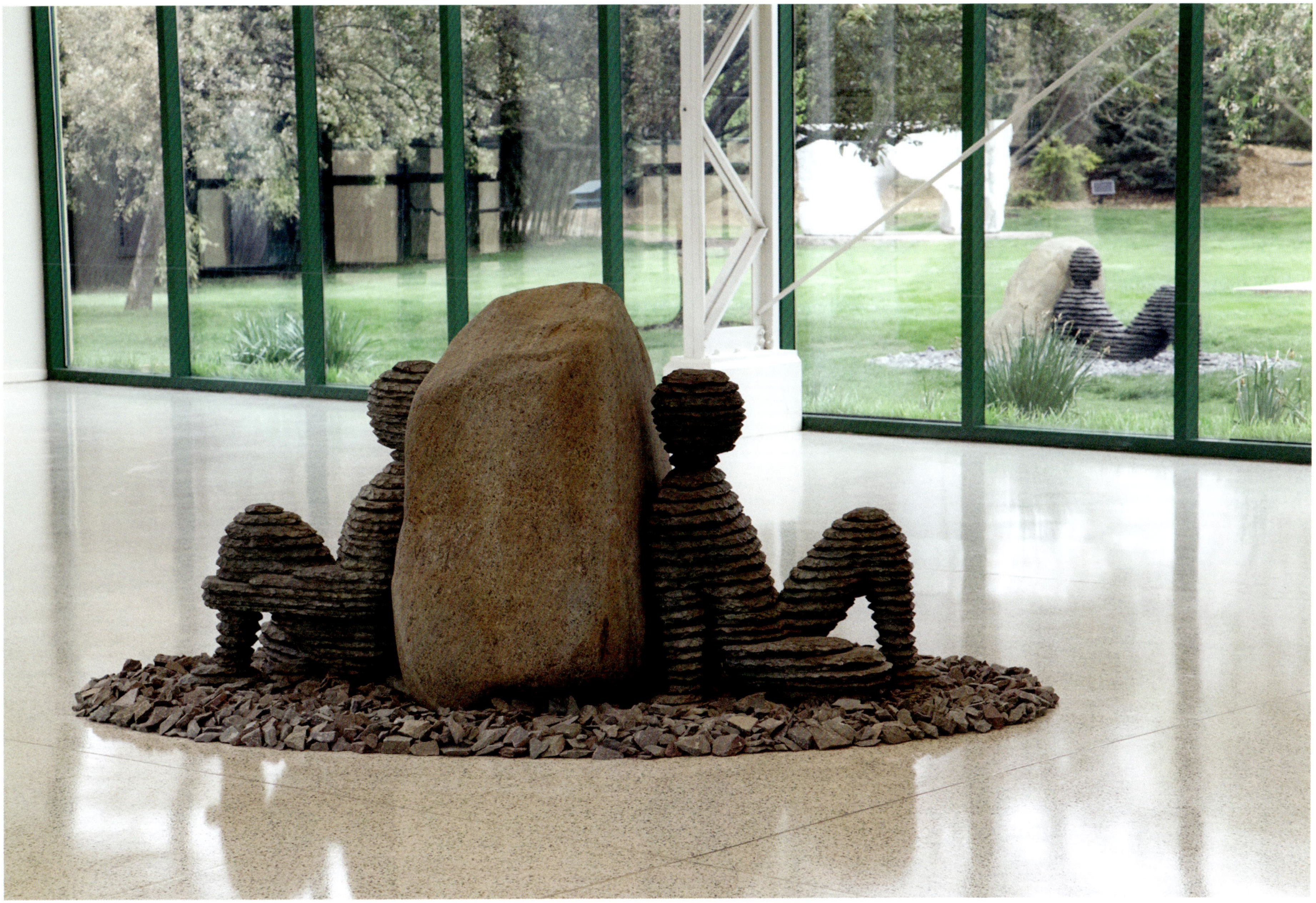

PLATE 85. *Gilalay & Ginnetoy*, 1998.
Bronze, boulder, and bluestone,
38 x 100 x 60 in. (96.5 x 254 x 152.4 cm).
Edition of 5. Private collection of Rebecca Vaadia and Sara Vaadia.

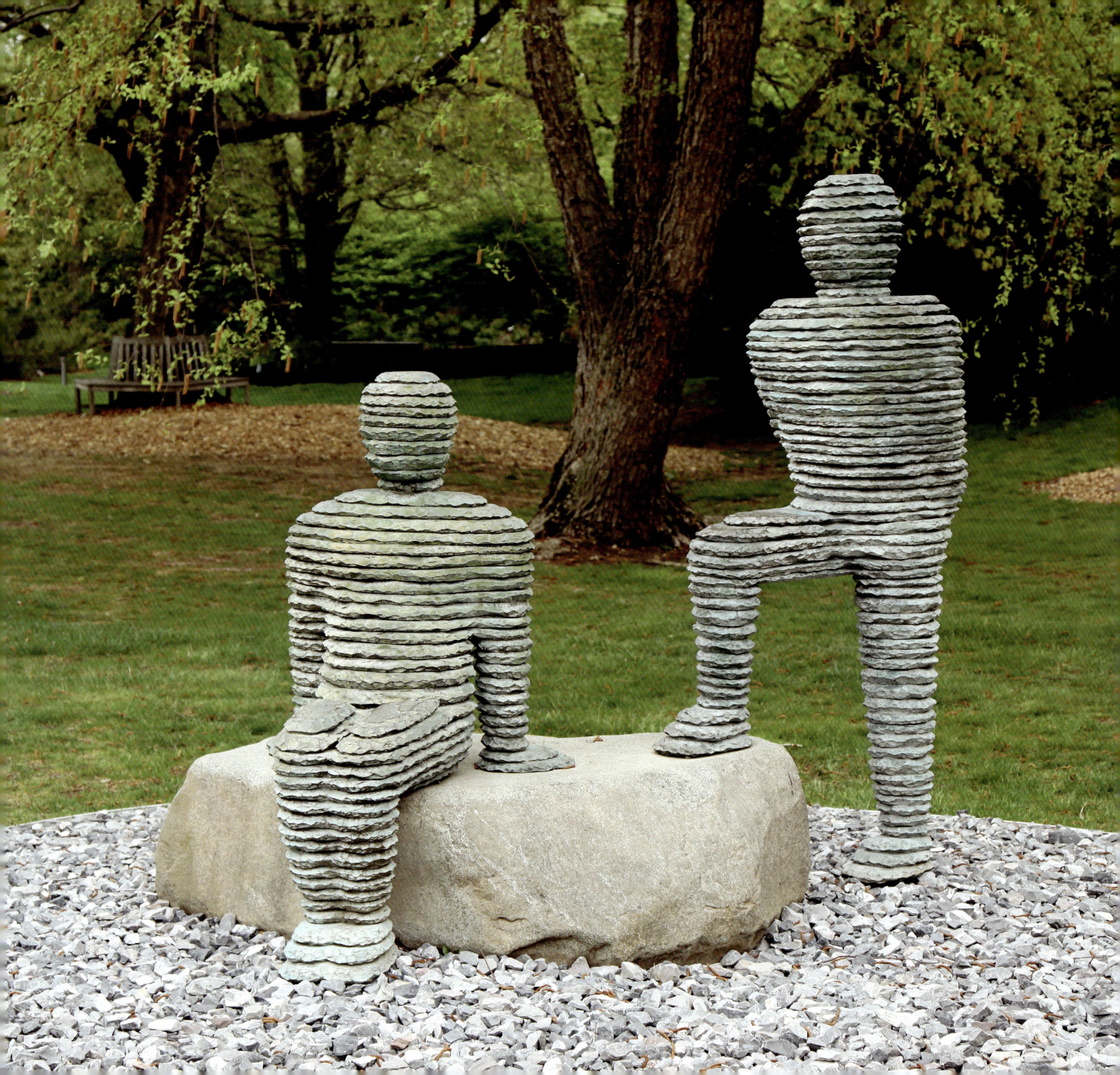

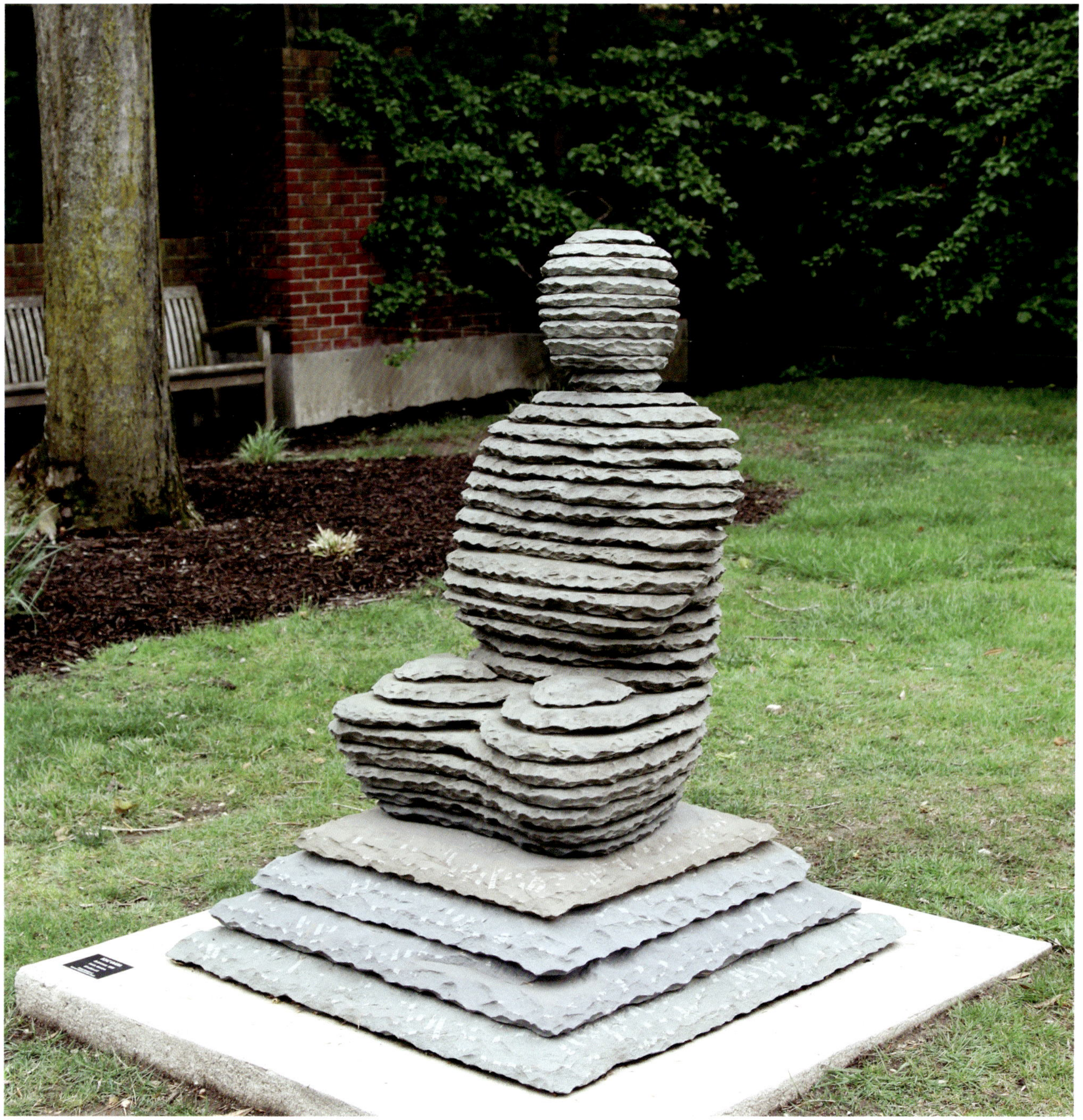

PLATE 87. *Ba'al-zevuv*, 1999.
Bronze and bluestone,
44 x 35 x 35 in. (111.8 x 88.9 x 88.9 cm).
Edition of 5. Private collection of Rebecca Vaadia and Sara Vaadia.

OPPOSITE

PLATE 86. *Ammi'el & Amaryahu*, 1999.
Bronze, boulder, and bluestone,
70 x 100 x 72 in. (177.8 x 254 x 182.9 cm).
Edition of 5. Private collection of Rebecca Vaadia and Sara Vaadia.

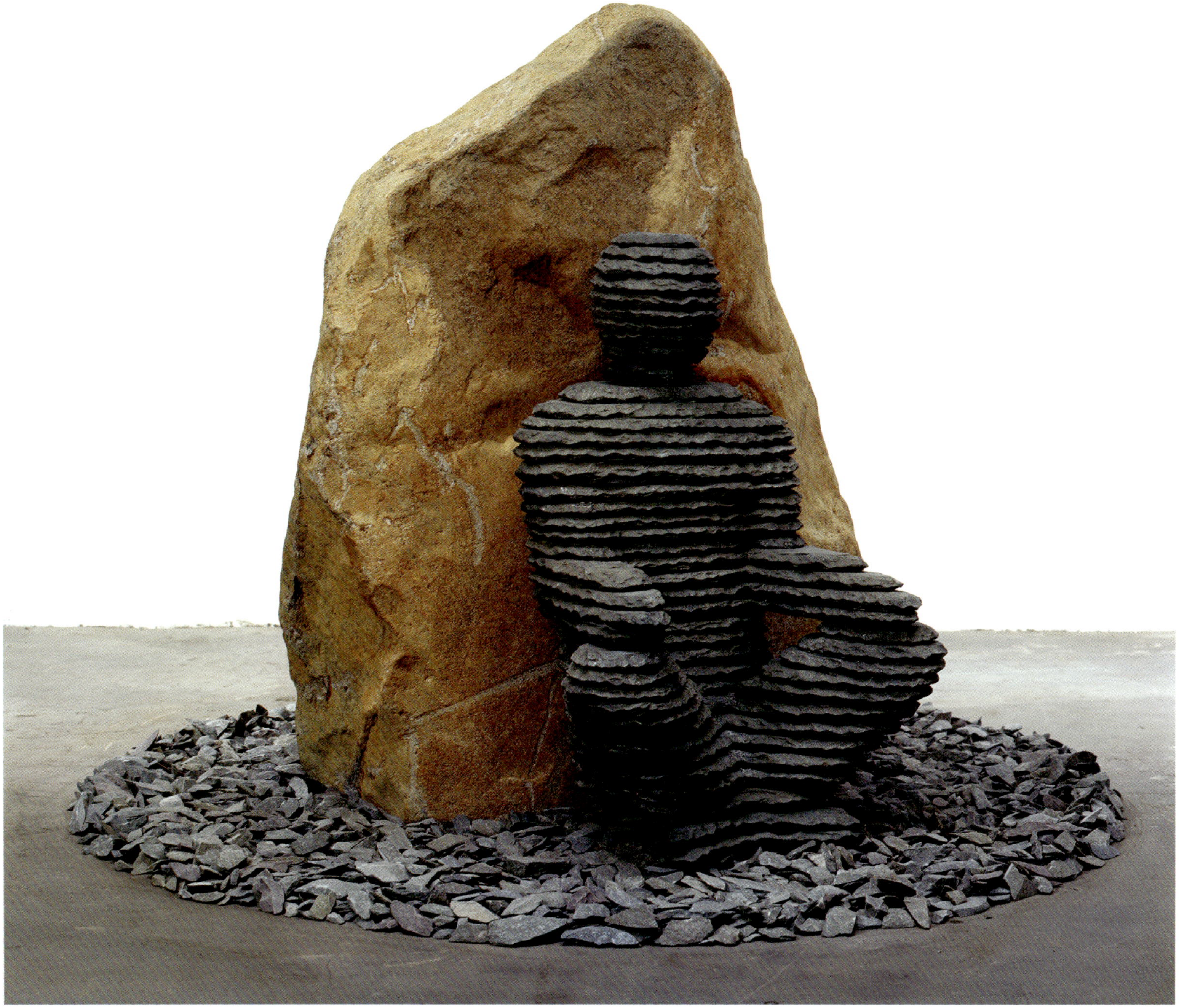

PLATE 88. *Eli'ezer*, 1999.
Bronze, boulder, and bluestone,
55 x 66 x 66 in. (139.7 x 167.6 x 167.6 cm).
Edition of 5. Private collection of Rebecca Vaadia and Sara Vaadia.

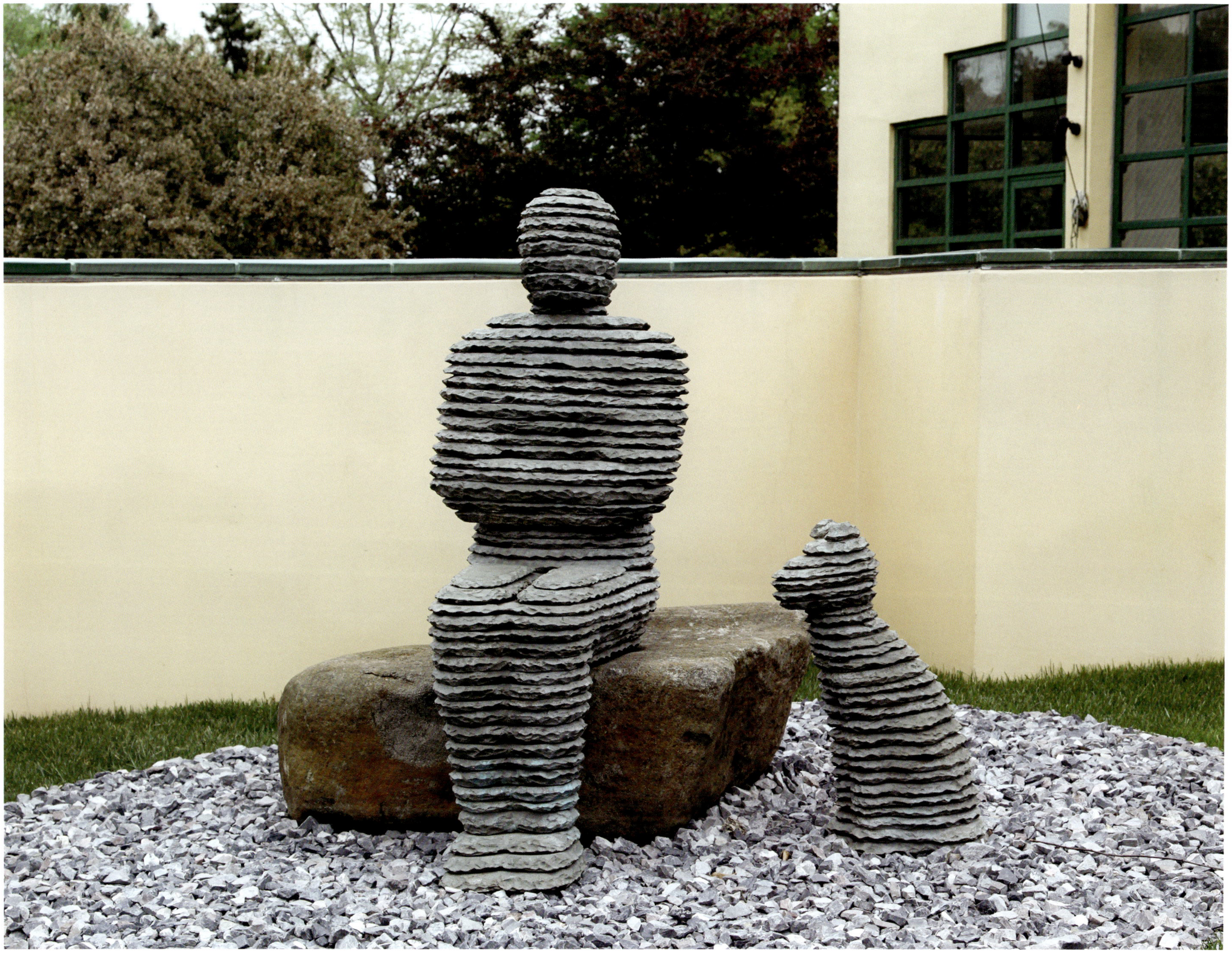

PLATE 89. *Asa with Dog*, 2000.
Bronze, boulder, and bluestone,
66 x 84 x 84 in. (167.6 x 213.4 x 213.4 cm).
Edition of 5. Private collection of Rebecca Vaadia and Sara Vaadia.

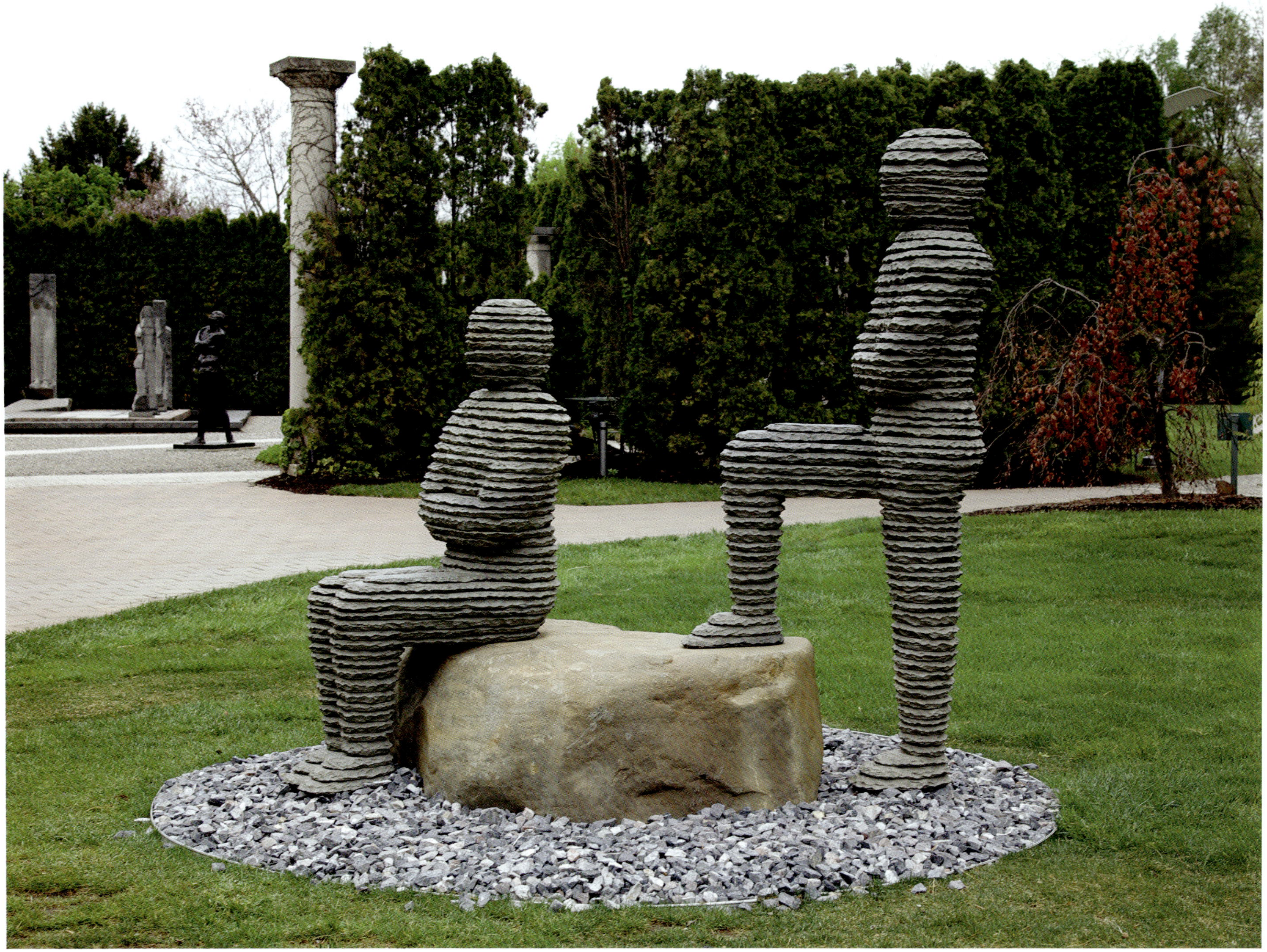

PLATE 90. *Asa & Yehoshafat*, 2000.
Bronze, boulder, and bluestone,
86 x 108 x 108 in. (218.4 x 274.3 x 274.3 cm).
Edition of 5. Private collection of Rebecca Vaadia and Sara Vaadia.

OPPOSITE
PLATE 91. *Avdon*, 2001.
Bronze and bluestone,
72 x 29 x 23 in. (182.9 x 73.7 x 58.4 cm).
Edition of 5. Private collection
of Rebecca Vaadia and Sara Vaadia.

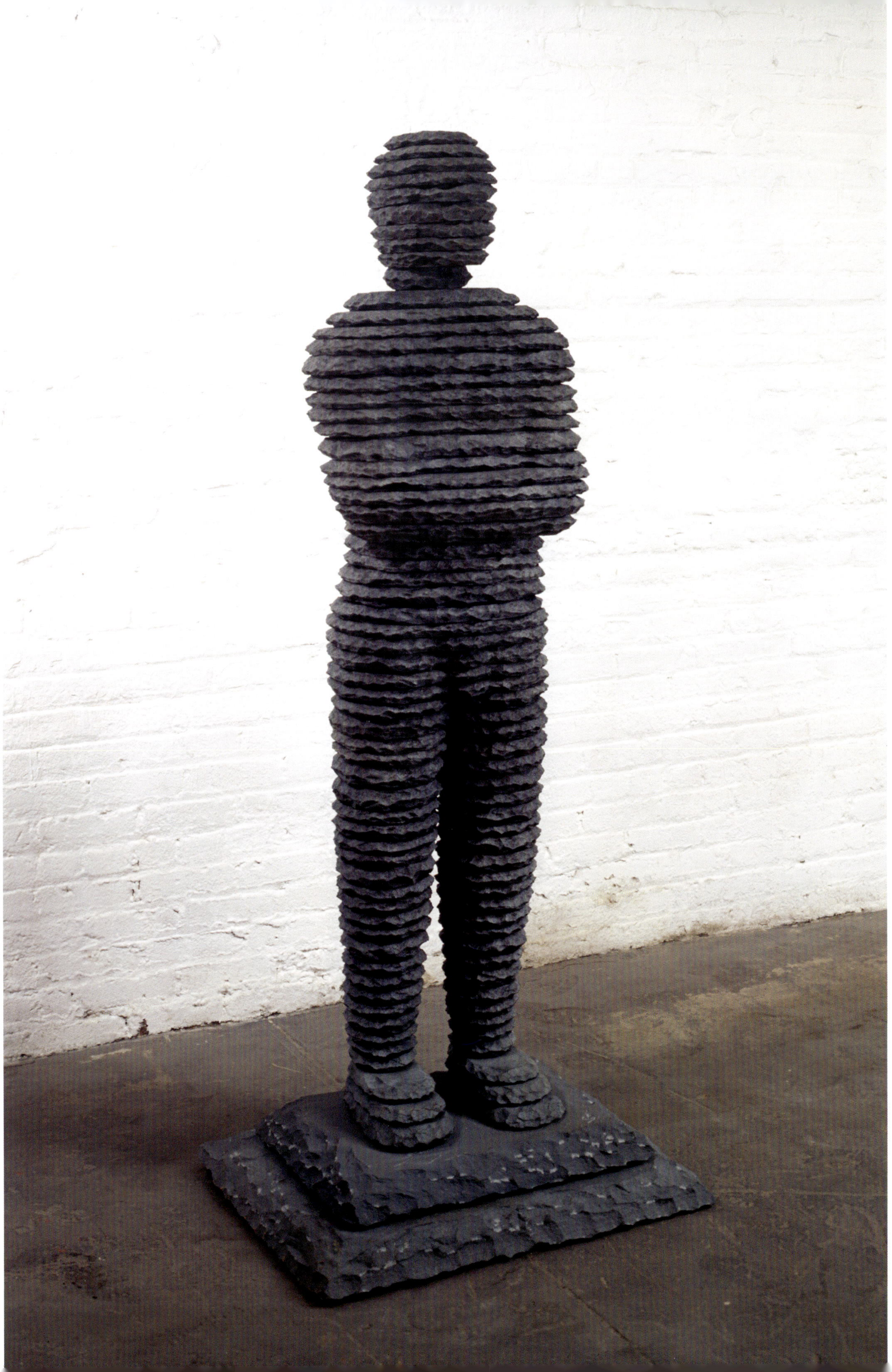

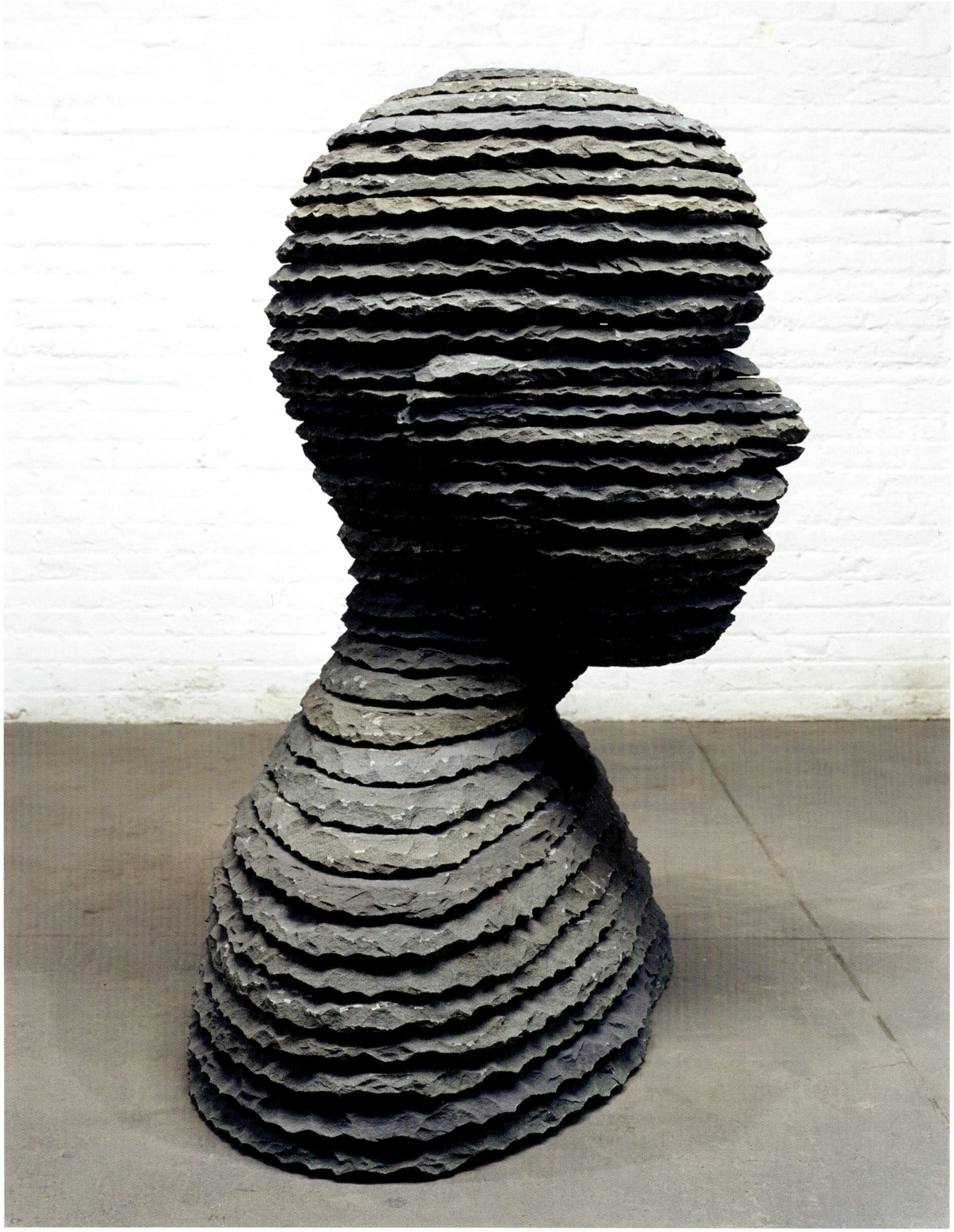

PLATE 92. *ZAMIR*, 2004.
Bluestone,
50 x 49 x 29 in. (127 x 124.5 x 73.6 cm).
Private collection of Rebecca Vaadia and Sara Vaadia.

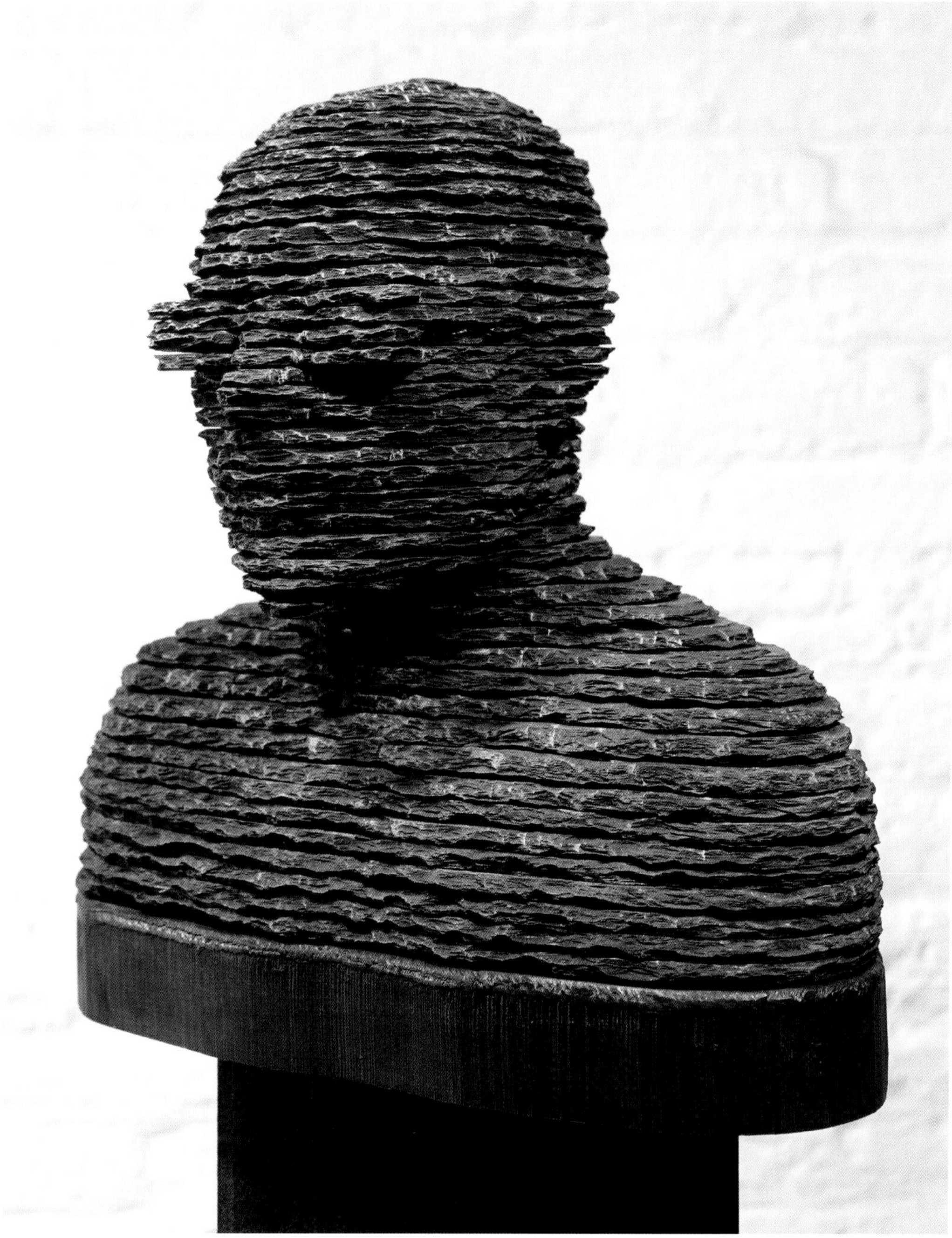

PLATE 93. *Boaz*, 2002.
Slate and steel pedestal,
10 x 10½ x 7 in. (25.4 x 26.7 x 17.8 cm).
Private collection of Rebecca Vaadia and Sara Vaadia.

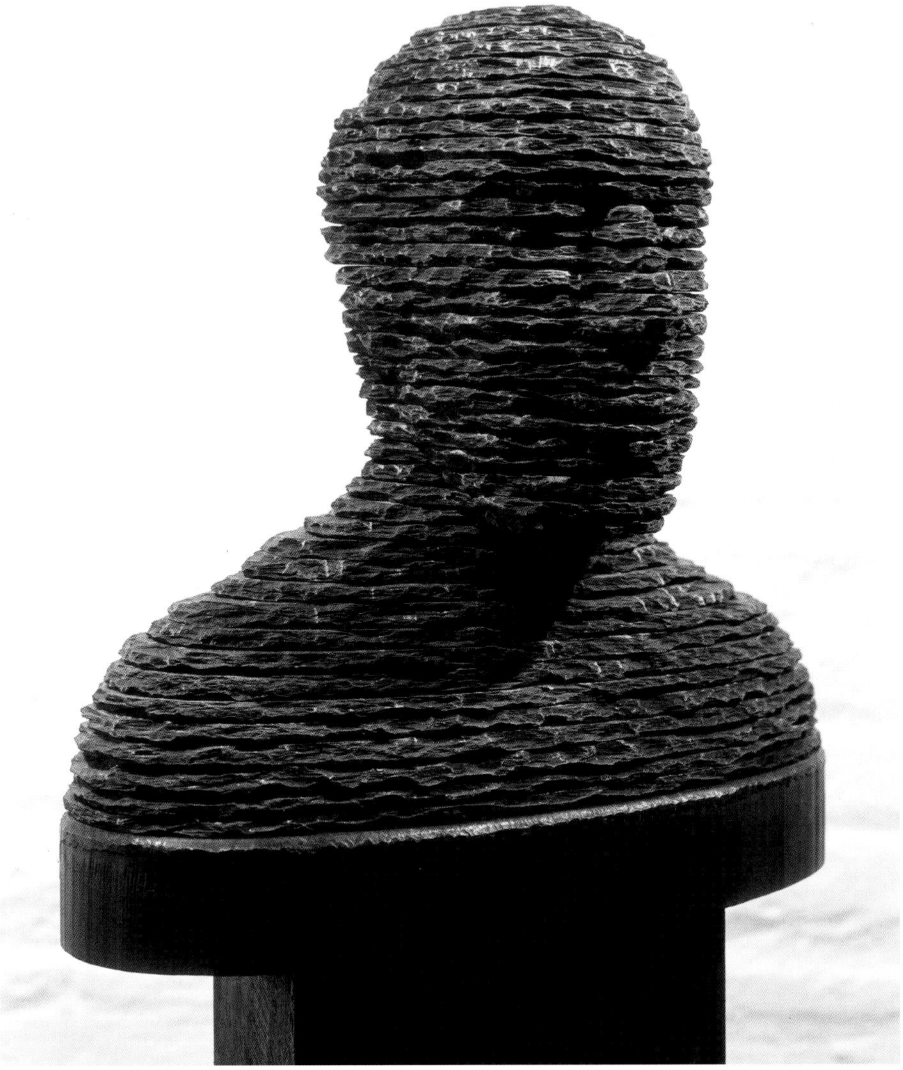

PLATE 94. *Raffael*, 2002.
Slate and steel pedestal,
9½ x 10¼ x 6¾ in. (24.1 x 26 x 17.1 cm).

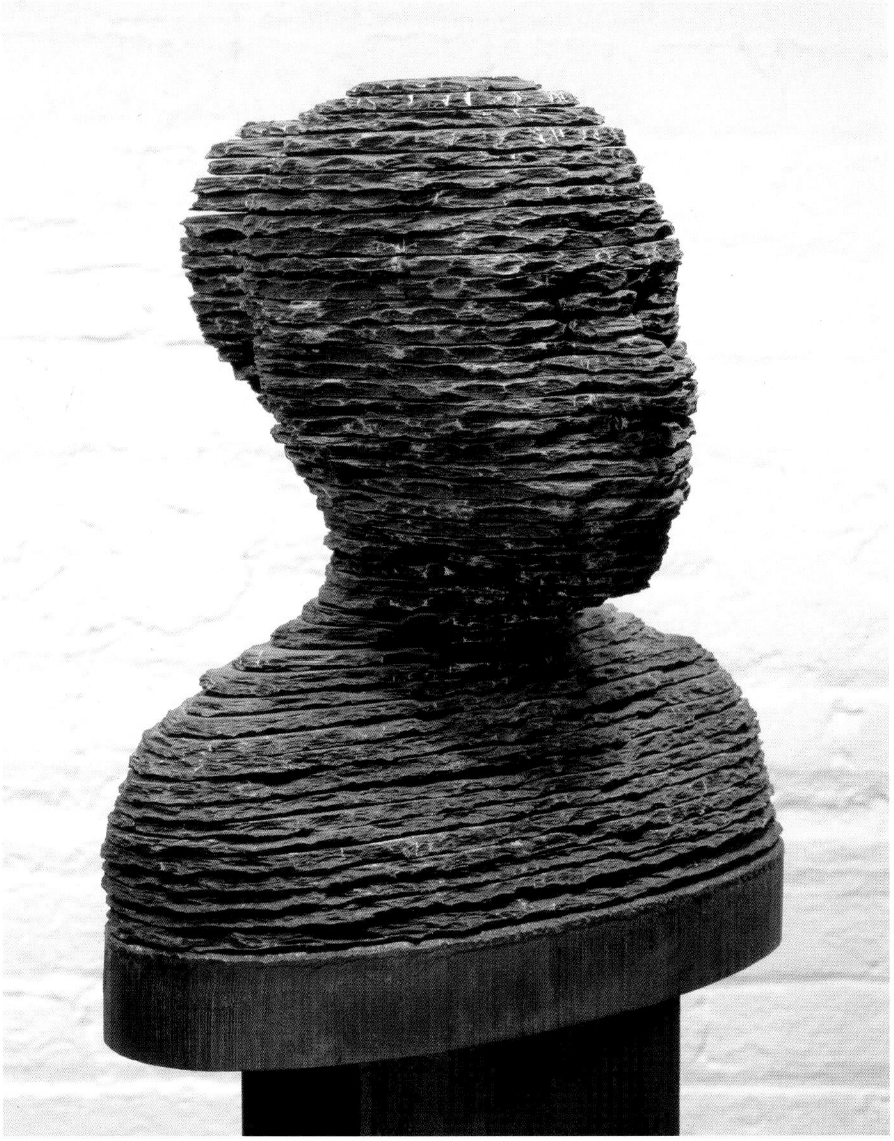

PLATE 95. *Leisa*, 2002.
Slate and steel pedestal,
10¾ x 11 x 8¼ in. (27.3 x 27.9 x 20.9 cm).

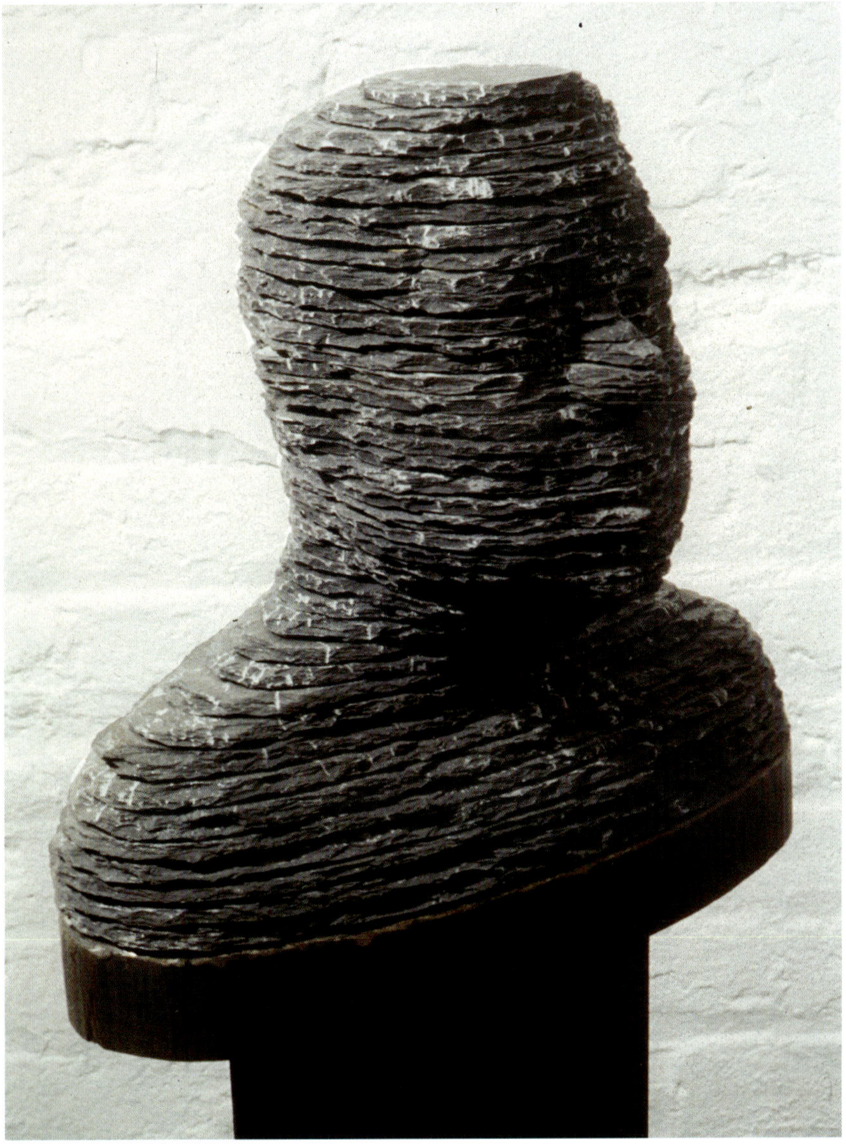

PLATE 96. *Rafi*, 2002.
Slate and steel pedestal,
10½ x 12 x 8 in. (26.7 x 30.5 x 20.3 cm).

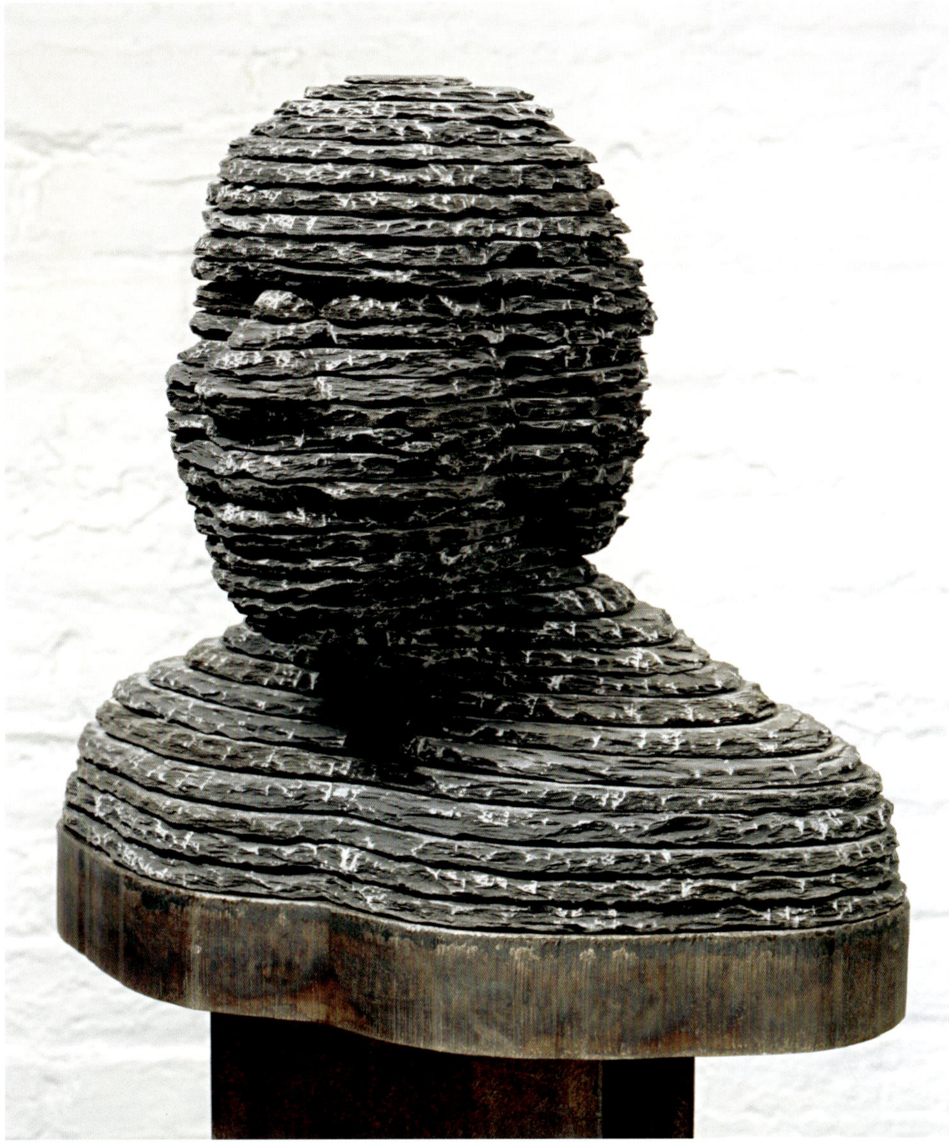

PLATE 97. *Dawne*, 2003.
Slate and steel pedestal,
10 x 12 x 8 in. (25.4 x 30.5 x 20.3 cm).

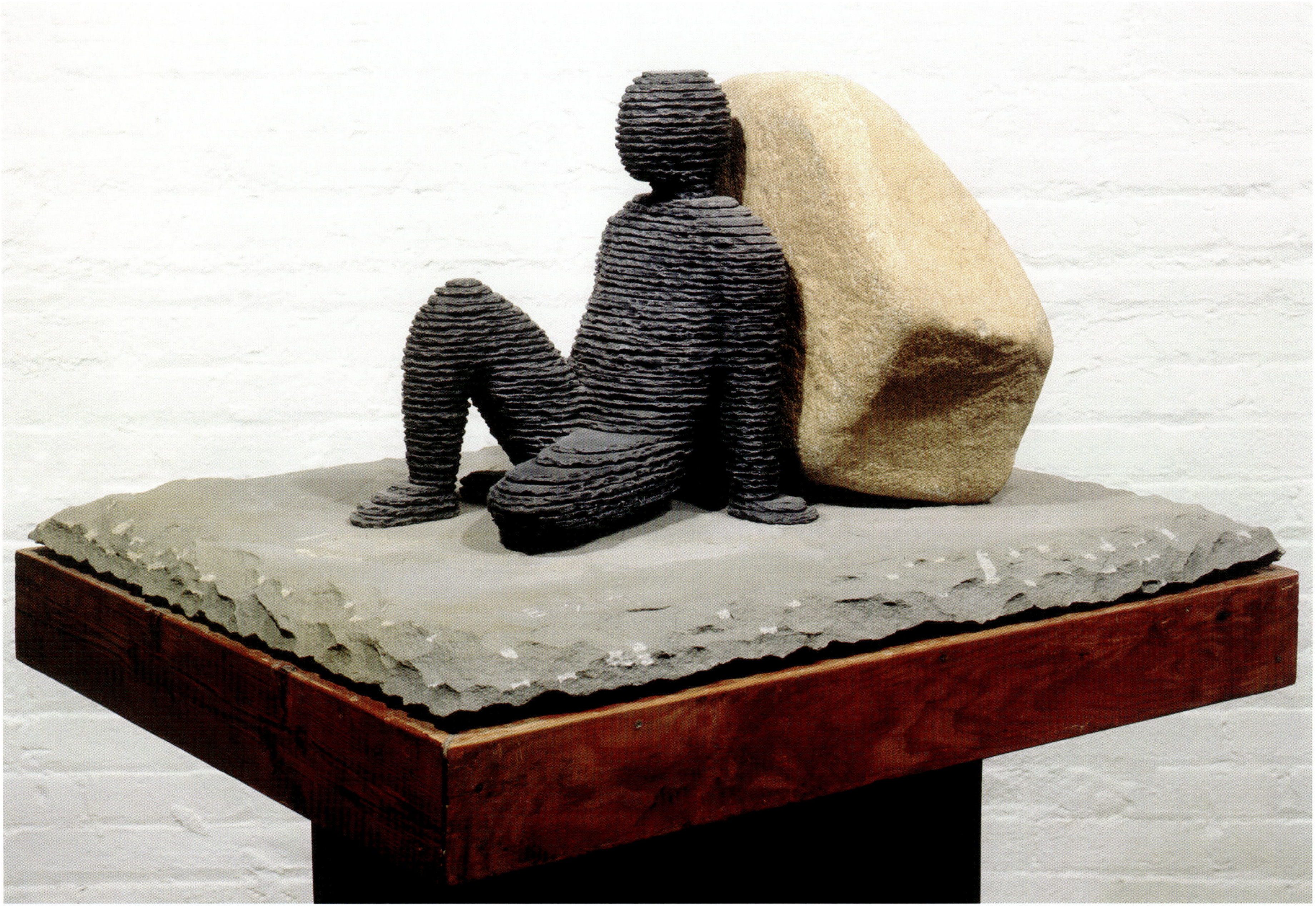

PLATE 98. *Efrayim*, 2003.
Bronze, boulder, and bluestone,
14 x 29 x 23 in. (35.6 x 73.7 x 58.4 cm).
Edition of 7. Private collection of Rebecca Vaadia and Sara Vaadia.

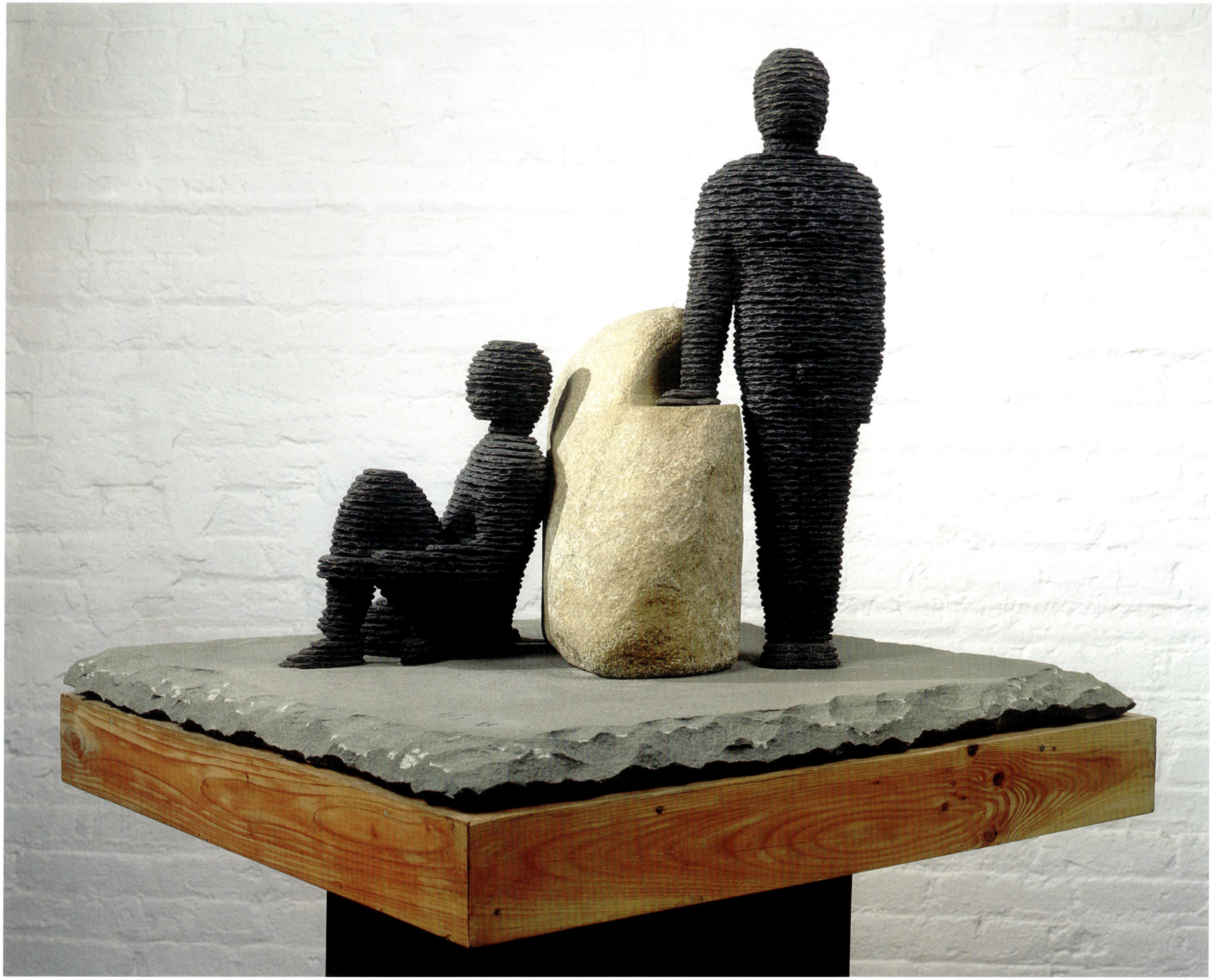

PLATE 99. *Ge'u'el & Binyamin,* 2002.
Bronze, boulder, and bluestone,
23 x 28 x 28 in. (58.4 x 71.1 x 71.1 cm).
Edition of 7. Private collection of Rebecca Vaadia and Sara Vaadia.

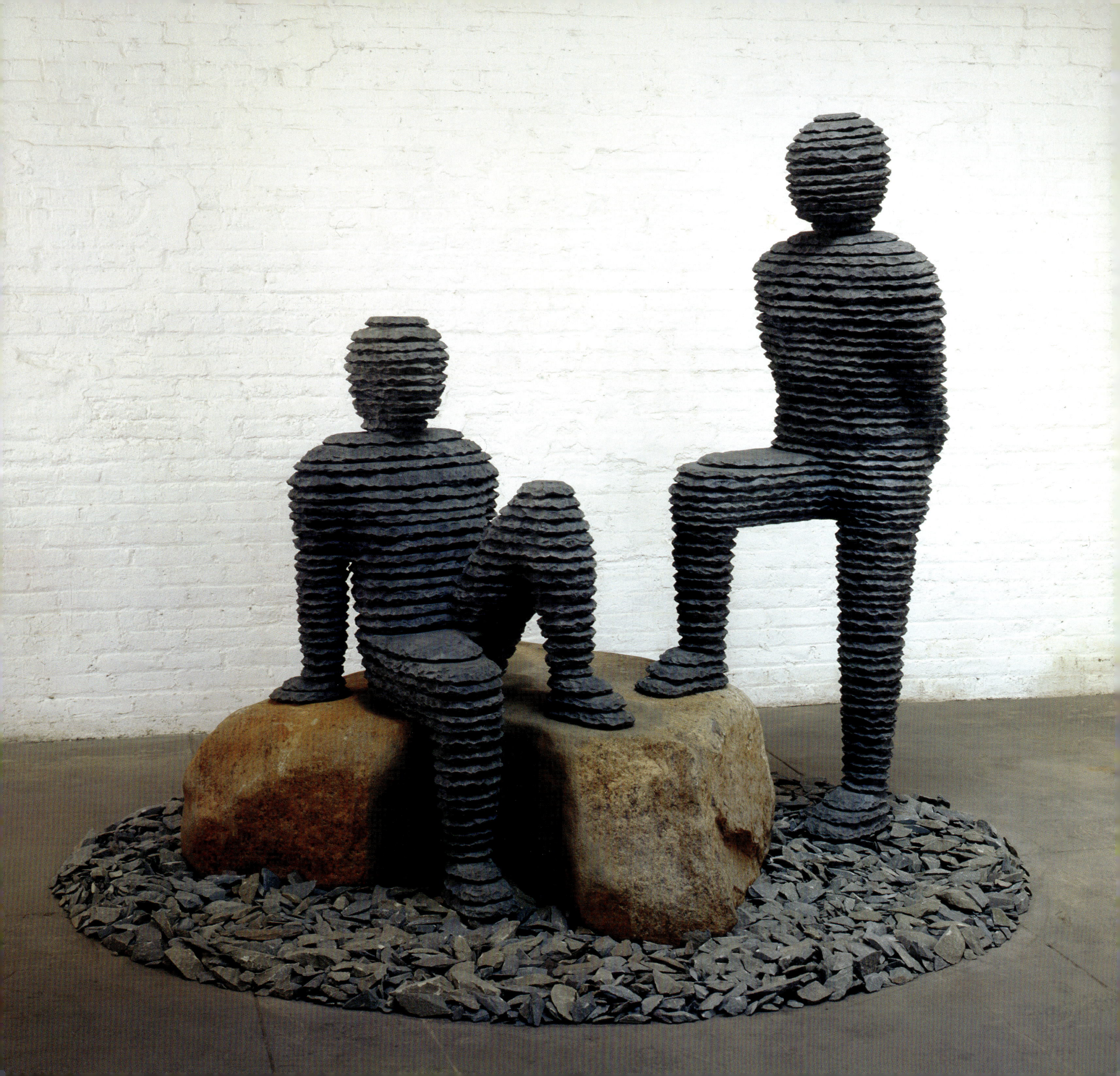

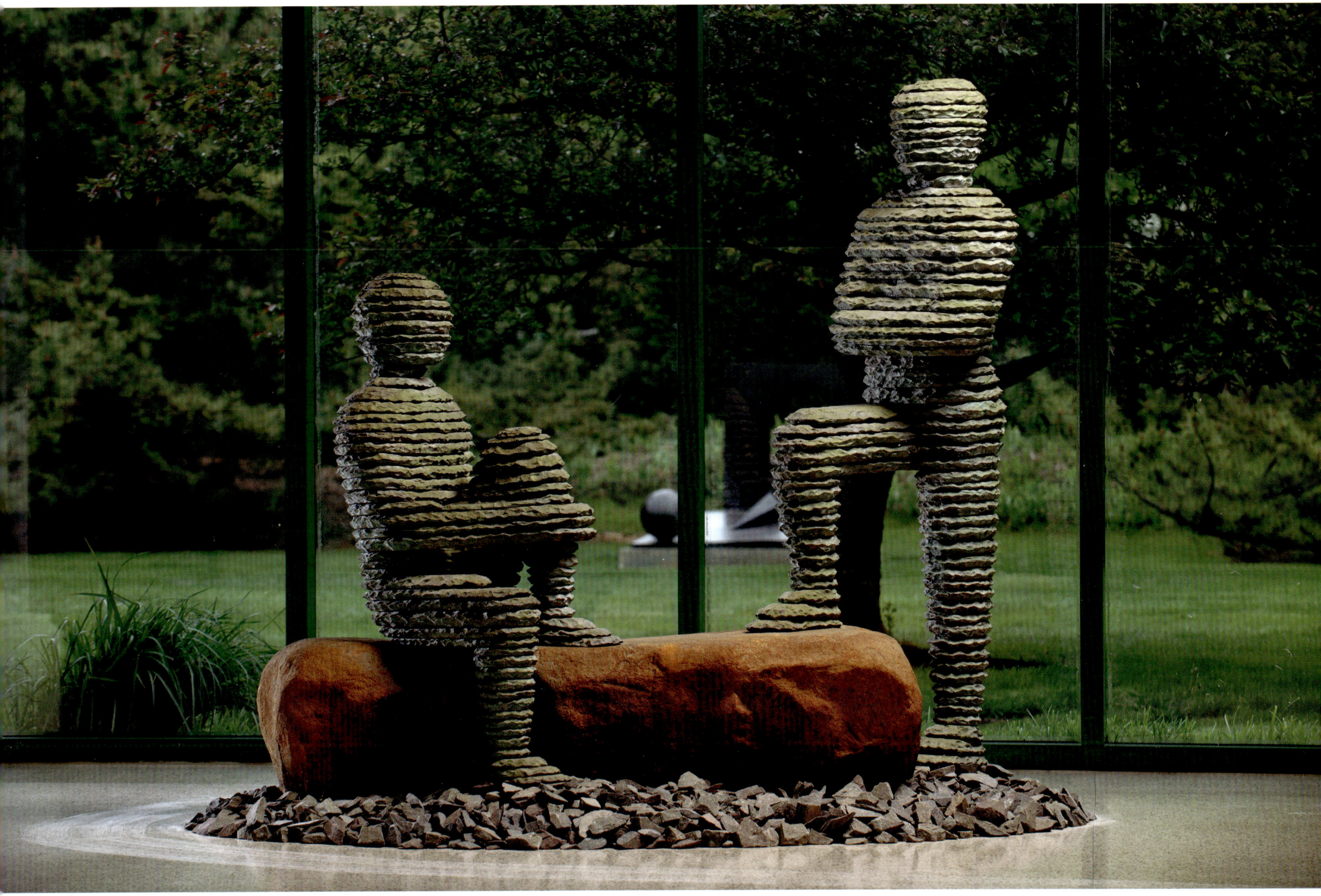

OPPOSITE

PLATE 100. *Asaf & Yo'ah*, 2001.
Bronze, boulder, and bluestone,
78 x 100 x 100 in. (198.1 x 254 x 254 cm).
Edition of 5. Private collection of Rebecca Vaadia and Sara Vaadia.

PLATE 101. *Yizhaq & Eli'av*, 2005.
Bronze, boulder, and bluestone,
72 x 92 x 70 in. (183 x 233.7 x 177.8 cm).
Edition of 5. Private collection of Rebecca Vaadia and Sara Vaadia.

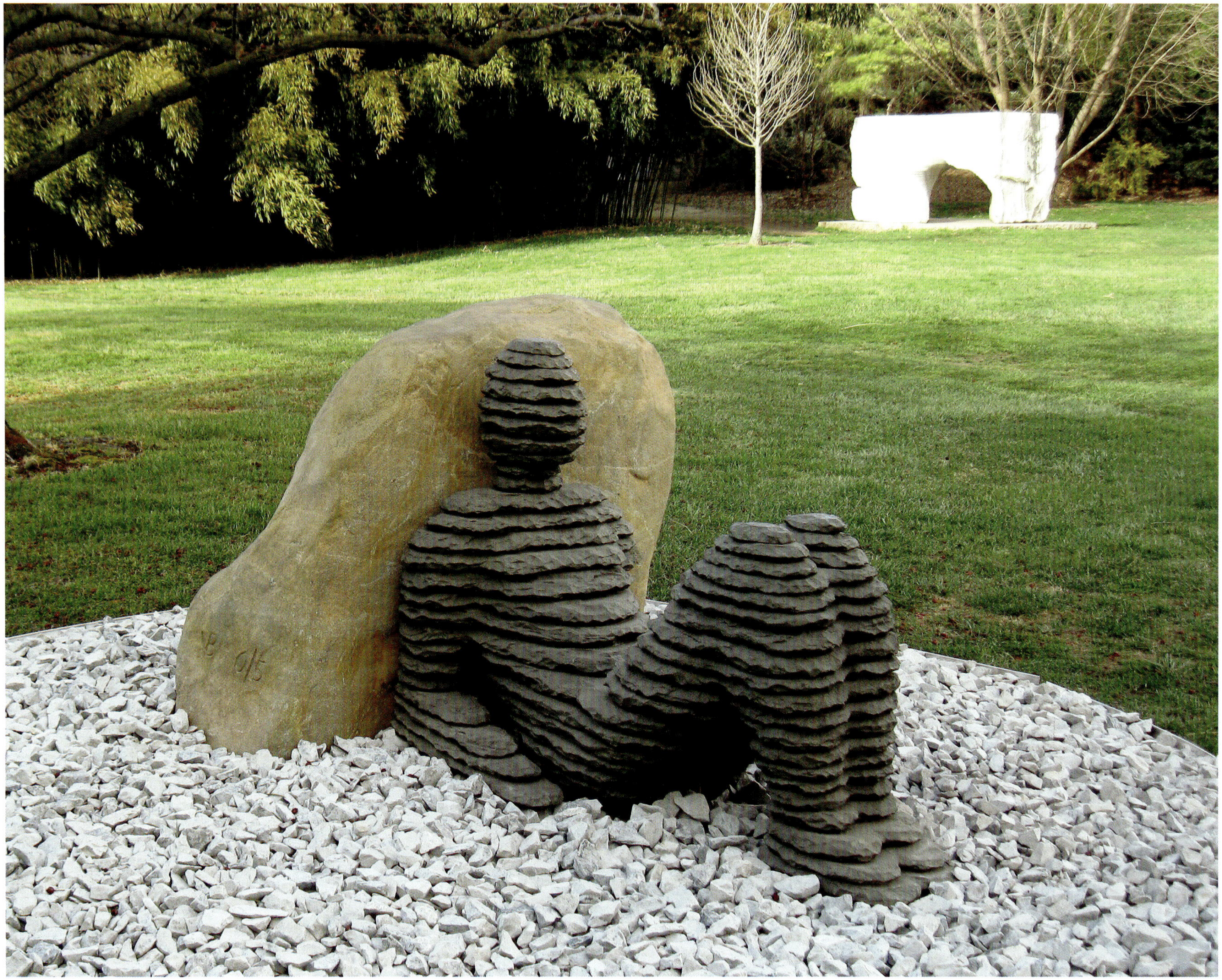

PLATE 102. *Ahiam 2nd*, 2006.
Bronze, bluestone, and boulder,
32 x 90 x 60 in. (81.3 x 228.6 x 152.4 cm).
Edition of 5. Private collection of Rebecca Vaadia and Sara Vaadia.

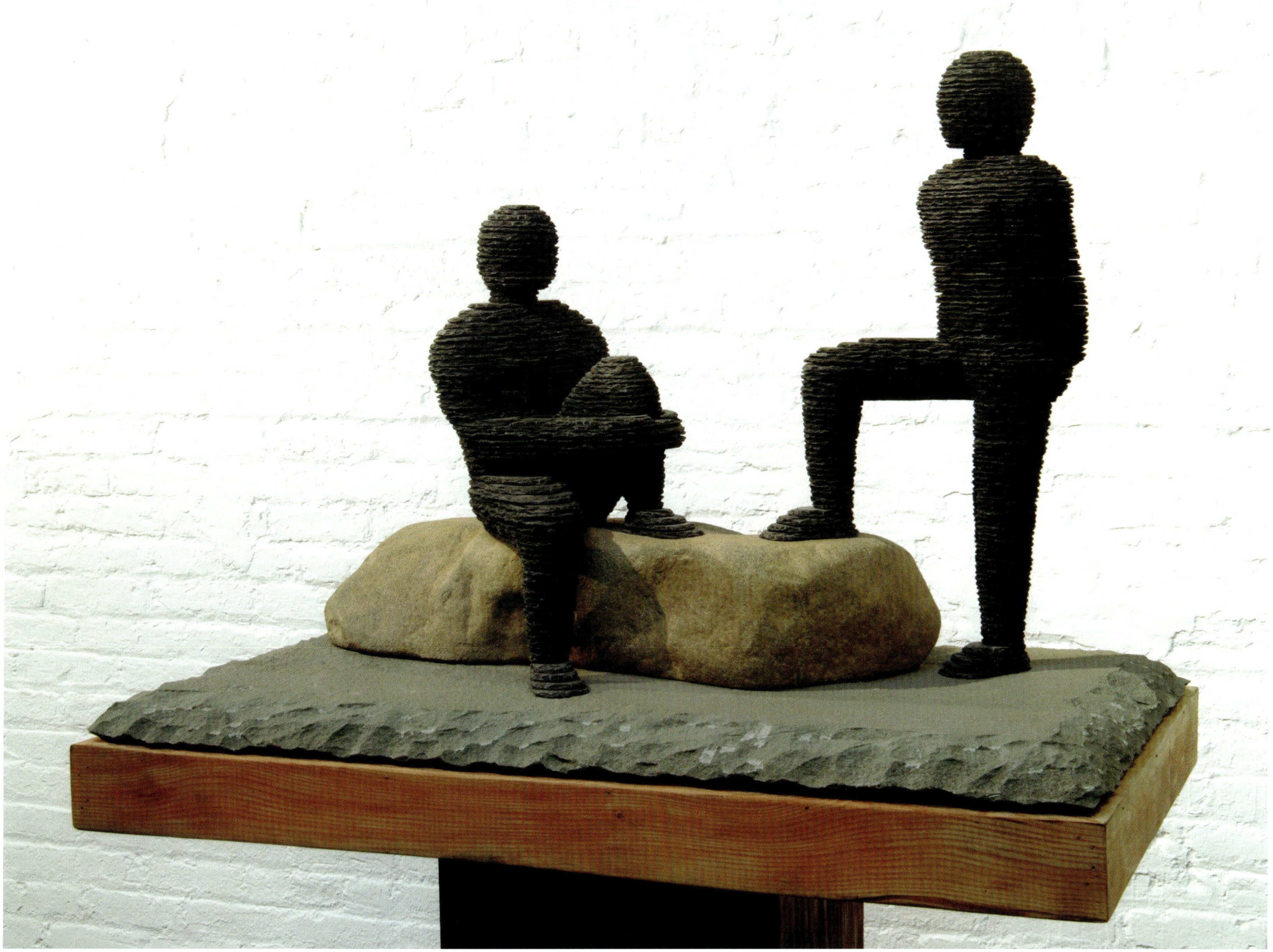

PLATE 103. *Ah'av and Ovadyahu*, 2006.
Slate, boulder, and bluestone,
26½ x 40 x 23½ in. (67.3 x 101.6 x 59.7 cm).

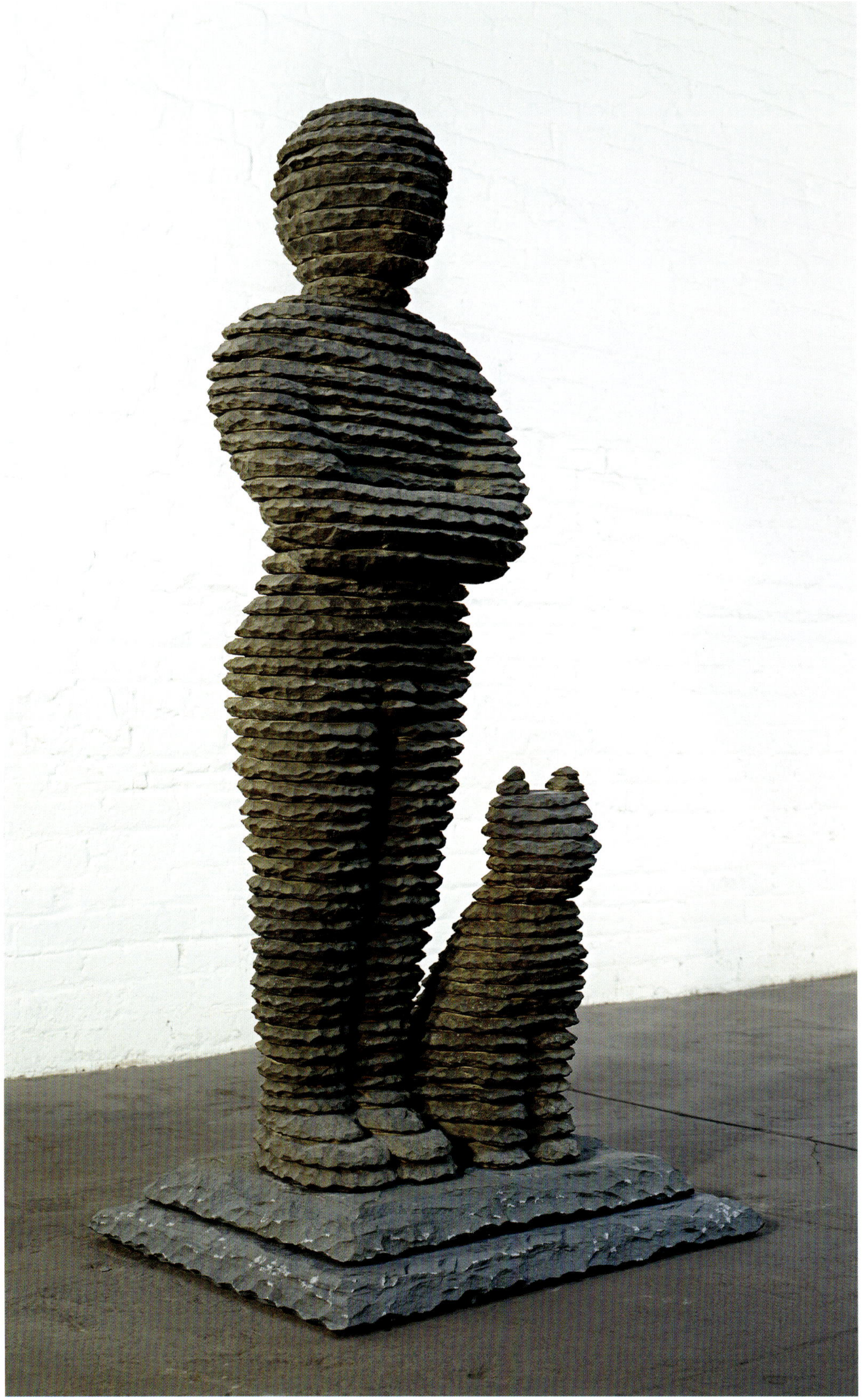

PLATE 104. *Baraq with Cat*, 2007.
Bronze and bluestone,
57 x 28 x 21½ in. (144.8 x 71.1 x 53.3 cm).
Edition of 5.

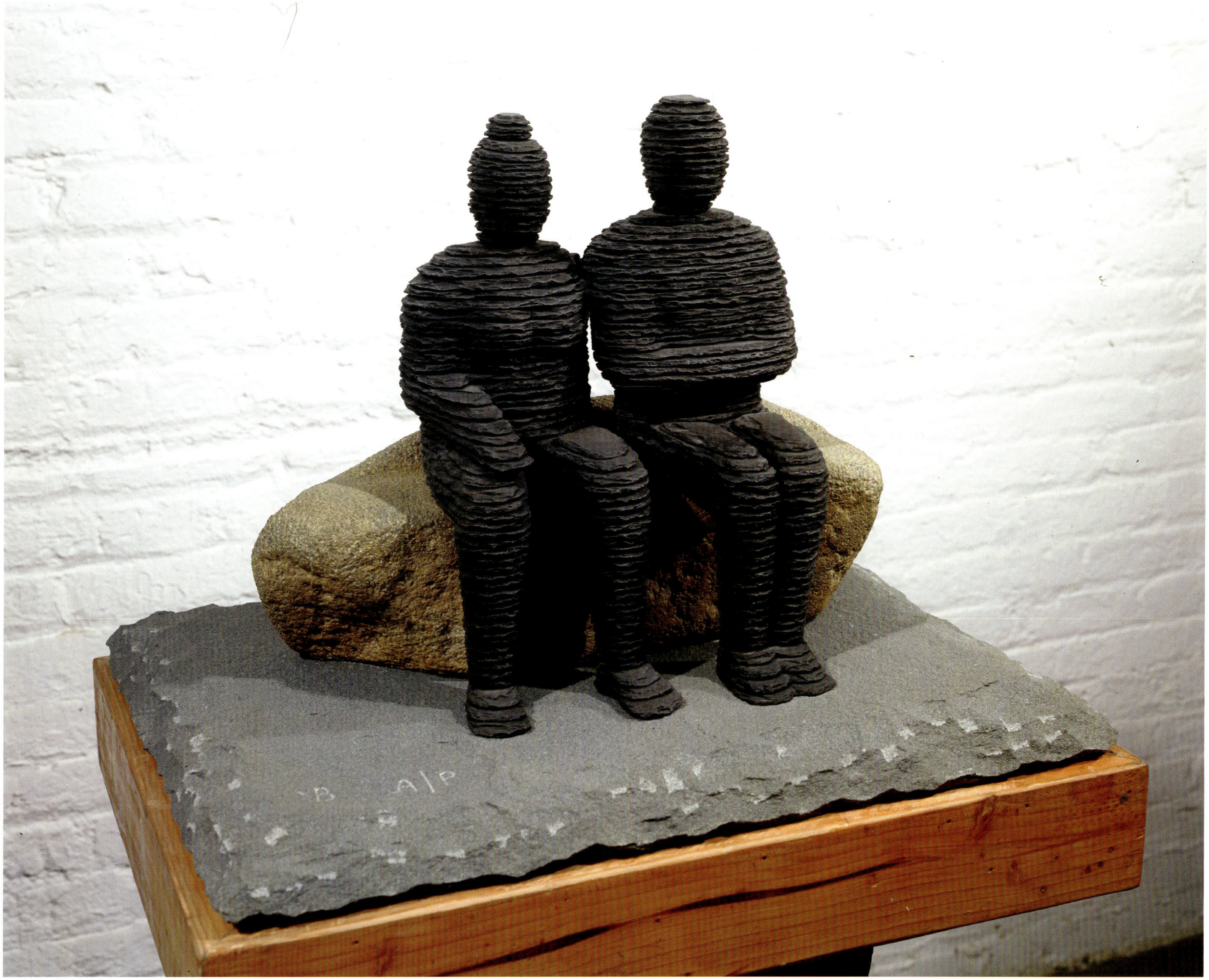

PLATE 105. *Yokheved & Amram*, 2009.
Bronze, boulder, and bluestone,
16 x 23 x 17 in. (40.6 x 58.4 x 43.2 cm).
Edition of 7. Private collection of Rebecca Vaadia and Sara Vaadia.

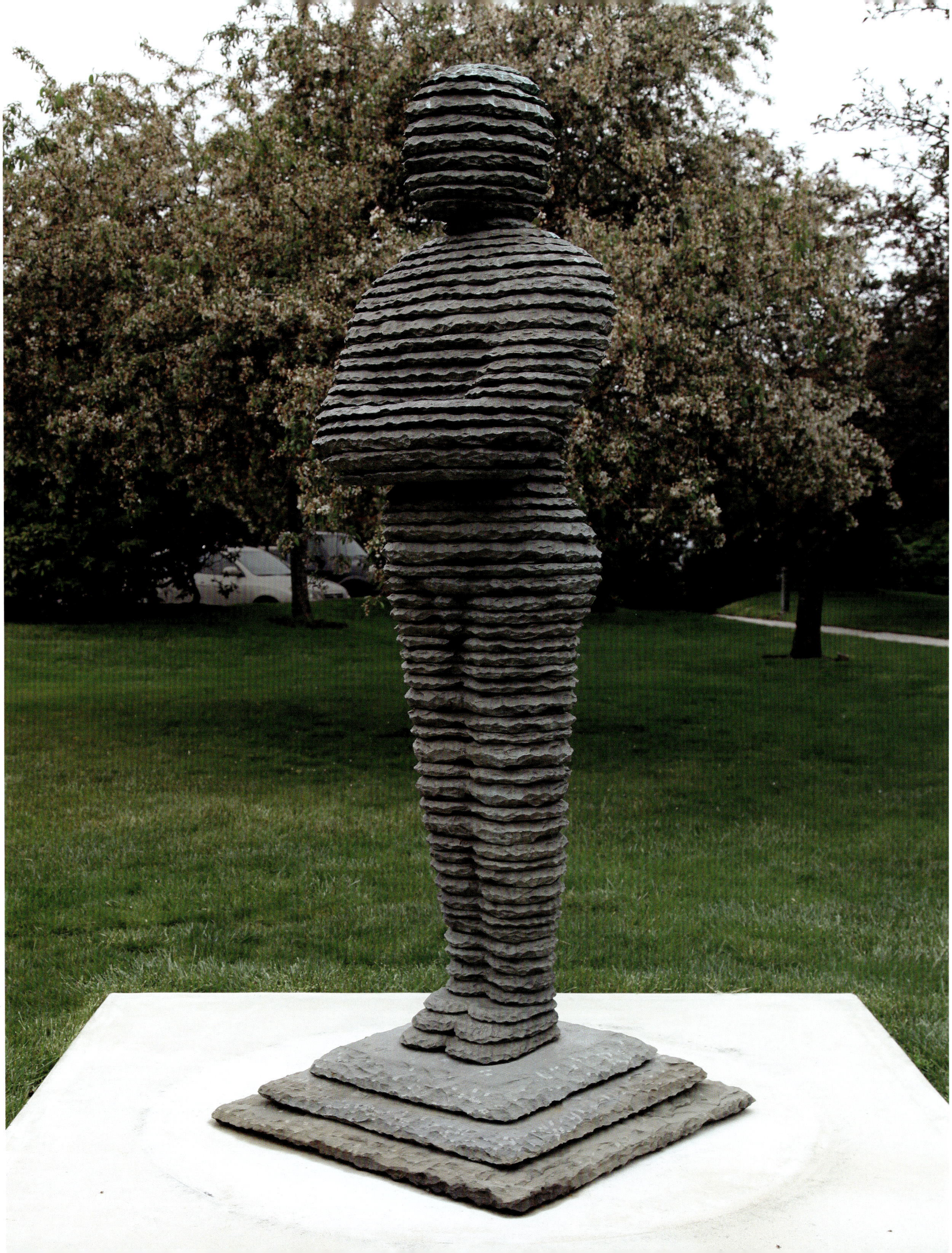

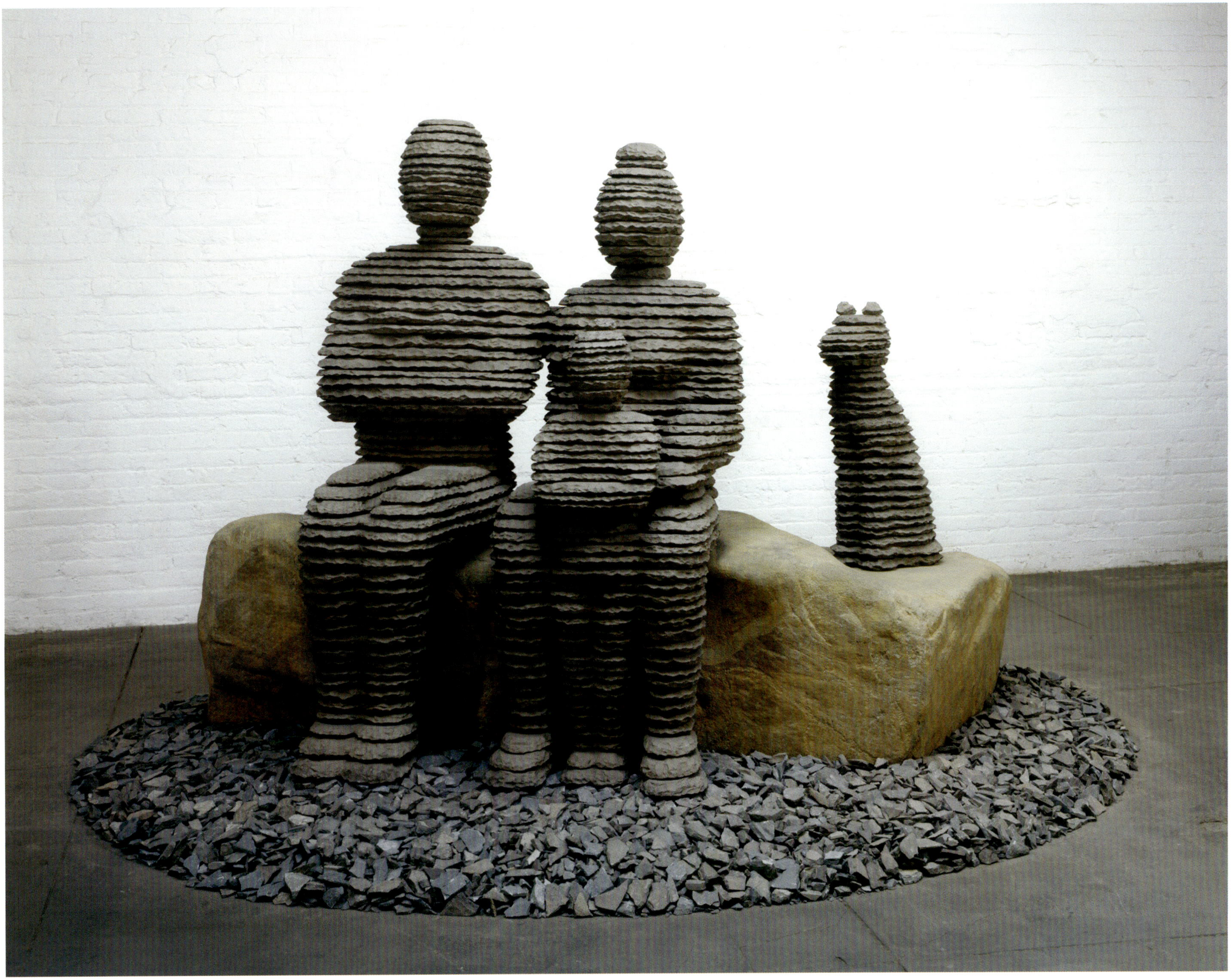

OPPOSITE

PLATE 106. *David*, 2010.
Bronze and bluestone,
91 x 36 x 36 in. (231.1 x 91.4 x 91.4 cm).
Edition of 5.

PLATE 107. *Family with Dog*, 2009.
Bronze, boulder, and bluestone,
76 x 120 x 100 in. (193 x 305 x 254 cm).
Edition of 5.

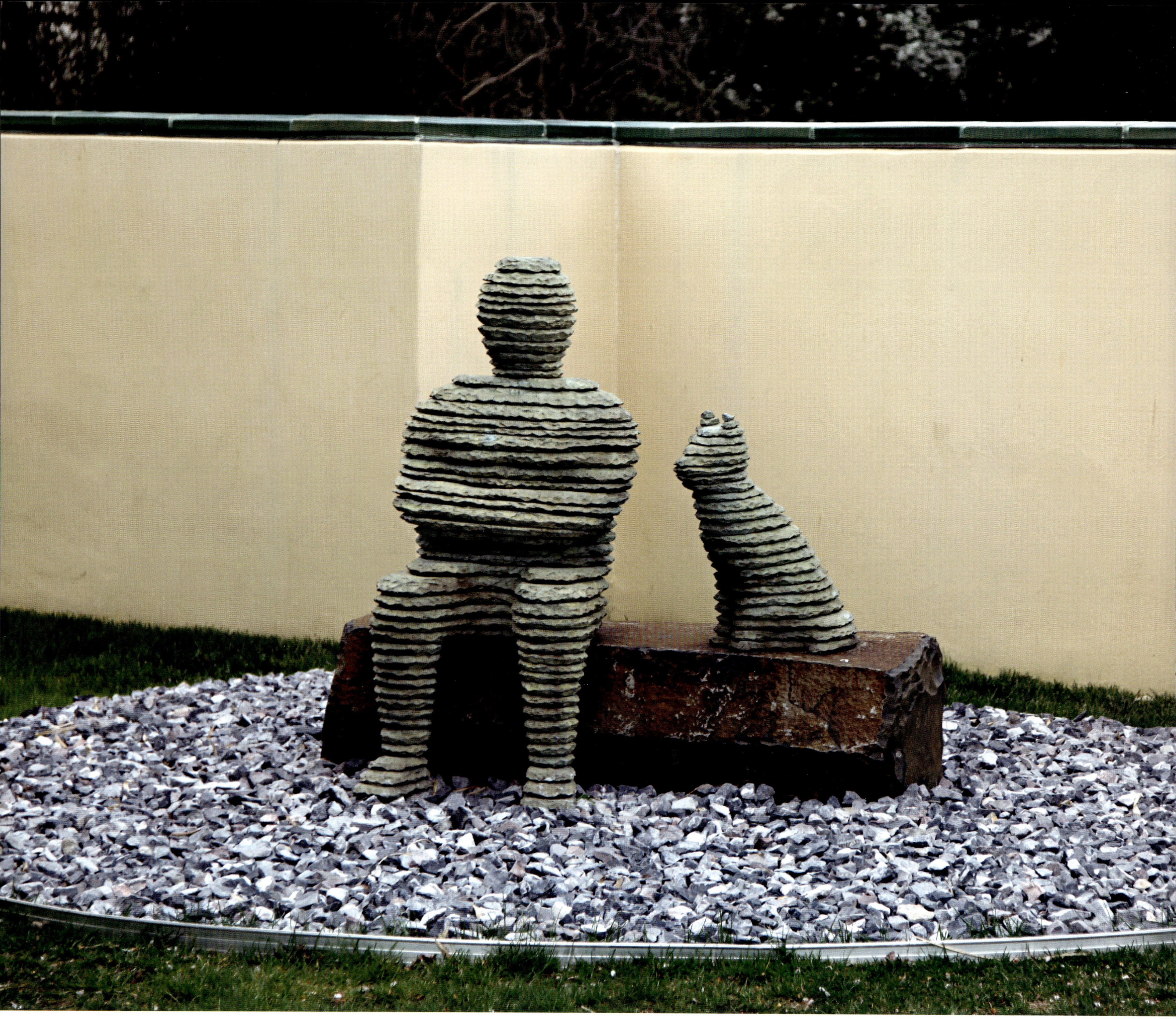

OPPOSITE

PLATE 108. *Ba'al with Cat*, 2009.
Bronze, basalt, and bluestone,
47 x 77 x 50 in.
(119.3 x 195.6 x 127 cm).
Edition of 5.

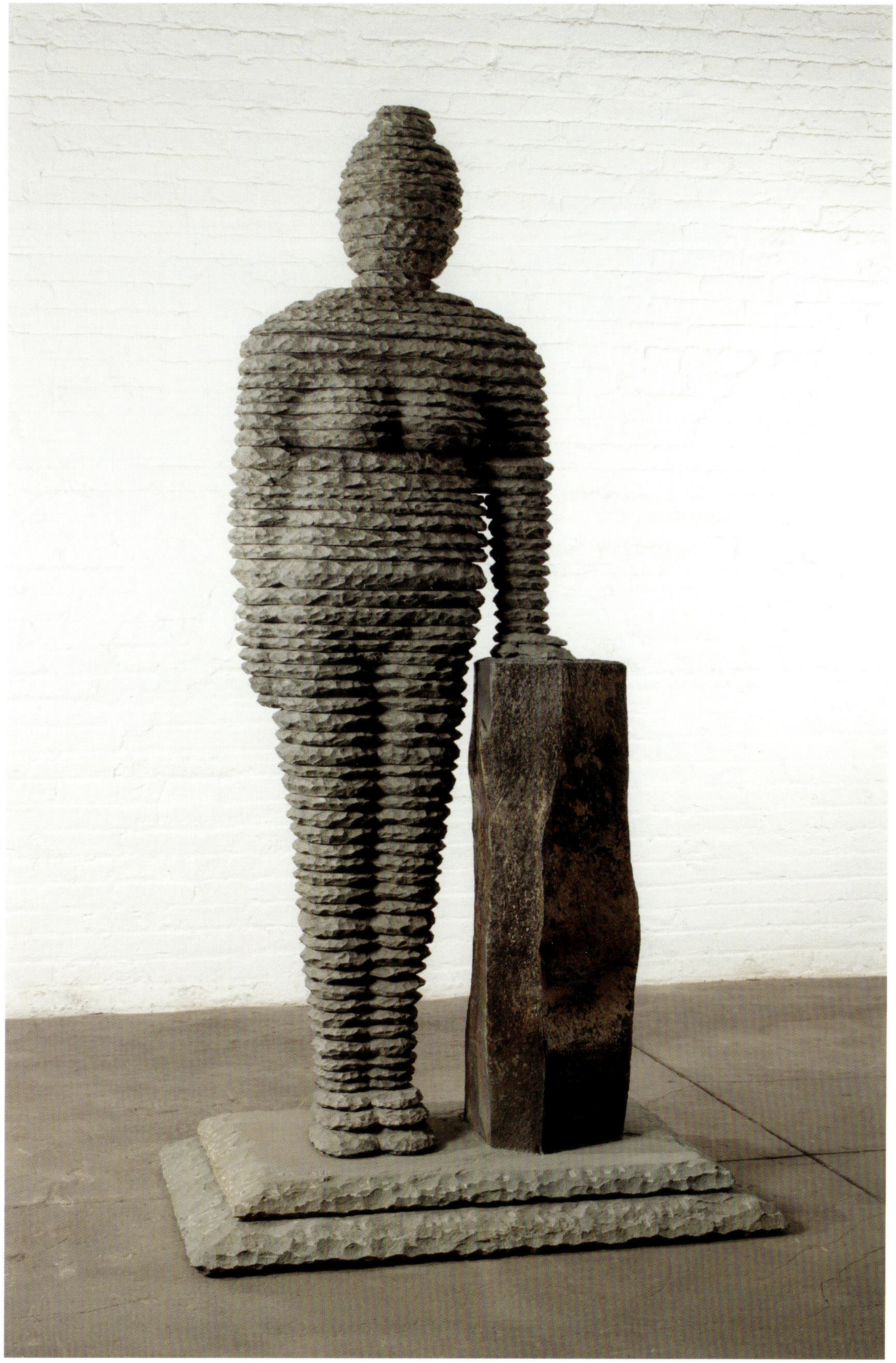

PLATE 109. *Hulda*, 2011.
Bronze, basalt, and bluestone,
79 1/2 x 41 x 29 in.
(201.9 x 104.1 x 73.7 cm).
Edition of 5.

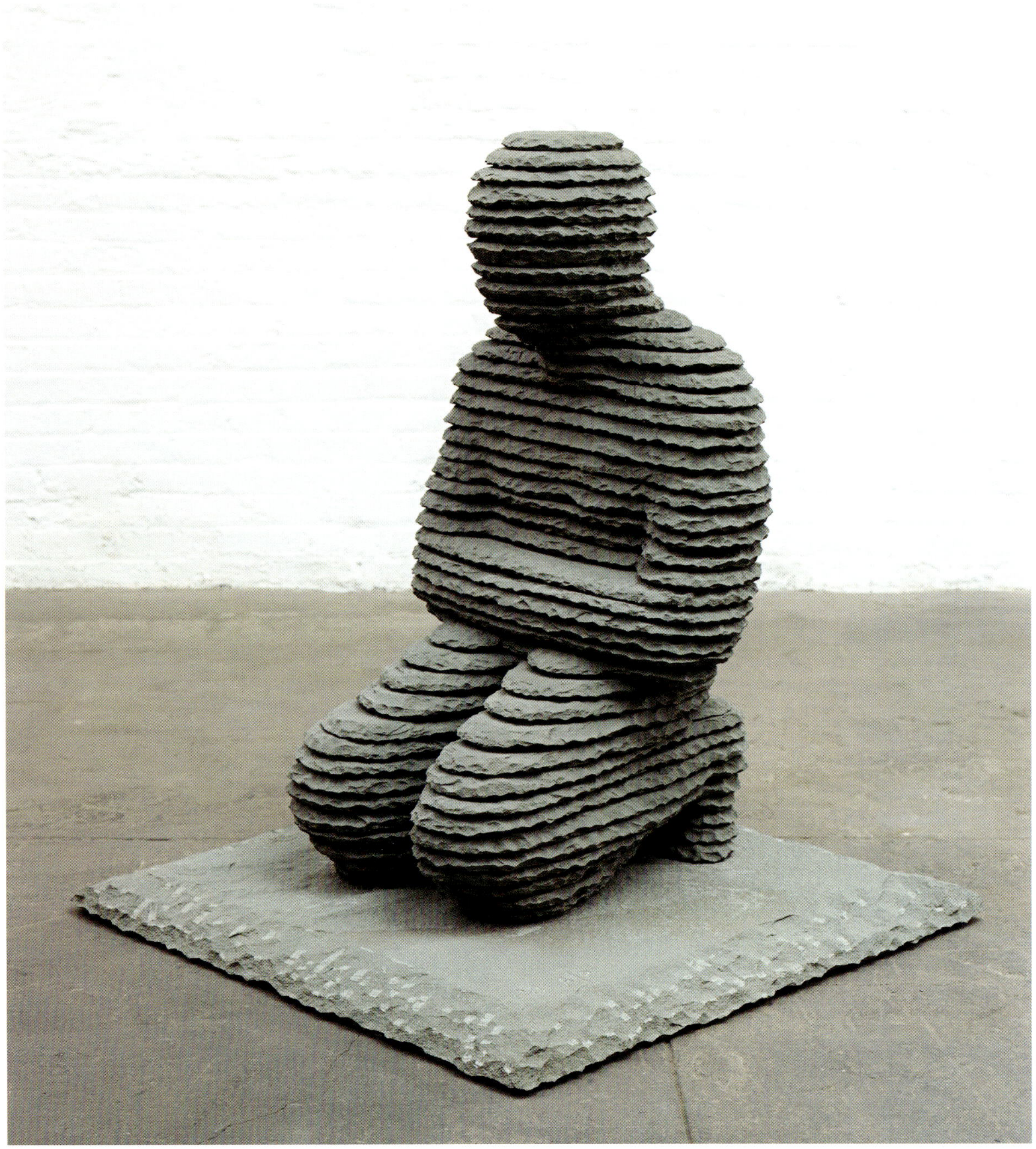

PLATE 110. *Ma'aseyahu*, 2012.
Bronze and bluestone,
43 x 35½ x 35½ in. (109.2 x 90.2 x 90.2 cm).
Edition of 5.

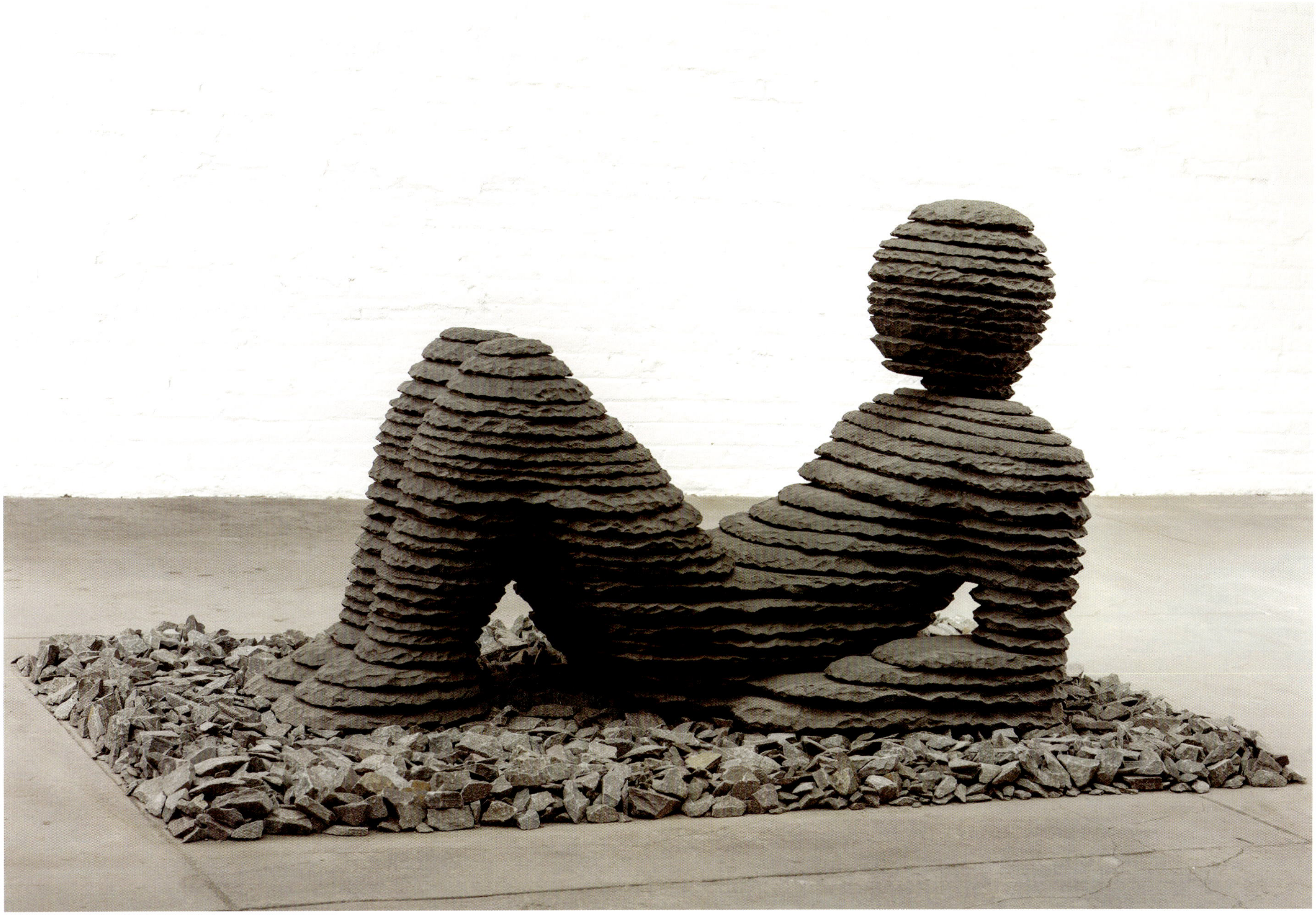

PLATE 111. *Natan*, 2014.
Bronze and bluestone,
38 x 80 x 48 in. (96.5 x 203.2 x 121.9 cm).
Edition of 5.

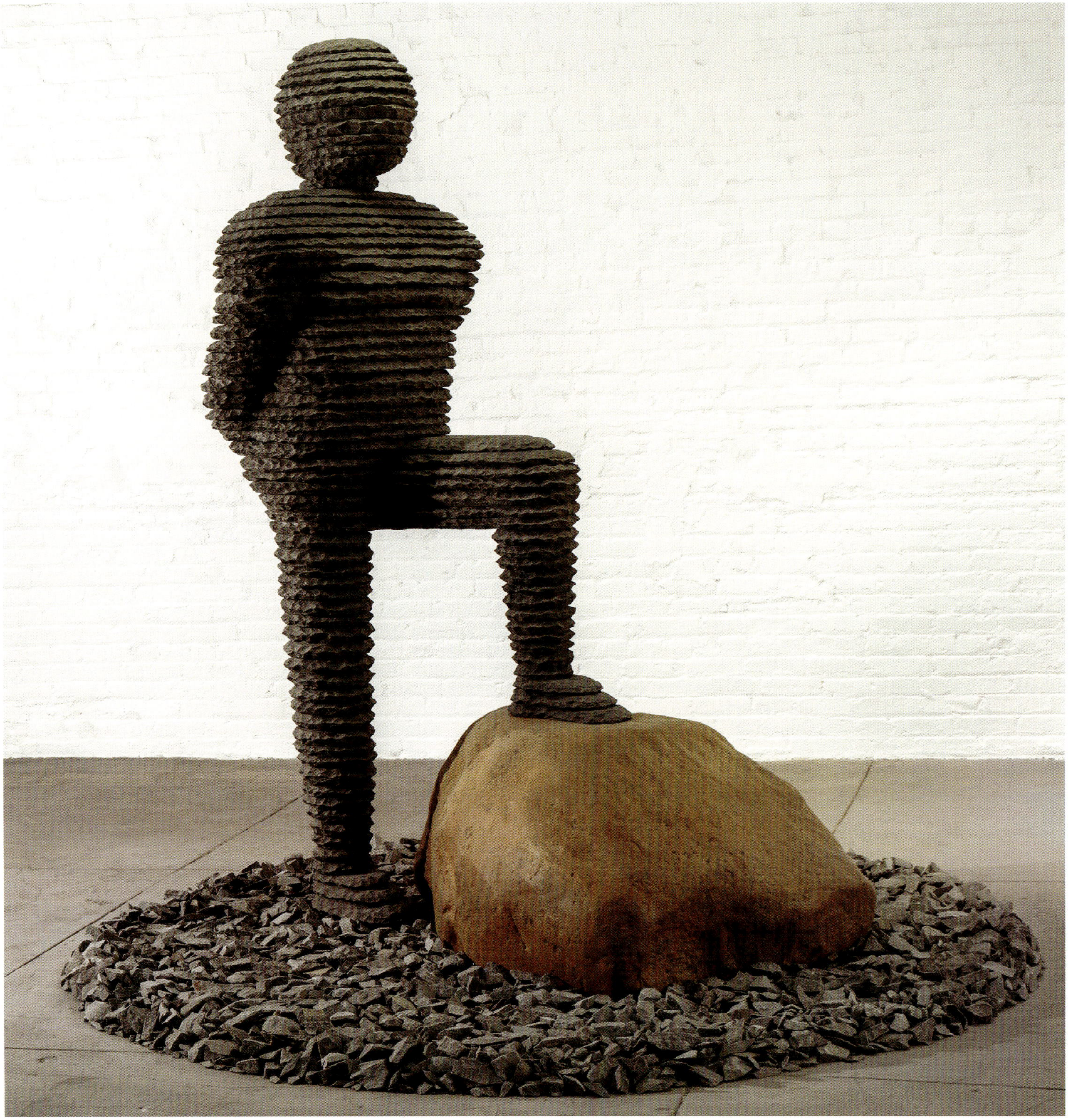

PLATE 112. *Havaqquq*, 2014.
Bronze, boulder, and bluestone,
90 x 90 x 90 in. (229 x 229 x 229 cm).
Edition of 5.

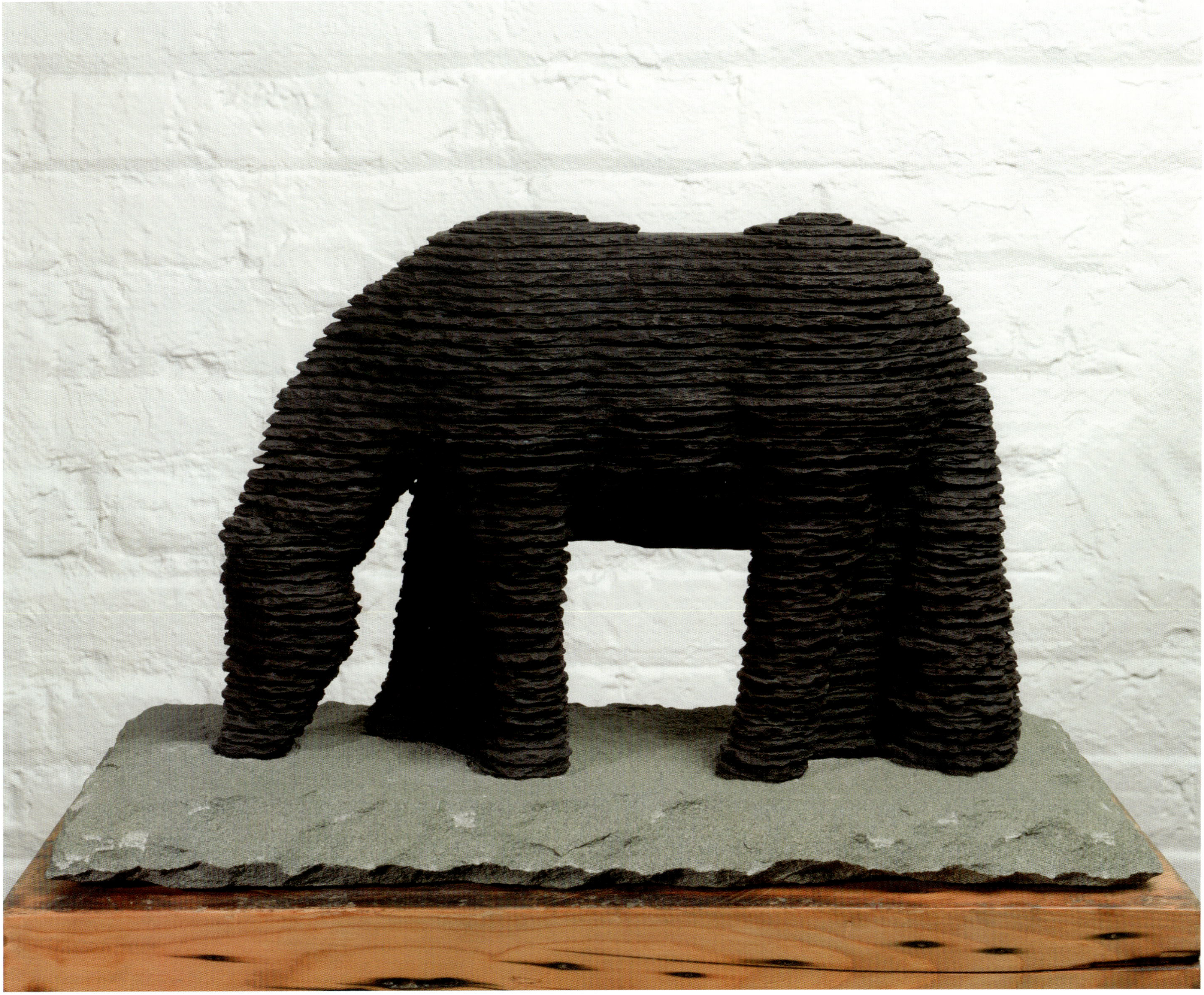

PLATE 113. *Grazing Horse*, 2014.
Bronze and bluestone,
$11^1/_2$ x 19 x 9 in. (29.2 x 48.3 x 22.9 cm).
Edition of 7.

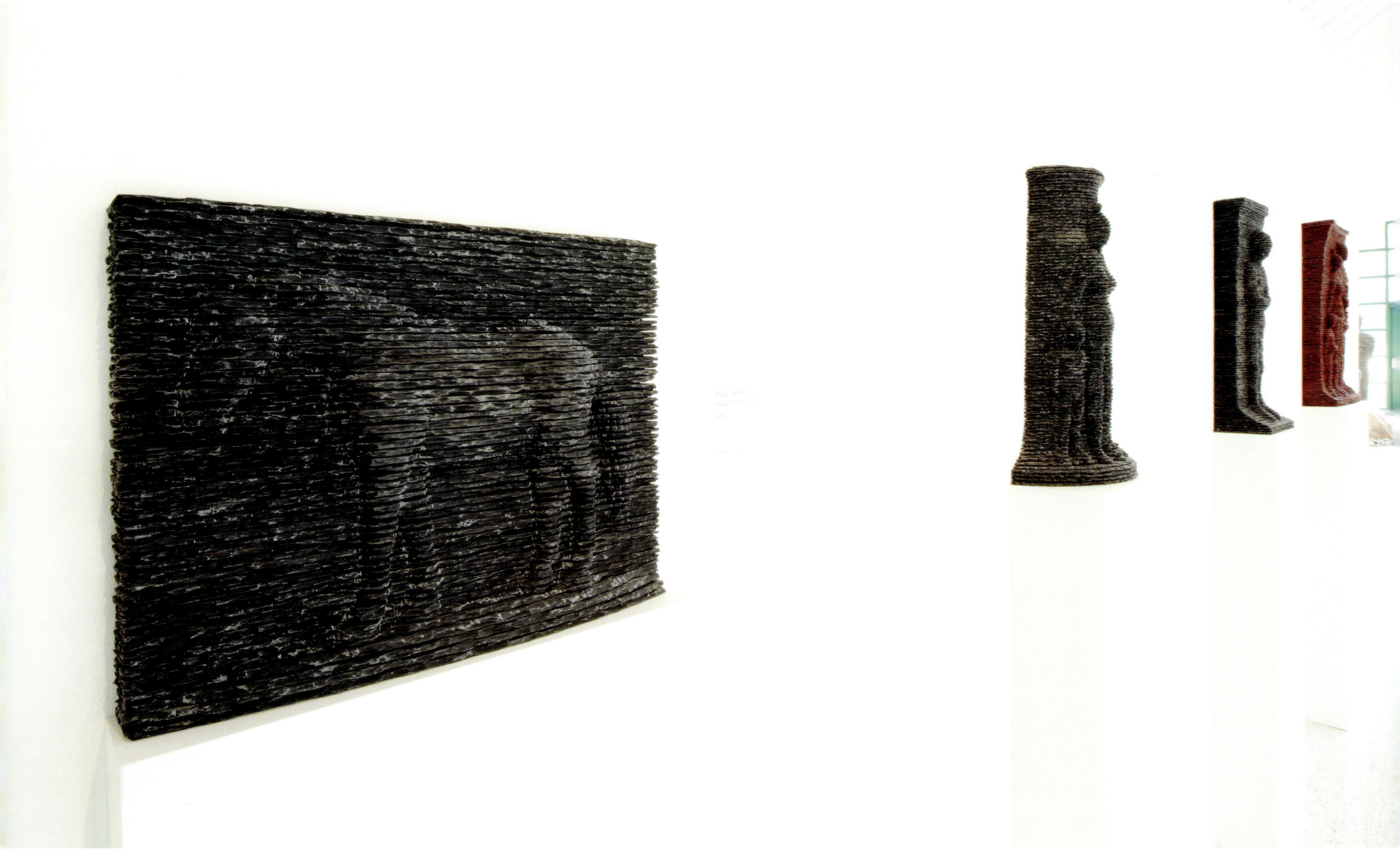

Bas-relief Works, 2014 to the Present

BOAZ VAADIA has always sought to innovate with techniques and materials, new and old, in the creation of new chapters in his work as a sculptor. Having worked on freestanding figurative works in stone, slate, and bronze for more than three decades, Vaadia has recently turned to bas-relief, a timeless genre of sculpture that dates back to ancient Greek, Roman, and Assyrian art. In his bas-relief works, Vaadia carves the slate to depths that retain the image of the natural contours of the figures in his compositions. However, one of the most distinguishing characteristics of Vaadia's reliefs is the use of layers of sedimentary stone that comprise the overall tableau. This exhibition debuts this new body of works. For the first time, we can see that Vaadia's use of layered stone brings a new innovation to an old medium. For Vaadia, these works point to a new direction and foreshadow intriguing possibilities that we all must patiently await.

Installation at
Main Museum Gallery,
Grounds For Sculpture,
Hamilton, NJ, 2016.

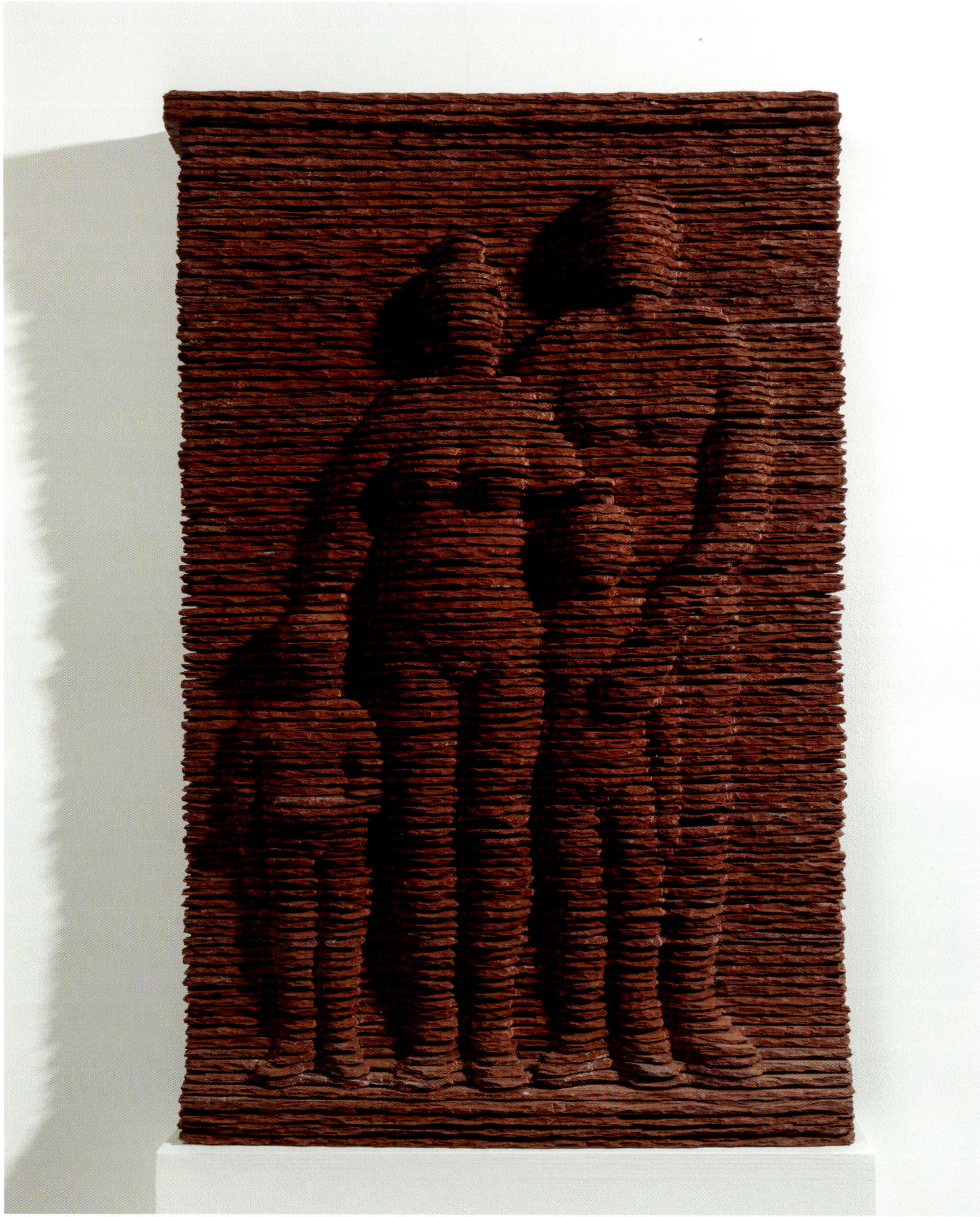

PLATE 114. *Family of Four* (Relief), 2014.
Red slate,
$28^{1}/_{2}$ x $18^{1}/_{2}$ x 5 in. (72.4 x 47 x 12.7 cm).

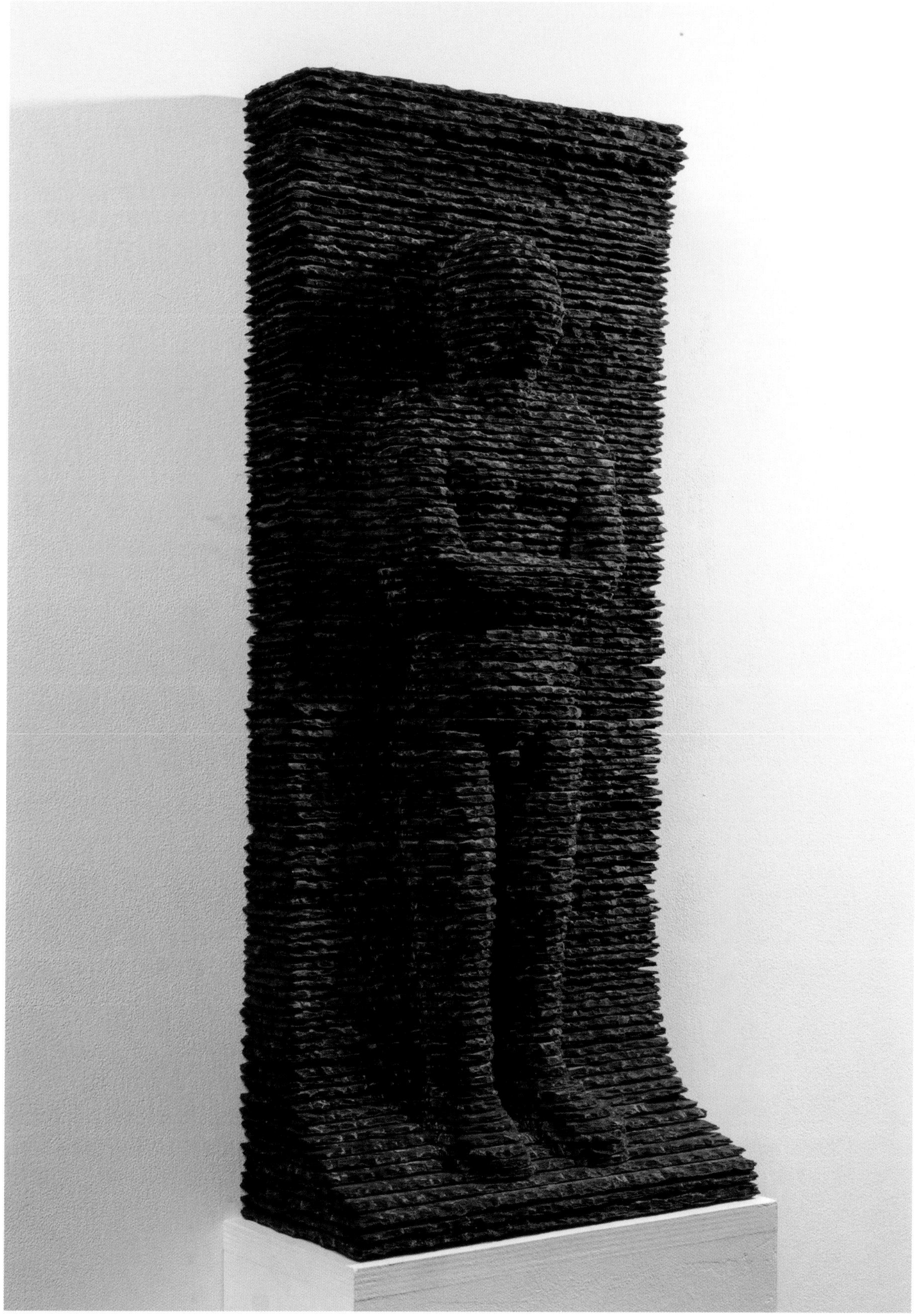

PLATE 115. *Man* (Relief), 2014.
Slate,
27 x 11½ x 5¾ in. (68.6 x 29.2 x 14.6 cm).

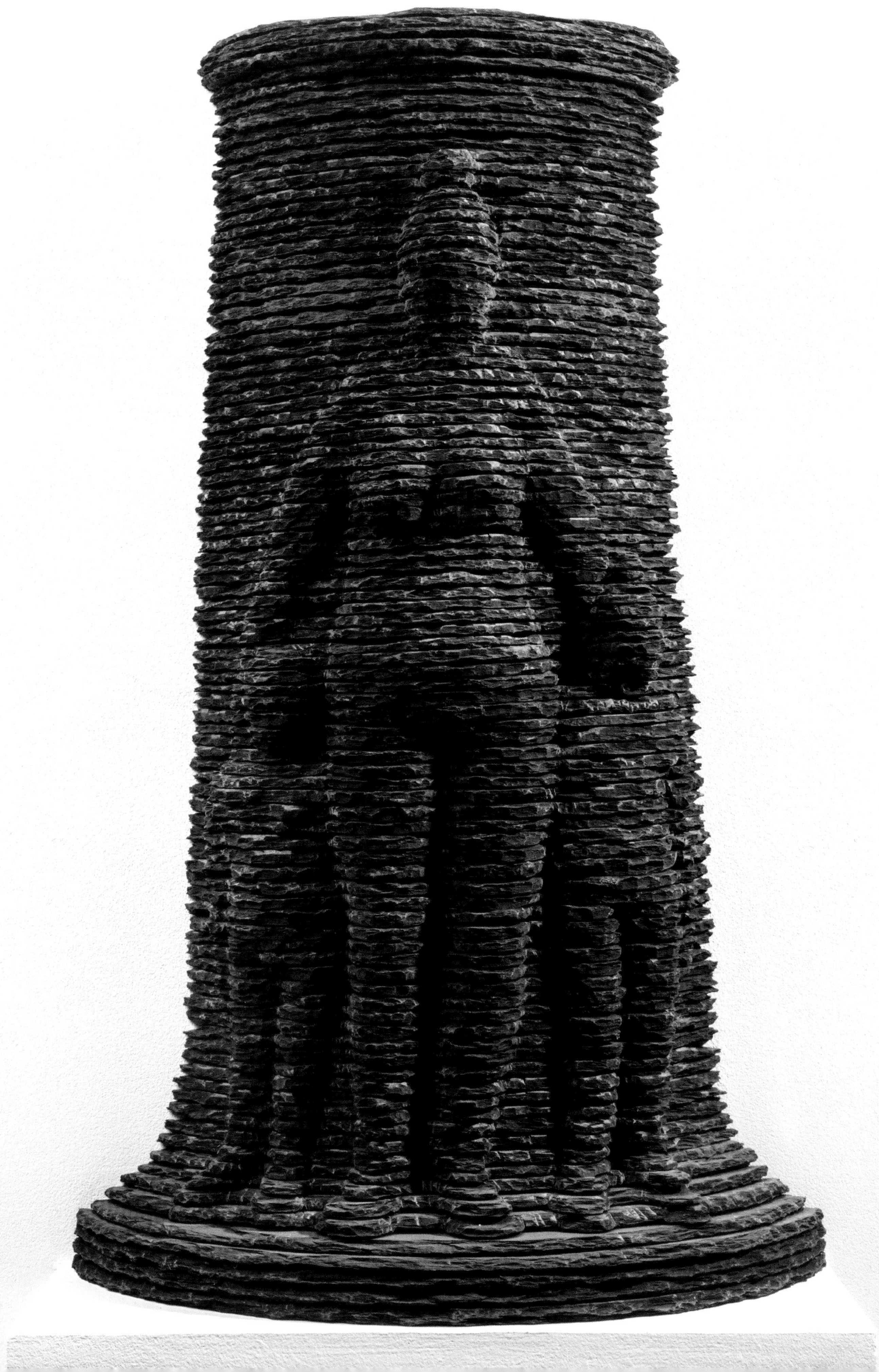

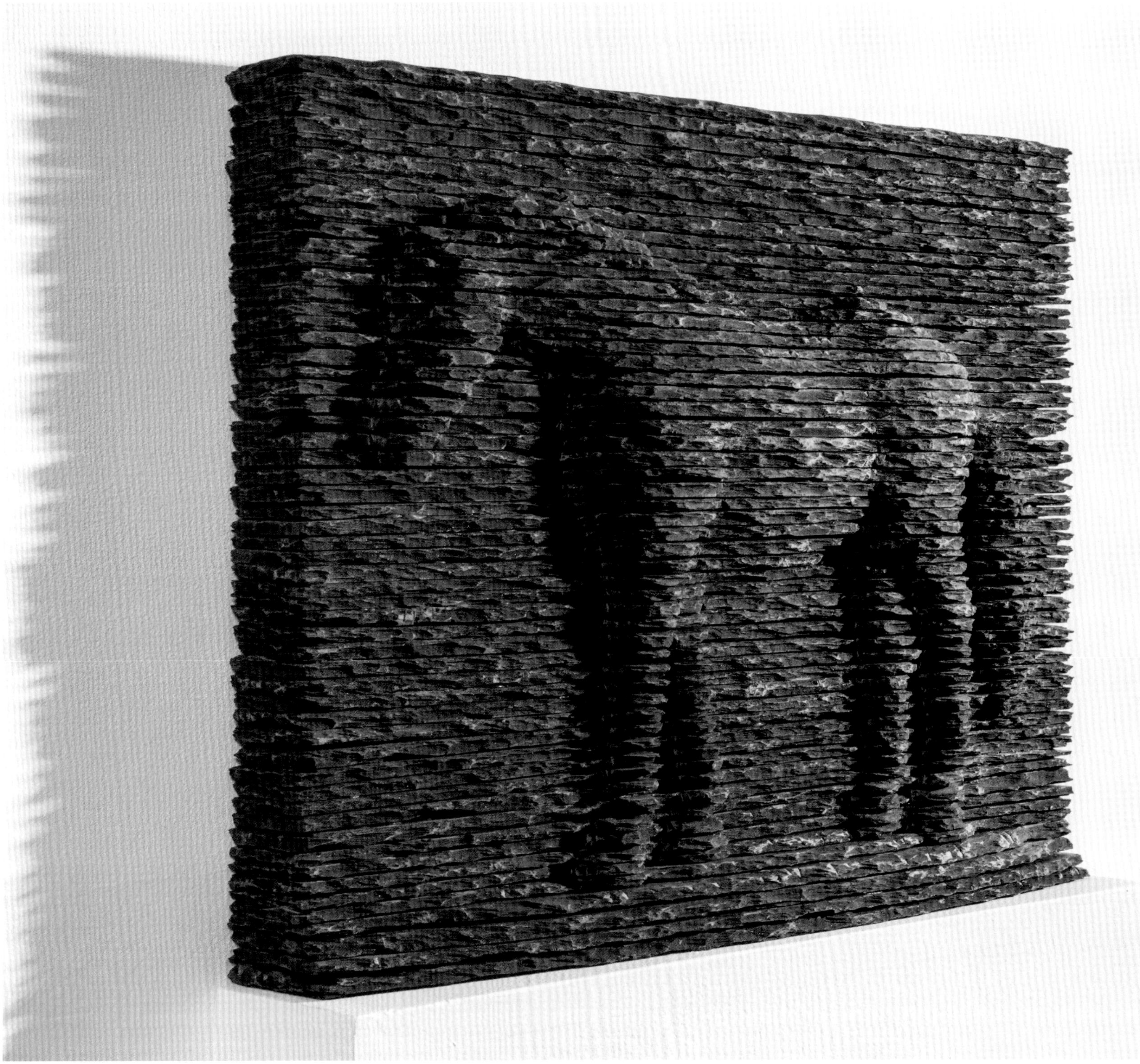

OPPOSITE

PLATE 116. *Mother and 2 Children* (Column Relief), 2014.
Slate,
$23\frac{1}{2}$ x $14\frac{1}{2}$ x 6 in. (59.7 x 36.8 x 15.2 cm).

PLATE 117. *Horse* (Relief), 2015.
Slate,
14 x 19 x $3\frac{1}{4}$ in. (35.6 x 48.3 x 8.2 cm).

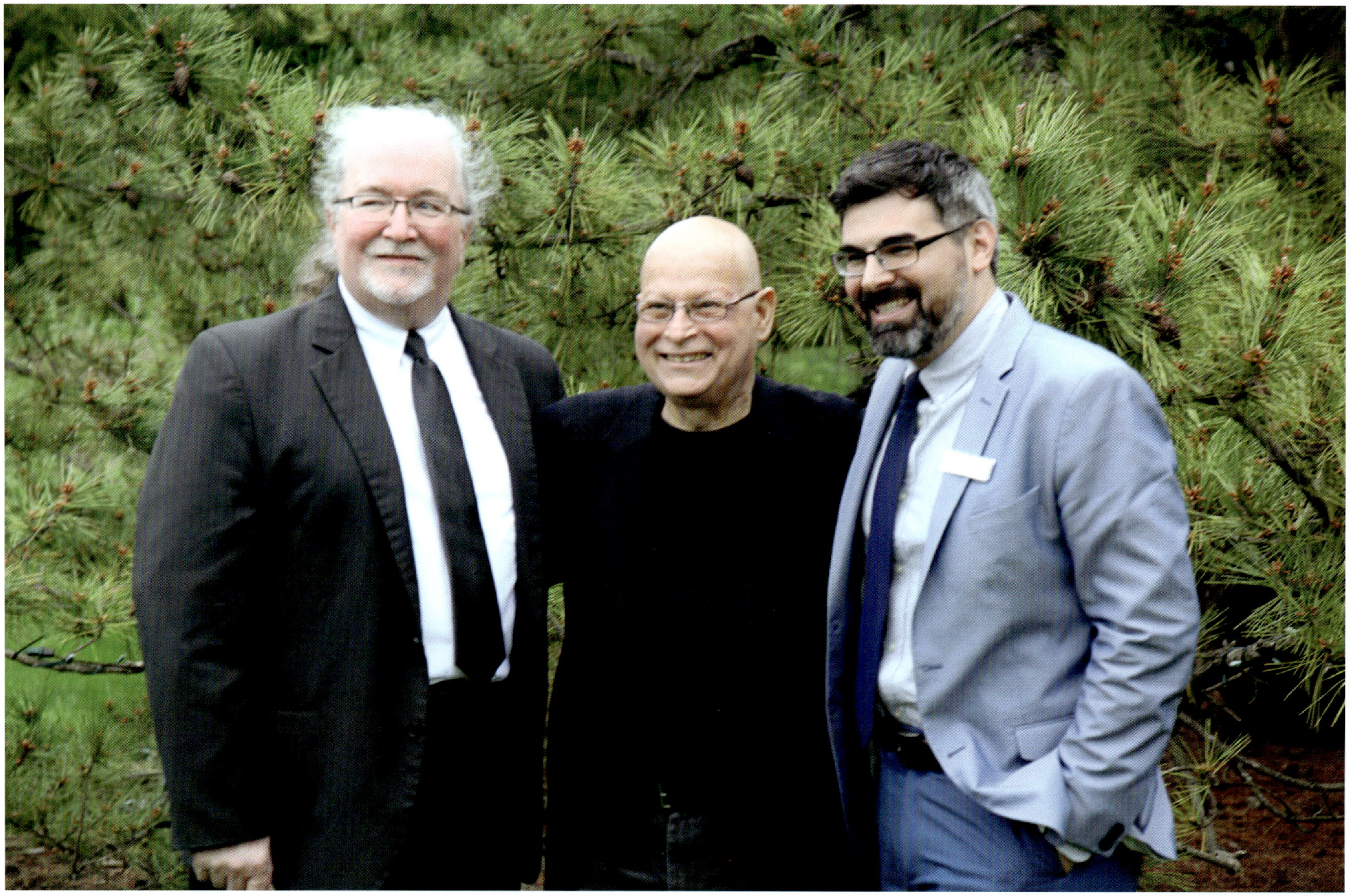

Grounds For Sculpture Curator Tom Moran, Sculptor Boaz Vaadia, and Grounds For Sculpture Director Gary Garrido Schneider at the *Boaz Vaadia: Sculpture* opening reception on April 29, 2016.

Exhibition Checklist

PLATE 1
Untitled, 1971.

PLATE 2
Untitled, 1973.

PLATE 3
Untitled, 1973.

PLATE 4
Untitled, 1973.

PLATE 5
Untitled, 1973.

PLATE 6
Untitled, 1973.

PLATE 7
Untitled, 1973.

PLATE 8
Untitled, 1973.

PLATE 9
Untitled, 1973.

PLATE 10
Untitled, 1973.

PLATE 11
Untitled, 1973.

PLATE 12
Untitled, 1974.

PLATE 13
Untitled, 1974.

PLATE 14
Untitled, 1974.

PLATE 15
Untitled, 1974.

PLATE 16
Untitled, 1974.

PLATE 17
Untitled, 1974.

PLATE 18
Untitled, 1974.

PLATE 19
Untitled, 1974.

PLATE 20
Untitled, 1974.

PLATE 21
Untitled, 1974.

PLATE 22
Untitled, 1974.

PLATE 23
Untitled, 1974.

PLATE 24
Untitled, 1974.

PLATE 25
Untitled, 1975.

PLATE 26
Untitled, 1976.

PLATE 27
Untitled, 1976.

PLATE 28
Untitled, 1976.

PLATE 29
Untitled, 1976.

PLATE 30
Untitled, 1976.

PLATE 31
Untitled, 1976.

PLATE 32
Untitled, 1976.

PLATE 33
Untitled, 1976.

PLATE 34
Untitled, 1976.

PLATE 35
Untitled, 1976.

PLATE 36
Untitled, 1976.

PLATE 37
Untitled, 1976.

PLATE 38
Untitled, 1976.

PLATE 39
Untitled, 1977.

PLATE 40
Untitled, 1977.

PLATE 41
Untitled, 1977.

PLATE 42
Untitled, 1977.

PLATE 43
Untitled, 1977.

PLATE 44
Untitled (maquette), 1977.

PLATE 45
Untitled (maquette), 1977.

PLATE 46
Untitled (maquette), 1977.

PLATE 47
Untitled (maquette), 1977.

PLATE 48
Untitled (maquette), 1977.

PLATE 49
Untitled (maquette), 1978.

PLATE 50
Untitled, 1978.

PLATE 51
Untitled, 1978.

PLATE 52
Untitled, 1978.

PLATE 53
Model for *The Left Pillar in the Porch of the Temple*, 1978.

PLATE 54
Untitled, 1978.

PLATE 55
Untitled, 1979.

PLATE 56
Untitled, 1979.

PLATE 57
Untitled, 1982.

PLATE 58
Untitled, 1977.

PLATE 59
Untitled, 1981.

PLATE 60
Untitled, 1981.

PLATE 61
Untitled, 1982.

PLATE 62
Untitled, 1982.

PLATE 63
Untitled, 1982.

PLATE 64
Untitled, 1982.

PLATE 65
Untitled, 1982.

PLATE 66
Untitled, 1982.

PLATE 67
Untitled, 1982.

PLATE 68
Untitled, 1983.

PLATE 69
My Precious Stones Series No. 2, Star of David Cut, 1983.

PLATE 70
My Precious Stones Series No. 5, Octagon Cut, 1983.

PLATE 71
Untitled, 1984.

PLATE 72
Untitled, 1984.

PLATE 73
Untitled, 1984.

PLATE 74
Untitled, 1983.

PLATE 75
Untitled, 1984.

PLATE 76
Solomon, 1985.

PLATE 77
Hanna & Shemu'el, 1988.

PLATE 78
Maakha and Rehavam, 1988.

PLATE 79
Shimshon and Delila, 1989.

PLATE 80
Zur with Dog, 1989.

PLATE 81
Milka & Tirza, 1990.

PLATE 82
Ahino'am with Dog, 1990.

PLATE 83
Avimelekh with Dog and 8 Lambs, 1991.

PLATE 84
Shimshon, 1998.

PLATE 85
Gilalay & Ginnetoy, 1998.

PLATE 86
Ammi'el & Amaryahu, 1999.

PLATE 87
Ba'al-zevuv, 1999.

PLATE 88
Eli'ezer, 1999.

PLATE 89
Asa with Dog, 2000.

PLATE 90
Asa & Yehoshafat, 2000.

PLATE 91
Avdon, 2001.

PLATE 92
ZAMIR, 2004.

PLATE 93
Boaz, 2002.

PLATE 94
Raffael, 2002.

PLATE 95
Leisa, 2002.

PLATE 96
Rafi, 2002.

PLATE 97
Dawne, 2003.

PLATE 98
Efrayim, 2003.

PLATE 99
Ge'u'el & Binyamin, 2002.

PLATE 100
Asaf & Yo'ah, 2001.

PLATE 101
Yizhaq & Eli'av, 2005.

PLATE 102
Ahiam 2nd, 2006.

PLATE 103
Ah'av and Ovadyahu, 2006.

PLATE 104
Baraq with Cat, 2007.

PLATE 105
Yokheved & Amram, 2009.

PLATE 106
David, 2010

PLATE 107
Family with Dog, 2009.

PLATE 108
Ba'al with Cat, 2009.

PLATE 109
Hulda, 2011.

PLATE 110
Ma'aseyahu, 2012.

PLATE 111
Natan, 2014.

PLATE 112
Havaqquq, 2014.

PLATE 113
Grazing Horse, 2014.

PLATE 114
Family of Four (Relief), 2014.

PLATE 115
Man (Relief), 2014.

PLATE 116
Mother and 2 Children (Column Relief), 2014.

PLATE 117
Horse (Relief), 2015.

Brief Biography

BOAZ VAADIA was born in Gat Rimon, Israel, in 1951. At the young age of 12, Vaadia decided to pursue his passion and become a sculptor. He studied sculpture at the Avni Institute of Art and Design in Jaffa, from which he graduated in 1971. In 1974, Vaadia received a major scholarship from the America-Israel Cultural Foundation to study in New York City. In 1975, Vaadia moved to New York City, where he studied at Pratt Institute and continued to pursue his career as a sculptor. He received The Beckmann Scholarship from the Brooklyn Museum Art School in 1976. Vaadia continued to work in the city, moving his studio permanently to Williamsburg, Brooklyn, in 1989, where it remains today.

As an internationally known sculptor, Vaadia has exhibited widely and placed his works in many public and private locations around the world. Notable permanent installations include among numerous others: in front of the Time Warner Building, New York City, and in Independence Park, Tel Aviv, as part of the Tel Aviv Centennial celebration. Notable temporary installations include eleven large sculptures throughout New York City; the White House Rose Garden, Washington, DC; and Berkeley Square, London, England. Vaadia's work is also in the permanent collections of significant international museums, including The Metropolitan Museum of Art and The Jewish Museum, New York City; the San Francisco Museum of Modern Art, California; the Norton Museum of Art, West Palm Beach, Florida; the Bass Museum of Art, Miami Beach, Florida; The Baker Museum, Naples, Florida; The Israel Museum, Open Museum at Tefen, and Tel-Aviv Museum, Israel; and The Hakone Open-Air Museum, Kanagawa Prefecture, and Tokyo Metropolitan Teien Museum, Japan.

Vaadia has received numerous awards, including a National Endowment for the Arts Grant, USA; The Utsukushi-ga-hara Open Air Museum Award, Nagano, Japan; the Aviv Award through the America-Israel Cultural Foundation; and in 2014, the Russian American Foundation named Vaadia "Person of the Year" in sculpture at a celebration held at The Metropolitan Museum of Art's Temple of Dendur.

In 2013, a 284-page monograph was published about Vaadia's work entitled *Boaz Vaadia Sculpture: 1971–2012*. Selected publications include, among others, articles in *ARTnews*, *Art & Antiques*, *The New York Times*, and *Sculpture Magazine*. Multimedia, including videos, as well as a more extensive résumé can be viewed at www.vaadia.com.

Selected Solo Exhibitions

2016	*Boaz Vaadia: Sculpture*, The Museum at Grounds For Sculpture, Hamilton, NJ
	Jim Kempner Fine Art Sculpture Garden, New York, NY
2015	Vered Gallery, East Hampton, NY
2014	Connaught Brown, London, England
	Jim Kempner Fine Art, New York, NY
2012	Baker Sponder Gallery, Boca Raton, FL
	Gail Severn Gallery, Ketchum, ID
2011–2012	The Sculpture Park at Moore in Aviator Park, Moore College of Art & Design, Philadelphia, PA
2011	Connaught Brown, London, England
	Jim Kempner Fine Art Sculpture Garden, New York, NY
2010	Eckert Fine Art, Kent, CT
2008	Connaught Brown, London, England
2007–2008	*Boaz Vaadia Sculpture in New York City*, eleven sculptures exhibited in Manhattan, seven of which were simultaneously in *Art and the Parks: Celebrating 40 Years*, New York, NY
2006	Connaught Brown, London, England
	Galerie Terminus, Munich, Germany
	Eckert Fine Art, Naples, FL

2005	Caldwell Snyder Gallery, San Francisco, CA; Courcoux & Courcoux Gallery, England
2004	Miriam Shiell Fine Art, Toronto, Canada
2003	Kraft Lieberman Gallery, Chicago, IL
	Imago Galleries, Palm Desert, CA
2002	Elaine Baker Gallery, Boca Raton, FL
2001	Fay Gold Gallery, Atlanta, GA
2000	Elaine Baker Gallery, Boca Raton, FL
1997	Imago Galleries, Palm Desert, CA
	Jaffe Baker Gallery, Boca Raton, FL
	Fay Gold Gallery, Atlanta, GA
1996	Buschlen Mowatt Gallery, Vancouver, BC
	Jaffe Baker Gallery, Boca Raton, FL
1995	Allene Lapides Gallery, Santa Fe, NM
1994	OK Harris Works of Art, New York, NY
1993	Fay Gold Gallery, Atlanta, GA
1990	OK Harris Works of Art, Birmingham, MI
	Hokin Kaufman Gallery, Chicago, IL
1988–1989	Sculpture Court Installation, The Jewish Museum, New York, NY
1986	OK Harris Works of Art, New York, NY
1985	Broadway Windows, New York University, New York, NY
1982	Elise Meyer Gallery, New York, NY
1980	Julie M. Gallery, New York, NY
1978	Sculpture Court, The Jewish Museum, New York, NY
1976	Hundred Acres Gallery, New York, NY
1972	Yad-Labanim Museum, Petah-Tiqva, Israel

Selected Group Exhibitions

2016	*Art New York*, Sponder Gallery New York, NY,
	Casterline Goodman Gallery, Aspen, CO
	Caldwell Snyder Gallery, San Francisco, CA
2015	*Art Silicon Valley*, Sponder Gallery, San Francisco, CA
	Art Southampton, Sponder Gallery, Southampton, NY
	Summer Group Show, Madison Gallery, La Jolla, CA
	Small Works, Jim Kempner Fine Art, New York, NY
	Rubber, Metal & Stone, Sarasota Sculpture Center at Alfstad & Contemporary, Sarasota, FL
	Imago Galleries, Palm Desert, CA
2014	*Art Wynwood*, Sponder Gallery, Miami, FL
	The Salon: Art + Design, Connaught Brown, New York, NY
	Eckert Fine Art, Pine Plains, NY
2013–2014	*Season of Sculpture: Season VII*, Bayfront Park on the Tamiami Trail, Sarasota, FL
2013	*Art Palm Beach*, Sponder Gallery, West Palm Beach, FL
	Caldwell Snyder Gallery, San Francisco, CA
2012	*Art Miami*, Jim Kempner Fine Art, Miami, FL
	Palm Springs Fine Art Fair, Eckert Fine Art, Palm Springs, FL
	Art MRKT Hamptons, Eckert Fine Art, Bridgehampton, NY

2011	*London Art Fair*, Connaught Brown, London, England
	Caldwell Snyder Gallery, San Francisco, CA
2010	*Fine Art Asia—Hong Kong International Art & Antiques Fair*, Caldwell Snyder, Wanchai, Hong Kong
	Onward, Beshart Gallery, Atlanta, GA
2009	*London Art Fair*, Connaught Brown, London, England
	The Art Palm Beach Modern and Contemporary Art Fair, Eckert Fine Art and Connaught Brown, Palm Beach, FL
2008	*Art I Love*, Fay Gold Gallery, Atlanta, GA
	Caldwell Snyder Gallery, San Francisco, CA
2007	*Our Artists*, Fay Gold Gallery, Atlanta, GA
	ARTSEASONS, Galerie Terminus, Cape Town, South Africa
2006	*Palm Beach*, Eckert Fine Art, Palm Beach, FL
	Sculpture from Calder to Bolla, Nohra Haime Gallery, New York, NY
2005	Chicago Contemporary & Classic, Kraft Lieberman Gallery, Chicago, IL
	ART London, Belloc Lowndes Fine Art, England
2004	Exhibition of gallery artists, Scott White Contemporary Art, Telluride, CO
	OFA, Kraft Lieberman Gallery, Chicago, IL
2003	*Art of the 20th Century*, Lillian Heidenberg Fine Art, New York, NY
	Brooklyn on 57th Street, Nohra Haime Gallery, New York, NY
	The Armory Show, Fay Gold Gallery, New York, NY
2002	*Art of the 20th Century*, Lillian Heidenberg, New York, NY
	Exhibition of gallery artists, Imago Galleries, Palm Desert, CA
	From Stone to Foam, Nohra Haime Gallery, New York, NY
2001	*Florida State University Sesquicentennial Sculpture Exhibition*, Florida State Museum of Fine Arts, Tallahassee, FL
	Kirkland International Outdoor Sculpture Exhibition, Kirkland, WA
2000	*Sculpture for the Outdoors IV*, Clark Gallery, Lincoln, MA

1999	*San Francisco International Art Exposition '99*, Atlanta, GA
	Exhibition of gallery artists, Imago Galleries, Palm Desert, CA
	XX/MM 20th Anniversary Exhibition, Fay Gold Gallery, Atlanta, GA
1998	*Milestones Israeli Sculptures 1948–1998*, The Open Museum, Tefen, Israel
	Art Museum 98, Elaine Baker Gallery, Boca Raton, FL
	Vancouver International Sculpture Project, Vancouver, BC
	Art International New York, Buschlen Mowatt Gallery, Vancouver, BC
1997	*Taipei Art Fair*, Taipei, Taiwan
	The International Fine Art and Antiques Fair for America, Washington, DC
1996–1997	Collector's Corner, Philharmonic Center for the Arts, Naples, FL
1996	Exhibition of gallery artists, Buschlen Mowatt Gallery, Vancouver, BC
	Bones and Champagne, Vered Gallery, East Hampton, NY
1995	*20th-Century Sculpture, Southern Region*, The Rose Garden, The White House, Washington, DC
	Imago Galleries, Palm Desert, CA
1994	*The 2nd Fujisankei Biennale*, Hakone Open Air Museum, Kanagawa Prefecture, Japan
	Israeli Sculpture in Tefen: The Last Decade, The Open Museum at Tefen, Israel
1993	*FIAC*, Paris, France
	Lillian Heidenberg Gallery, New York, NY
1992	*4th Rodin Grand Prize Exhibition*, Utsukushi-ga-hara Open Air Museum, Nagano, Japan
1991	*Centrepieces*, Norton Center, Centre College, Danville, KY
	Art at Gateway Center, Second Annual Sculpture Exhibition, Prudential Insurance Company of America, Newark, NJ
1989	*Best of Season*, Helander Gallery, Palm Beach, FL
1986–1987	*Other Gods: Containers of Belief*, traveling exhibition: Everson Museum of Art, Syracuse, NY; Fondo Del Sol, Washington, DC; Wallace/Wentworth Gallery, Washington, DC; The Los Angeles Municipal Gallery, Los Angeles, CA, with The Craft and Folk Museum, The Contemporary Arts Center, New Orleans, LA

1985–1986	*Contemporary Pedestal Sculpture*, traveling exhibition: The Moody Gallery of Art, University of Alabama, Tuscaloosa, AL; University Galleries, University of South Florida, Tampa, FL; Huntsville Museum of Art, Huntsville, AL
1985	*Sculptors Turn to Stone*, Arch at Grand Army Plaza, Brooklyn Art Palace, Brooklyn, NY
1984	*80 Years of Sculpture in Israel*, The Israel Museum, Jerusalem, Israel
	Sculpture in Architecture: A Group Show of Works by Eleven Contemporary Artists, Germans Van Eck Gallery, New York, NY
1983	*The Third Annual Holiday Invitational Exhibition*, A.I.R. Gallery, New York, NY
1981	*Are You Experienced?* Vrije University of Brussels, Belgium

Outdoor Installations and Public Art

2017	Permanent installation of *Ma'aseyahu and Haziel*, Point Leo Sculpture Park, Victoria, Australia
2016	Permanent installation of *Asa & Yehoshafat with Dog*, Main Street Square, Houston, TX
2015	Long-term installation of *Ah'av, Asa & Yehoshafat with Dog*, *Ba'al & Yizhaq*, and *Yo'ah with Dog*, Rockford, IL (on loan)
	Long-term installation of *David*, Poydras Corridor Sculpture Exhibition—Sculpture for New Orleans, New Orleans, LA (on loan)
2014	Permanent installation of *Amaryahu with Cat*, University Medical Center of Princeton, Plainsboro, NJ
	Permanent installation of *Family with Dog* and *Ah'av* (on long-term loan), Illinois Wesleyan University, Bloomington, IL
2013–2014	Temporary installation of *Ah'av*, *Maakha & Rehavam*, *Family with Dog*, *David*, *Assa & Yehoshafat with Dog*, and *ZAMIR*, *Season of Sculpture: Season VII*, Bayfront Park on the Tamiami Trail, Sarasota, FL (on loan)
2013	Long-term installation of *Ba'al with Cat* and *Yizhaq with Cat*, *Downtown Abstractions, Art in Public Places – Stamford Downtown*, Stamford, CT (on loan)
	Long-term installation of *Ba'al* and *Ammi'el*, Waterfront Promenade, Yonkers, NY (on loan)
	Temporary installation of *Asaf & Yo'ah*, Novo Nordisk Inc., Princeton, NJ

2011–2012	Long-term installation of *Family with Dog*, *Gilalay & Ginnetoy*, and *Yo'ah with Dog*, The Sculpture Park at Moore in Aviator Park, Logan Square, Philadelphia, PA (on loan)
	Long-term installation of *SARA*, *REBECCA*, and *MEIR*, Pratt Institute Sculpture Park, Brooklyn, NY (on loan)
	Long-term installation of *Ammi'el & Amaryahu*, Village Green, Summit, NJ (on loan)
2010–2012	Long-term installation of *Asa & Yehoshafat*, Frist Center for the Visual Arts, Nashville, TN (on loan)
	Long-term installation of *Daniyyel with Dog* and *Asa with Dog*, Rockland Center for the Arts, West Nyack, NY (on loan)
2009	Permanent installation of *Asa & Yehoshafat*, Independence Park, Tel Aviv, Israel
2008	Permanent installation of *Ginnetoy 2nd*, University of Nevada, Reno, NV
	Temporary installation of *Ba'al & Yizhaq*, The Village Green, Cashiers, NC (on loan)
2007–2008	*Boaz Vaadia Sculpture in New York City*, eleven sculptures exhibited in Manhattan, seven of which are simultaneously in *Art and the Parks: Celebrating 40 Years*, New York, NY (on loan)
2006	Temporary installation of *Asa & Yehoshafat*, Promenadepl, Munich, Germany (on loan)
	Temporary installation of *Ammi'el*, Berkeley Square, London, England (on loan)
	Permanent installation of *Yo'ah with Dog*, The Hilton Garden Inn, Staten Island, NY
2005	Long-term installation of *Ammi'el* and *Ba'al*, DeCordova Museum and Sculpture Park, Lincoln, MA (on loan)
2004	Permanent installation of *Asaf and Yo'ah*, Time Warner Center, South Tower entrance, New York, NY
2003–2005	Long-term installation of *Shaul* and *Rahel and Binyamin*, Nassau County Museum of Art, Roslyn Harbor, NY (on loan)
2001	Long-term installation of *Amryahu*, *Avi* and *Zadoq and Shim'on*, Florida State University Sesquicentennial Sculpture Exhibition, Tallahassee, FL (on loan)
	Kirkland International Outdoor Sculpture Exhibition, Kirkland, WA

2000 Permanent installation of *Eli'ezer*, Hall Office Park, Frisco, TX

1998 Permanent installation of *David and Yonatan*, Chicago Symphony Sculpture Garden at Ravinia, Chicago, IL

Temporary installation of *Amaryahu* and *Ammi'el & Amaryahu*, Vancouver International Sculpture Project – Third Biennial, Vancouver, BC (on loan)

1997 Permanent installation of *Meshullemet and Menashshe*, The Baker Museum, Naples, FL

1996 Permanent installation of *Milka & Tirza*, All Souls School, New York, NY

1995 Temporary installation featuring *Zur with Dog*, *20th-Century American Sculpture*, The White House Rose Garden, Washington, DC (on loan from the Norton Museum)

Permanent installation of *Piltay & Pashhur*, Tokyo Metropolitan Teien Museum, Japan

1993 Permanent installation of outdoor sculpture *Yakhin*, in front of The Monterey apartment building, New York, NY

1992 Permanent installation of *Moriyya*, Hakone Open Air Museum, Kanagawa Prefecture, Japan

Utsukushi-ga-hara Open Air Museum, Nagano Prefecture, Japan

Permanent installation of sculpture *David Haggit & Adoniyya*, Arlington County Beautification Program, Rosslyn, VA; sited at 1300 N. 17th Street; a public–private partnership between Arlington County and La Salle partners; sculpture commissioned by La Salle Partners through an invited competition with a selection panel consisting of Arlington County officials, developers, art professionals, and a landscape architect

1990 *Hofstra Museum Outdoor Sculpture*, installation, Hofstra University, Hempstead, NY

1981 Temporary installation, The Manhattan Psychiatric Center, Ward's Island, New York, NY

1979 Temporary installation, Battery Park, New York, NY

1977 Temporary installations of two sculptures along the Appalachian Trail, Bear Mountain and Palisades Interstate Park, New York, NY

Selected Collections

The Baker Museum, Naples, FL
Bass Museum of Art, Miami Beach, FL
Best Products Inc., Richmond, VA
Cargill Inc., Minneapolis, MN
Charles A. Wustum Museum of Fine Arts, Racine, WI
Flint Institute of Arts, Flint, MI
Hakone Open Air Museum, Kanagawa Prefecture, Japan
The Israel Museum, Jerusalem, Israel
The Jewish Museum, New York, NY
La Salle Partners, Arlington, VA
Lufthansa Airlines, East Meadow, NY
The Metropolitan Museum of Art, New York, NY
Museum of Modern Art, San Francisco, CA
Norton Museum of Art, West Palm Beach, FL
Open Museum at Tefen, Israel
Paine Webber Inc., Puerto Rico
The Related Companies, New York, NY
Tel-Aviv Museum, Israel
Tokyo Metropolitan Teien Museum, Japan
Vero Beach Art Museum, Vero Beach, FL
Richard Brown Baker, NY
Patty and Jay Baker, FL
Larry Belger, MO
Howard Brown, MD
Philippe Brugere-Trelat
Lois Kohn-Claar and Gary Claar, NY
Mitchell Draizin, NY

The Home of Bob and Terry Edwards, FL
Pauline and John Gandel, Australia
Richard Gelfond, NY
Avram Gray, FL
Ambassador Kathryn Hall and Craig Hall, CA
Rand Hoch, FL
Elton John, GA
Mr. and Mrs. Samuel Johnson, WI
Dr. Arthur and Anita Kahn, NY
David Klein, MI
Kogan Family Trust, CO
Laura Lemle, PhD, NY
Mr. and Mrs. Noah Liff, TN
Scott and Simone Lutgert, FL
The Manney Collection, New York, NY
Martin Z. Margulies, FL
Samuel and Barbara Masket, CA
Elyce and Mark Metzner, IL
Eric P. Meyer, Switzerland
Edward J. Minskoff, NY
Richard Nicotra, NY
Jorge M. Perez, FL
Marcia Riklis, NY
Stephen M. Ross, NY
Dr. Beth Sackler, NY
Joan C. Sall, PA
Bob and Polina Schlott, NE
Gad and Suzan Shaanan, CA
Dr. Bob Shillman, CA
Dana and Andrew Stone, NY
Mr. and Mrs. Donald Tober, NY
Edna and Stanley Tuttleman, PA
Larry and Lisa Wilens, NY
Mr. and Mrs. Raymond Zimmerman, TN

Grants, Fellowships, and Awards

2014	12th Annual Russian Heritage Month Honoree, Russian American Foundation, New York, NY
2012	Aviv Award, The America-Israel Cultural Foundation, New York, NY
1992	Utsukushi-ga-hara Open Air Museum Award, Japan
1988	National Endowment for the Arts, Washington, DC; grant
1977	America the Beautiful Fund, Palisades Interstate Park NY; grant and residency
1976–1977	Beckmann Scholarship, Brooklyn Museum Art School, Brooklyn, NY
1975–1976	America-Israel Cultural Foundation, New York, NY; grant

Selected Bibliography

Astor, Maggie. "Neighborhood Sculptor Makes His Mark on Morningside." *Columbia Spectator*, October 10, 2007.

Castro, Jan. "Balancing Families in Stone: A Conversation with Boaz Vaadia." *Sculpture Magazine*, June 2008.

Davis, Brendan. "Boaz Vaadia." *Art Interview Online Magazine*, 2006.

Drucker, Stephen. "Waxing Purple: In Manhattan a Passion for Color Inspires a Design Where Every Detail Counts." *Architectural Digest*, December 2004.

Garnett, Adrienne. "Preview." *South Florida Times*, 2005.

Gilbert, Debora. "Boaz Vaadia in Manhattan." *WG News + Art*, November 2007.

Gould, Genia. "Sculptor Harvests Brooklyn Boulders as Materiel for Art." *The New York Times*, July 2, 2000.

Lasky, Julie. "Mostly True Grit." *The New York Times*, June 27, 2013.

Micucci, Dana. "Force of Nature." *Art & Antiques*, April 2008.

Pollack, Barbara. "Boaz Vaadia – Review." *ARTnews*, September 2003.

Steiner, Wendy, Anthony Brown, and Ivan C. Karp. *Boaz Vaadia: Sculpture 1971–2012*. Easthampton, MA: Hudson Hills Press, 2013.

Photograph Credits

David Allyon: plate 53

John Berens: fig. 16, plates 77, 81, 82, 83, 88, 91

Ken Ek: pp. 6, 7, 8, 10, 14, 36, 72, 110, plates 2, 28, 29, 55, 56, 57, 58, 59, 60, 71, 72, 73, 84, 101

Steven Greaves: pp. 2–3

Rachel Lazar: fig. 5

Faith McClellan: plate 102

Adam Reich: front cover, p. 1, fig. 14, plates 92, 96, 98, 99, 100, 103, 104, 105, 109, 110, 111, 112, 113, 114, 115, 116, 117

Dax Sommerfeld: fig. 15, plate 7

Vincent Tiley: p. 116

Boaz Vaadia: back cover, p. 4, figs. 1, 2, 4, 9, 10, 11, 12, 13, 17, plates 1, 51, 64, 65, 66, 67, 69, 70, 76, 79, 80, 85, 86, 87, 89, 90, 106, 108

Boaz Vaadia Studio Archive: p. 42, figs. 3, 8, plates 3, 4, 5, 6, 8, 9, 10, 11, 12, 13, 14, 15, 16, 17, 18, 19, 20, 21, 22, 23, 24, 25, 26, 27, 30, 31, 32, 33, 34, 35, 36, 37, 38, 39, 40, 41, 42, 43, 44, 45, 46, 47, 48, 49, 50, 52, 54, 61, 62, 63, 68, 74, 75, 107

Kim Turner Vaadia: plate 78

Ellen Page Wilson: plates 93, 94, 95, 97

Boaz Vaadia: Sculpture is supported in part by Quaker Bridge Mall, A Simon Mall; The Consulate General of Israel in New York; Baker Sponder Gallery; Imago Galleries; Jim Kempner Fine Art; Vered Gallery; the New Jersey State Council on the Arts/Department of State, a Partner Agency of the National Endowment for the Arts; The Geraldine R. Dodge Foundation; and the Johnson Art and Education Foundation; and many others.

GROUNDS FOR SCULPTURE

QUAKER BRIDGE MALL
A SIMON MALL

CONSULATE GENERAL OF ISRAEL IN NEW YORK

NATIONAL ENDOWMENT FOR THE ARTS
A great nation deserves great art.

NEW JERSEY STATE COUNCIL ON THE ARTS

THE GERALDINE R. DODGE FOUNDATION

First Edition

Published in the United States by The Artist Book Foundation
115 East 57th Street, 11th floor, New York, New York 10022

Distributed in the United States, its territories and possessions, and Canada by
ACC Distribution
www.accdistribution.com/us

Distributed outside North America by ACC Distribution
www.accdistribution.com/uk

Publisher and co-founder: L. Pell
Co-founder: H. Gibbs Taylor, Jr.
Production manager: David Skolkin
Design: Irene Cole
Editor: Deborah Thompson
Proofreader: Marisa Crumb
Printed and bound by Friesens

Manufactured in Canada

ISBN 978-0-9962007-4-5

Library Of Congress Cataloging-in-Publication Data

Names: Steiner, Wendy, 1949- | Grounds For Sculpture, organizer, host institution.
Title: Boaz Vaadia : sculpture / essay by Wendy Steiner ; foreword by Tom Moran.
Other titles: Boaz Vaadia (Grounds For Sculpture)
Description: First Edition. | New York : The Artist Book Foundation, 2016.
Identifiers: LCCN 2016030989 | isbn 9780996200745
Subjects: LCSH: vaadia, boaz, 1951---exhibitions.
Classification: LCC NB237.V25 A4 2016 | DDC 730.92--DC23
LC record available at https://lccn.Loc.Gov/2016030989

COVER: *Horse* (Relief), 2015. Slate, 14 x 19 x 3¼ in. (35.6 x 48.3 x 8.2 cm). Photograph by Adam Reich.

PAGE 1: *Zamir*, 2004. Bluestone, 50 x 49 x 29 in. (127 x 124.5 x 73.7 cm). Private collection of Rebecca Vaadia and Sara Vaadia. Photograph by Adam Reich.

PAGES 2–3: *Asaf and Yo'ah*, 2000. Bluestone and boulder, 78 x 110 x 80 in. (198.1 x 279.4 x 203.2 cm). Private collection. Permanent installation, Time Warner Center, South Tower, New York, NY. Photograph by Steven Greaves.

PAGE 4: *Natan Toviya and Havaqquq*, 2013. Bluestone and boulder, 91 x 120 x 132 in. (231.1 x 124.5 x 335.3 cm). Private collection. Photograph by Boaz Vaadia.

PAGE 6: Installation at Main Museum Gallery, Grounds For Sculpture, Hamilton, NJ, 2016. Photograph by Ken Ek.